LOOKING EAST IN WINTER

To His Beatitude Archbishop Anastasios of Tirana, dear friend and brother; and in memory of Olivier Clément: two witnesses to the gifts of the Eastern Church to the whole Christian world

LOOKING EAST IN WINTER

Contemporary Thought and the
Eastern Christian Tradition

ROWAN WILLIAMS

BLOOMSBURY CONTINUUM
LONDON · OXFORD · NEW YORK · NEW DELHI · SYDNEY

BLOOMSBURY CONTINUUM
Bloomsbury Publishing Plc
50 Bedford Square, London, WC1B 3DP UK
29 Earlsfort Terrace, Dublin 2, Ireland

BLOOMSBURY, BLOOMSBURY CONTINUUM and the Diana logo are
trademarks of Bloomsbury Publishing Plc

First published in Great Britain 2021

A catalogue record for this book is available from the British Library

Library of Congress Cataloguing-in-Publication data has been applied for

ISBN: HB: 978-1-4729-8924-6; eBook: 978-1-4729-8923-9;
ePDF: 978-1-4729-8922-2

2 4 6 8 10 9 7 5 3 1

Typeset by Deanta Global Publishing Services, Chennai, India
Printed and bound in Great Britain by CPI Group (UK) Ltd, Croydon CR0 4YY

To find out more about our authors and books visit www.bloomsbury.com
and sign up for our newsletters

CONTENTS

INTRODUCTION

During the last quarter of a century, Western theology has become conspicuously more aware of the intellectual seriousness of its counterpart in the Eastern Christian world. From being a slightly exotic subject in academic eyes, linked with issues to do with 'spirituality' or with the less frequented byways of patristics, the latter has increasingly been recognized as a credible and significant conversation partner in forming a response to a number of contemporary theological issues, especially around anthropology: the resources offered by the Eastern tradition for reflecting on humanity and the environment, emotion and reason, the ambiguities of individualism and other questions have been widely acknowledged. More broadly, there is a fuller awareness of how the exploration of these questions opens up further issues about 'ontology' – what a theologian might say about the fundamental contours of being; understanding more fully what can be said about the human constitution in its relation with God has implications for what we say about reality or truthfulness, about the nature of knowing and seeing. Once it is granted that knowing and seeing are activities that are to be learned, scrutinized and refined in the diagnostic light of a tradition of spiritual practice, it becomes impossible simply to go on theologizing with an unexamined set of assumptions about how reality is apprehended.

Hence this book begins with a lengthy examination of one influential set of sources for absorbing that tradition of practice: the eighteenth-century anthology of spiritual texts known as the *Philokalia*. This is not an uncontroversial choice: there are Orthodox theologians who regard the *Philokalia* – at least

1

as it is often used and read these days – as being dangerously inflected by a dualistic 'spiritualism', a world-denying ethos for which the body and the human community (even the church community) are secondary concerns.[1] The dangers are not hard to spot in countless texts in this collection; but pervading these writings is also an underlying cluster of themes which, when drawn together, point in a very different direction. As is often noted, the dominant presence in the *Philokalia* simply in terms of quantity of citation is Maximos the Confessor, the great seventh-century theological genius of the Byzantine Church, increasingly acknowledged as a Christian thinker on the level of Augustine for range and sophistication, as well as for his consistent grounding of theological argument in reflection on the experience of contemplation. Earlier material in the collection, especially from the controversial figure of Evagrios Pontikos at the end of the fourth century,[2] is clearly to be read in the light of Maximos's clarifications and elaborations. And if the reading I am proposing in these pages is correct, Maximos helps us read Evagrios to some extent 'against' himself: Evagrios was recognized as an analyst of spiritual practice almost unparalleled in the early centuries, but there is no denying the powerful legacy of dualism in his work, as well as a general theological perspective that has unsettled 'mainstream' theologians ever since. I have taken these Maximian cues for reading Evagrios with an eye to deliberately pushing back at the cliché that the spiritual climate Evagrios represents is ultimately not friendly to the religion of the Incarnation – a view

---

[1] See, for example, Christos Yannaras, *Against Religion: The Alienation of the Ecclesial Event*, tr. Norman Russell (Brookline, MA, Holy Cross Orthodox Press 2013), pp. 188–99, and Nikolaos Loudovikos, *Analogical Identities: The Creation of the Christian Self* (Turnhout, Brepols 2019), e.g. pp. 95–9, 148–51. See also below, pp. 11–12, for Alexander Schmemann's sceptical attitude towards contemporary enthusiasm for the *Philokalia*.

[2] Evagrios is notoriously associated with the legacy of the great third-century Origen of Alexandria, and more particularly with those aspects of Origen's thought that were seen as emphasizing the radical independence of soul and spirit from body, and affirming the existence of created spirits prior to their embodiment at birth.

I have myself expressed in the past, I'm afraid:[3] the introductory chapter seeks to redress an imbalance.

What emerges from reading the philokalic tradition in a strongly 'Maximian' light is a model of what human engagement with reality, finite and infinite, involves that affirms (a bit counter-intuitively, given the criticisms already mentioned) not only the centrality of a stark critique of the myth of untouchable inner 'selfhood' but also the intrinsic role of bodily located modes of knowledge in charting the human vocation. But another and equally important element in this Maximian reading is the ultimate grounding of what is said about human subjectivity in trinitarian theology. All sorts of themes converge on the focal reality of *logos*: in eternity, divine *logos* is the identity-in-difference of the divine as the limitless source of all. The next few chapters of the book trace these themes in a little more depth. Beyond finite reality, we recognize an infinite returning-to-itself of this limitless source – a limitless returning that does not and cannot exhaust the limitless source's action in generating/'breathing out' divine life into an other. In the vocabulary of the tradition, the Word is that which the Father generates, yet this is not a static mirroring of 'one' to 'another', as the Father is always already the one who 'breathes' Spirit, the Spirit that eternally holds open the space in which the Word lives, and will also, in the finite world, realize the life of the Word within history. This is what infinite being simply *is*; and finite being is thus sustained by an eternal act that has this shape and no other. Hence we can say that resting upon, and being animated and directed by, Word and Spirit are the most important truths about all finite being and in a very distinctive sense the most important truths about human existence. To mature as a human is to grow more fully into this foundational reality. So our theological discussion of knowing, praying, acting, whatever else, is shaped by this; and what it means to become fully a created person is shaped by the eternal 'filial' reality of the

[3] As in *The Wound of Knowledge: Christian Spirituality from the New Testament to St John of the Cross*, 2nd edn (London, Darton, Longman and Todd 1990), pp. 67–9.

divine Word whose agency is entirely response to the gift from the eternal Source. Thinking through the trinitarian basis of our doctrine of the human helps us to understand how the classical language of the 'deification' promised to the created subject does not entail any de-humanizing or de-creation of the human agent, because this deification is about the effect of adoptive grace coming to inhabit finite agency and anchor it wholly in the filial responsiveness and so the intimacy and liberty that belongs to the eternal Word. Clarifying these connections helps to establish the continuity between scriptural and patristic theologies that can easily be missed if we fail to see how theological language about being gifted with 'divine' dignity is grounded in the eternal life of the one who in his earthly life calls the divine Source 'Abba'.

This section of the present book (chapters 2–5), then attempts to move from some very broad ontological considerations back to considerations of the life and growth of the finite heart/ spirit. But – mindful again of some of the critiques of philokalic theology that we have mentioned – this life and growth cannot be thought or spoken of without attention to the common life of humanity. So the section that follows (chapters 6–10) offers a variety of approaches to what the sanctified common life involves, beginning with a sketch of the 'liturgical humanism' sketched by one notable modern Orthodox thinker. This leads into a survey of how the Eastern Christian tradition, especially in nineteenth- and twentieth-century Russia, understands the authoritative handing-on of Christian truth in the community: the doctrine of 'tradition' thus developed both grows out of and in turn deepens and extends the basic anthropological themes sketched earlier. If the human subject/agent is as the spiritual tradition affirms, then this has implications for how doctrinal truth is both learned and transmitted in the Church, and these implications sharply challenge both Catholic and Protestant discourses about tradition and authority (and indeed a good many more conventional Orthodox approaches as well). The insights that arise about the nature of a community living in response to grace naturally generate further questions about specific patterns of power, justice and shared social goods in human relations more generally: if this is what restored and life-giving relations look like, how are they worked for, and to what extent realized, in human society overall? And this leads into the question of what a theologically informed politics might look like if we begin from an anthropology determined by liturgy and contemplation.

That being said, the intersection of the Church and human society at large is not a simple matter. It is not that the Church is a human organization striving for success and influence, let alone trying to win elections; nor is it an organization devoted to cultivating 'private' virtue or holiness, or to providing a satisfying spiritual gloss to unchallenged human comforts and compulsions. Christian history is littered with the evidence of these disastrous corruptions. The Eastern Christian tradition is not exempt; but it has also, especially in Russia, developed a distinctive vehicle for thinking about the tensions between the judgements of human society and the priorities of God's kingdom through the narratives of 'holy folly', first in the context of traditional hagiography, but, since the nineteenth century, in an assortment of very untraditional fictional narratives, from Dostoevsky onwards. The notion that holiness might, paradoxically, be visible in what seem to be absurd, subversive, parodic behaviours is a subtle one:[4] it has its roots both in a Christological insight about the unrecognizability of the holy in a diseased world and in a strong sense of the causeless grace of God. All this may seem a long way from our starting point in the monastic counsels of Evagrios and others; but in fact the diagnoses offered by the philokalic tradition presuppose that our habitual vision of the world is deeply skewed by self-serving 'passion', and that what we think is rational may be quite the

---

[4]It is close to the method utilized by the Catholic novelist Flannery O'Connor in her depictions of what can only be called a parodic holiness, which possesses a kind of bizarre authenticity simply by undermining complacent morality and religiosity; on this, see, for example, Rowan Williams, *Dostoevsky: Language, Faith and Fiction* (Waco, TX, Baylor University Press/London, Continuum 2008), p. 6, and some of the discussion in Michael Mears Bruner, *A Subversive Gospel: Flannery O'Connor and the Reimagining of Beauty, Goodness, and Truth* (Downers Grove, IL, IVP Academic 2017).

opposite, if we are serious in thinking through what we mean by reason in the light of a fully theological and trinitarian scheme.

In this perspective, the outrageous risk represented by martyrdom can be called a reasonable act – indeed a form of that 'rational [*logike*] worship' commended by St Paul (Romans 12.1). The chapter on the theological writings of Mother Maria Skobstova of Paris examines what this very unconventional monastic figure – with some discernible elements of 'holy folly' in her behaviour – has to say about Christian love in action and about the reasonableness of unconditional solidarity with human suffering. Her articulate refusal to understand Christian love of neighbour as an option, a duty or an achievement arises from her conviction that life in the Body of Christ simply expresses itself in such love. She has some strikingly bold things to say about maternity as a paradigm for Christian love because the bond between mother and child once created is one that is irreducibly material and is simply there, independent of acts of choice; and this is grounded in the same conviction of the plain 'givenness' of solidarity in Christ's Body. As elsewhere in these studies, the paradoxical conclusion is that certain sorts of attention to the material are the best way into understanding 'spirit' – to the extent that they draw attention away from the conscious performances of ego and will. For Mother Maria, it was essential to affirm that the love that characterizes the Christian community is more than an individual performance or even a 'culture' of individual performances, but at some level is simply an aspect of what we *are* within the filial life of Christ. Hence the importance for her of bypassing any prudential account 'in advance' of what love might demand of us or who the neighbour might turn out to be. Just as our theological anthropology is flawed if we try to identify certain *aspects* of humanity as bearing the image of God (with the implication that their absence or apparent absence nullifies any claim to human dignity), so here: to decide which neighbour has a claim is implicitly to decide which does *not* have a claim. As with Dietrich Bonhoeffer, who explores some related themes in his late ethical fragments, this is not to argue for either a 'situationist' moral programme or for a melodramatic and unreal sense of unrestricted emotional involvement or unlimited guilt; it is to grasp that the imperative of love requires the most rigorous and self-forgetting attention to the specific circumstances we confront moment by moment.

It is in this light that we can formulate something of what can be said about the eschatological hope of Christians, the subject of the final chapter here. If it is true that finite being is summoned to a communion with infinite trinitarian being in which the act and purpose of that infinite love is no longer an *object*, an external force, but a permeating or saturating presence, the end that is hoped for is that 'non-dual non-identity' which our habitual categories of speech accommodate with such difficulty, but which is already real in the incarnate Word. And this is why it matters – following the lead of theologians like John Zizioulas and Christos Yannaras, converging on this despite their differences of emphasis – to look at the 'routine' elements of Christian practice in an eschatological light: they are not to be understood just as a set of religious behaviours, but as moments where finite and infinite, present and eschatological future overlap in such a way that the world is seen afresh, seen in that 'dispassionate' light evoked by the spiritual tradition of Evagrios and Maximos; not a programme or an ideology, but an epiphany. This is a recurrent theme in recent Orthodox thinking, discernible in the liturgical theologies of Schmemann and Clément, and – more globally and forcefully still – in Christos Yannaras's eloquent denunciation of the reduction of the 'ecclesial event' to religiosity.[5]

---

[5] Christos Yannaras, *Against Religion: The Alienation of the Ecclesial Event*, tr. Norman Russell (Brookline, MA, Holy Cross Orthodox Press 2013). See, for example, pp. 106–7: 'In tradition the participants in the ecclesial event discern whether the gospel, the good news of their hopes, has any realistic capital in terms of existential *meaning* and perspective, or whether it consists of "cleverly devised myths" (2 Peter 1.16), ideological programs and religious pseudo-consolations ... Knowledge of the witness of the Gospels is an event and experience of *relation* ... Only the experience of participation in the things signified (and not simply information about the events) saves the ecclesial event from its alienation into a product of ideology.'

Ultimately the question raised here is one of how theology may be steered back to this basic issue of our actual rootedness in the eternal life of *logos*, and more particularly in the life of the Logos made flesh in which is manifest the calling and destiny of creation itself. Beginning from the practical reflections of monastic writers on how we allow the act of the trinitarian God to suffuse our creatureliness in contemplation, we shall be trying to see how the defining doctrinal themes of the Christian tradition make sense within, and make sense *of*, the practices of shared faith. The result is not a systematic but – I hope – a coherent theological approach to prayer, the nature of the Church and the imperatives of public and social witness. The book's title picks up an image used by the great fifth-century writer Diadochos of Photike (see below, p. 18): looking east in winter we feel the warmth of the sun on our faces, while still sensing an icy chill at our backs. Our divided and distorted awareness of the world is not healed instantly. But we are not looking at this phenomenon from a distance: we do truly sense the sun on our faces; and we have good reason to think that the climate and landscape of our humanity can indeed be warmed and transfigured. And, as Yannaras so stresses, this is the promise that the Church must embody if it is to be credible in what is at the moment a notably wintry world.

PART ONE

PROLOGUE

I

THEOLOGIZING THE LIFE
OF THE SPIRIT: THE WORLD
OF THE *PHILOKALIA*

'The ascetical writings collected in the *Philokalia*[1] have a tremendous success in some esoteric groups that are supremely indifferent to the life, death and resurrection of Jesus Christ.' So wrote Fr Alexander Schmemann, one of the most creative of twentieth-century Orthodox theologians, in that profound and luminous little book, *The World as Sacrament*.[2] The sentiments are very characteristic; they can be found reiterated in a number of places in Schmemann's Journals[3] as part of a general and deeply felt suspicion of monastic elitism and a precious and self-conscious spirituality that deserved all of the Nietzschean polemic against a religion that created unreal feelings for unreal objects and so took away the essential distinctive sign of Christianity – the eschatological joy of the sacraments, announcing the transfiguration of this world. Thus you will find him deploring 'the reduction of everything in Orthodoxy to the "Fathers" and

---

[1] I have used the four-volume Greek text published by Astir in Athens; quotations in English are from the four volumes so far published of the translation under the general editorship of G. E. H. Palmer, Philip Sherrard and Kallistos Ware: *The Philokalia: The Complete Text Compiled by St Nikodimos of the Holy Mountain and St Makarios of Corinth* (London, Faber & Faber 1979, 1981, 1984 and 1995). References in the text are to the volumes and page numbers of this translation.

[2] (London, Darton, Longman and Todd 1966), p. 138; the work is better known in the United States under its alternative title, *For the Life of the World*.

[3] *The Journals of Father Alexander Schmemann, 1973–1983* (Crestwood, NY, St Vladimir's Seminary Press 2000).

"Spirituality"! ... The triumph nowadays of a sectarian "only"! Only the Fathers, only "Dobrotolubie" [that is, the Slavonic version of the *Philokalia*], only typikon [the texts of liturgical services]. Boredom, mediocrity and lack of seriousness and talent in it all.'[4]

It is apparently a severe indictment of the world of spiritual vision and counsel we are examining – and perhaps it is one that would be shared by other theologians impatient with spiritual preciousness and wary of what might seem to relativize or sidestep the sacramental reality of life in the Church. But it may be possible to show that what is being criticized by Schmemann is a way of approaching these texts that systematically avoids their broad theological vision, reducing them to just that limited and self-enclosed 'spirituality' he always claimed not to understand. Schmemann's own theology of the sacramentality of the world in Christ is, I should want to argue, exactly where we should begin in rereading the *Philokalia*, and exactly where a thoroughgoing theological reading will lead us back again.

But there is of course a double risk in addressing this subject. Apart from the danger of presumption in dealing with it outside the specific context of spiritual practice and the acquisition of discernment, there is the obvious risk involved in someone formed largely by Western spiritual and intellectual currents attempting to trace the chief features of these Eastern sources. In all that follows, the reader must bear these dangers in mind. But in a context where spirituality and doctrine are still regarded as separate matters by so many, it may not be a waste of time to try to show how the contemplative practice to which the *Philokalia* is a guide both presupposes and reinforces a set of beliefs about God and creation. For the authors of the *Philokalia*, revelation was essentially the gift of a wisdom that opened up fresh possibilities for human action – or, more accurately, that restored possibilities lost by human sin and ignorance. The person examining himself or herself in the light of these texts is a person learning how to

---

[4] *Journals*, p. 130.

live truthfully in the world as it really is; and such truthful living is not possible without both the self-manifestation of God and the self-giving of God into human activity. There is no 'spirituality' free of doctrine, and the fashionable modern opposition between spirituality and religion is meaningless in the context of the *Philokalia*.[5] The health and maturity of the human spirit are dependent on purified awareness, 'watchfulness', *nepsis*, the key concept of the *Philokalia*, and such awareness is necessarily a matter of being alert to false and imprisoning accounts of who and what the human subject is – and of who and what God is.

One other introductory observation. In what follows, I have concentrated a good deal (though not exclusively, especially in the later parts of this chapter) on the earlier texts in the *Philokalia*, simply because they are the ones in which the vocabulary and thought-world of the later selections are most vividly mapped out. Many of the most copious texts in the later sections add little to the substance of the theological analysis of the human subject and of the development of contemplation outlined earlier; some are, in effect, recastings of earlier ones (such as those of John Klimakos).[6] Where they add significantly to the theology of the whole corpus is in two areas: the practical outworkings of the underlying concepts of hesychastic prayer, and (especially in the texts from Gregory Palamas) some fresh and bold proposals for better understanding the character of divine action and relation.

I

Given what has just been said about the need for awareness of false accounts of the human and the divine, a good place to start is with the idea of nature in the *Philokalia*. For anything to be

[5] For some reflections on this issue in relation to recent discussions, see Rowan Williams, 'The Spiritual and the Religious: Is the Territory Changing?' in Rowan Williams, *Faith in the Public Square* (London, Bloomsbury 2012), pp. 85–96.
[6] The most marked instance of this is the paraphrase of the Macarian Homilies made by Symeon Metaphrastes, vol. III of the Greek text, pp. 171–234, vol. III of the English translation, pp. 285–353.

13

natural is for it to be as God intends, to be in the state in and for which God created it. Hesychios (I, p. 194) summarizes the classical view of this idea towards the end of his treatise *On Watchfulness and Holiness* (#179): the natural state of human beings is the 'beauty, loveliness and integrity' of the first creation. Quoting Athanasius's *Life of Antony*, Hesychios accepts the identification of holiness with the 'natural' state, which is clear perception. But the condition we experience as habitual is the opposite of clear perception: it is a state of bondage to images that are seen or sensed as objects for the mind's satisfaction. The intelligence[7] can receive impressions in two basic ways, defined by Mark the Ascetic (*On the Spiritual Law*, #87, I, p. 116) as 'passionate' or 'objective' (*monotropos*, literally 'in a single or simple mode'; the significance of this notion of 'simple' perception will be apparent in our later discussion). We may perceive objects either as related to the unreconstructed needs of the human self or as related to the single intelligible purpose of the creator. It is a distinction rooted in the analyses offered by Evagrios, whose treatise on 'discrimination' (otherwise familiar outside the philokalic tradition as *On Thoughts*)[8] had distinguished between thinking of the things of the world with and without desire and had (#7, I, pp. 42–3; cf. #4, p. 40) elaborated this concept further in terms of the differences between angelic, diabolical and human awareness. The angel knows the 'essence' of things – though 'meaning' might be a better rendering: how they work in the providence of God in the natural order and how they serve the purpose of God in the historical order as well. The demon is aware of a thing only as something to be acquired and used for profit. Human awareness is initially and primitively just the registering of the image of an object without either meaning or

---

[7] I have decided to use 'intelligence' to render *nous* rather than the 'intellect', preferred by the English translators, on the grounds that 'intellect' has for most readers a narrower and more conceptually focused sense than 'intelligence'.

[8] Edited by Paul Gehin and Claire Guillaumont, *Sur las pensées*, Sources Chrétiennes 438 (Paris, Les Éditions du Cerf 1998).

craving attached. So what watchfulness entails is awareness of the moment at which this bare 'human' consciousness becomes diabolical, becomes bound to the acquisitive mode of perceiving; and the implication is that what will stabilize the mind is the infusion of angelic awareness, seeing the things of the world in their true – that is, symbolic – significance and using them accordingly (cf., for example, Maximos, *First Century on Love* #92, II, p. 63). This is a 'natural' state in that it relates human consciousness to the real significance of things. And this allows us to say that the world as it is has nothing in it that is intrinsically evil, whether in soul or body: everything has the capacity to convey the divine intelligence and so to be related to human intelligence in its proper state (Maximos, *Second Century on Love* #76ff., II, pp. 78–9). For the human intelligence – and thus the life that intelligence organizes – to be natural is to perceive the world as comprehensively significant; and because the world is significant in relation to God, it cannot take its significance from its potential for self-directed or self-serving human use.

This concept may illuminate the Maximian doctrine (e.g., *First Century on Love* #71, II, p. 60) that our love is properly directed towards the nature of other human beings, since this is one and the same for all. Love cannot be dependent on circumstance or attitude; we do not love perfectly if our love depends on someone's positive relation to us, but only when we accept the variety and instability of how others treat us or regard us. In this attitude we follow the example of Christ, who suffered for all; like him we can offer hope to all, even if we cannot dictate their response to this offer. Behind this in turn lies the conviction that God's love in general must be a love for human nature in its pristine glory: with the righteous, such love affirms and rewards a nature exercising its own proper gifts; with the unrighteous, it shows compassion for the loss of 'natural' dignity (ibid., #25, p. 55). In other words, as with the world of things, so with the world of other human subjects: the significance of other human beings depends not on what they do, least of all on what they do to make me secure or comfortable, but on what they intrinsically are. It may seem at first as though Maximos is commending an essentially impersonal kind of love, love for humanity in general; but in fact the exact opposite is the case. Love depersonalizes when it treats the neighbour as significant primarily in relation to myself; it is rightly directed towards the unique reality of the person when it sees the other in relation to God – as, in the proper sense, symbolic, a living sign of the creator, irreducible either to generalities or to the other's specific significance and usefulness for me.

Thus a coherent and subtle picture is built up of the natural activity of human intelligence. As Maximos says at the end of the *First Century on Love* (#97, p. 64), the restored human consciousness is either looking at human affairs without craving and the desire to dominate, or looking at the principles and processes of the world in their God-given order, or opening itself to the light of the Trinity. It is, in other words, receptive to what is actually there, to the human and the non-human world in their primordial relation to God, and to God as the source of the web of significance, of meaningful interaction and interdependence, which makes the universe a system of mutual gift and enlightenment. And in Maximos's scheme, this process is evidently connected with the conviction that we cannot know God 'in essence' but only by participating in his act or energy (e.g., *First Century*, #96, 100, p. 64, *Third Century*, #22–7, pp. 86–7). To know the 'essences' of things is simply to know their meaning in relation to God's action in the universe; but God's 'significance' is what it is, dependent on no contingent and particular thing. To know God can only be to know him in his character as the giver of significance through his action of self-bestowing – in what is revealed of his life in Trinity and in his acts of creation and providential sustaining. The not-knowing that is central to the true contemplative enterprise is here both a 'referral' of the meaning of all things to God and an acknowledgement that God's 'meaning' is within himself alone. When we turn to the texts from Gregory Palamas in the later parts of the *Philokalia*, it is important to remember that the famous distinction drawn by him between the ineffable divine 'essence' and the 'energies' through which God communicates with creation is not primarily a solution to a metaphysical problem (there are many complications in treating it as such)[9] but a way of codifying this vision of a world in which all meanings rest on a divine act whose own meaning can never be specified with reference to anything else, whose being is never therefore to be thought of as functional to any specific created agenda or narrative.

To return for a moment to the matter of humanity's natural state, it is clear that the early philokalic authors understand this as a capacity for non-passionate (non-acquisitive, non-self-directed) awareness of the world comparable in some sense to God's perception of the world (which is by definition disinterested, since God needs nothing from the world and is not given either being or intelligibility in terms of or in relation to the world). This capacity is obscured; indeed it could be said that the essential character of sin or fallenness in the *Philokalia* is our inability to see the world, including our fellow-humans, without 'passion', without the compulsion: that is, to see them in terms of our own supposed needs and fantasies. It is Diadochos of Photike who, in his treatise *On Spiritual Knowledge*, gives one of the most suggestive accounts of what the Fall effects. We discover, says Diadochos, in the course of our growth in illumination by the Spirit, that human sensation is primitively one and undivided (#25, 29, I, pp. 259, 260–1). In unfallen humanity, the variations of bodily sensation among the five senses are due only to the varying needs of the body – that is, they are diverse aspects of a single disposition of receptivity (the *monotropos* condition already noted in the vocabulary of Mark the Ascetic). The body's receptivity is not separate from that of the intelligence. But in the fallen state, perception has become divided. This division is not, it seems, simply a division of body from soul or sensible

[9] An excellent treatment can be found in Reinhard Flogaus, *Theosis bei Palamas und Luther: Ein Beitrag zum Ökumenischen Gespräch* (Göttingen, Vandenhoeck and Ruprecht 1997), ch. 2.

from intellective, but a division between self-oriented and other-oriented perceiving. Both bodily sense and intelligence are split between their natural openness to things as they are (to the 'symbolic' world, to use the Evagrian phrasing mentioned earlier) and the compulsion to obscure this true perception through selfish will, through the 'passionate' consciousness that replaces the reality with a simulacrum, a passion-laden perception that is designed to serve the self's agenda.

Thus, for Diadochos, the gift of the Holy Spirit in baptism and the life of grace thereafter is the restoration of simplicity. 'The form imprinted on the soul is single and simple' (ibid., #78, I, p. 280). The morally complex and spiritually strenuous condition of the baptized person is not a sign that there are two 'powers' at work still within us (Diadochos is determined to avoid any suggestion of the alleged Messalian model of two spirits within the believer), but the somewhat paradoxical mark of the gradual process by which simplicity establishes itself as normal. Continuing battle is a different matter, he says, from captivity (#82, p. 283). At first, in the new world of the Spirit, we cannot think good thoughts without being aware of their opposite: this is the continuing legacy of Adam's split consciousness.[10] We know the good in contrast to the destructive possibilities that we cannot forget (because they have been so habitual to us). In one of Diadochos's characteristically vivid images, we are like a man facing east at dawn in winter: the sun rises and warms him in front while he is still aware of the chill at his back. But the illustration shows that this is not a picture of two powers fighting within the soul, but a phase in the steady expansion of grace to fill soul and body. The renewed perception given to the believer allows us to be confident that a process is in hand that is out of our control but directed

---

[10] It is interesting to compare this with the theology of the Anglican layman Charles Williams, who, in his idiosyncratic but powerful and original essay, *He Came Down from Heaven* (London, Faber 1938), writes of the Fall of Adam and Eve: 'They knew good; they wished to know good and evil. Since there was not – since there never has been and never will be – anything else than the good to know, they knew good as antagonism' (p. 19).

firmly towards a new wholeness. In another memorable image, Diadochos speaks (#89, p. 288) of baptismal grace as the divine artist's monochrome sketch; it is for us in conscious collaboration with the Spirit to fill in the colours. And, 'when the full range of colours is added to the outline, the painter captures the likeness of the subject, even down to the smile'.

The artist is painting the likeness of the divine original: if we pursue the metaphor in detail, its implication is that God is painting a self-portrait in the elements of human nature, beginning with the act of decisive liberation that makes the whole enterprise possible, continuing with the distinctive and complex way in which human freedom energized by the Spirit in turn becomes an image of divine freedom, and so of divine love also. What the fuller implications of this picture might be for a theology of the trinitarian life is something to which we shall be returning, but for now the point is that we are habitually held back in what might rather awkwardly be called the natural process of becoming natural. The capacity we possess in virtue of our humanity, according to Evagrios, the capacity for passion-free or passion-neutral perception, is naturally oriented towards the 'symbolic' consciousness of specific things and persons in their relation to God. And as a result of Adam's divided perception, the introduction into human awareness of the perception of the world as symbolic only of the self's imagined needs, we need restoration. Habituated to this false awareness of the world, we have become forgetful of our nature and have to be awakened and to keep awake; as Mark the Ascetic observes (*On the Spiritual Law* #61–2, I, p. 114), forgetfulness is a form of ontological deficiency, a step towards self-destruction, a state of mind that is not only absorbed in unreal objects but is itself a shadow existence. Forgetting your nature is death; awareness is the condition for life. When Christ's gracious action has opened the way to 'natural understanding' (Mark, *Letter to Nicolas the Solitary*, I, p. 149), the dual habits of contrition and gratitude keep before us the nature we had almost lost and preserve us from defeat by the passion of lust and anger, which – to use an awkward but helpful phrasing – de-realize other

19

things and *persons*, making them either objects for possession and manipulation or objects of hatred and fear. Keeping the commandments so as to preserve baptismal purity, not out of hope for reward (e.g., Mark, *On Those Who Think That They Are Made Righteous by Works*, #23, #57), is the precondition for that openness to the full life of the Spirit in contemplative vision that is the fully natural state of human life. 'He who seeks the energies of the Spirit, before he has actively observed the commandments, is like someone who sells himself into slavery and who, as soon as he is bought, asks to be given his freedom while still keeping his purchase money' (ibid., #64, p. 130). As Maximos argues (*Second Century on Love* #4ff., II, p. 65), practical virtue, obedience to the commandments, detaches our intelligence from 'passionate' thinking; we are trained to respond to the world around us without allowing our self-serving instinct to distort. But this is only a step towards the radical receptivity to God's life that is experienced in 'undistracted prayer', pure *eros* towards God (ibid., #6, II, pp. 65–6). In other words, obeying the practical precepts of God's commandments, the acquiring of virtuous habit, keeps us alert to our true nature in such a way that we both guard against the entry into the intelligence of passionate perceiving and keep the door open to the Spirit's work that activates the deepest potential of the intelligence, the Christ-reflecting potential (about which, again, more later).

There is, incidentally, what may seem to be a surface contradiction between this picture and that suggested by the *Gnomic Anthology* of Ilias the Presbyter, a work probably from around 1100, where there is a sequence of texts on the relation between ascetic practice and contemplation (*Anthology* IV, esp. 33–60, III, pp. 52–5) apparently implying that some arrive at contemplation by way of asceticism and some come first to contemplation and move on to asceticism (see in particular #57: 'Where people of greater intelligence are concerned, contemplation precedes [*proageitai*] ascetic practice, whereas in the case of the more obtuse, ascetic practice precedes contemplation'). However, the translation is misleading here. It is quite clear from the whole section that contemplation is the superior state and that – as Maximos and others had insisted – *praktike* alone cannot take us beyond the ethical realm and deliver renewed spiritual vision. It is also clear that the contemplative habit cannot be arrived at without the steady presence of *praktike* (cf., for example, #77, III, p. 57). Thus the verb (*proago*) translated 'precede' in the controverted passage (#57, III, p. 55) has surely to be read as 'takes precedence' or 'is more highly valued or preferred' – i.e., not in a temporal sense. The properly enlightened value contemplation more highly, the 'more obtuse' prefer the more manageable or measurable activity of asceticism – and are accordingly more at risk of never realizing what they are called to and equipped for. In an intriguing anticipation of Teresa of Avila at the end of the *Interior Castle*, Ilias (#56) contrasts the ascetic who wants to 'depart and be with Christ' so that their struggles may be at an end, with the mature contemplative who is content to live in the present moment, both because of the joy it contains and because of the good that may be done to others.[11] The contemplative is the person who has arrived at the place where they stand in the world, the person present to the God who is present in all times and places; the 'pure' ascetic is the person who refuses the present for the future. This refusal has its place, dialectically, in the process of growth – so much is clear from any texts in this tradition – but the point of it is the return to present actuality as seen and sensed 'in God'.

II

The natural state of the human intelligence is thus a level of 'mindfulness' that is essentially opposed to the irrationality of passion. 'Irrationality' here means simply out of alignment with what is truly the case – arbitrary, 'mindless' love or hate, or a desire

---

[11] See Teresa's *Spiritual Testimonies* 17 and 37 (in Kieran Kavanaugh, OCD, and Otilio Rodriguez, OCD, trans.: *The Collected Works of St Teresa of Avila*, vol. 1 (Washington, Institute of Carmelite Studies 1976), pp. 329 and 341).

for what is not needed (Maximos, *Second Century* #16, II, p. 67). What is natural is, once again, receptivity to what is, grounded in the conscious acknowledgement of what one is oneself. And if I recognize myself as God's image, my intelligence as participating in the contemplative perceiving exercised by God towards the world, I recognize both the possibility of 'innocent', passion-free perception and the calling to enlarge this towards Evagrios's 'angelic' awareness, the unified and symbolic consciousness that connects us with the inner life of the contingent world. The merely human in Evagrios's schema is naturally open to the angelic or supernatural.

But the vocabulary is fluid in this area. Mark (*On Those Who Think* ... #90, I, p. 132) characterizes the restored natural state as one in which we acknowledge not only that we are in the image of God but also that we are ourselves the source of our own difficulties: natural awareness is mindfulness of our fragility, our capacity not only for dispassionate knowledge but also for passion. Natural awareness includes the knowledge that we may become unnatural in our intelligence, forgetting that our troubles arise from within (even if they are activated by the demonic forces) and projecting them on to others so that conflict and resentment arise. Self-awareness means that we become ready to receive what is 'above nature', the fruits of the Spirit. It is clear that any search here for a tightly consistent lexicon of nature and supernature is misplaced. Natural intelligence is simply truthful intelligence. In the unfallen state of 'nature' this would mean an openness to passion-free relation to the world, which would lead into the perception of the causes of things, the structure of divine wisdom embodied in creation. But the division of consciousness has made this state problematic: we have been lured into passionate perception. Natural awareness now is the awareness of inner dividedness, the coexistence of the possibility of passion-free, unselfish knowing and acting with the possessive fantasizing that enslaves intelligence and traps us in forgetfulness and unreality, and thus ultimately in death. The practice of the commandments teaches us to identify and fight against selfish and forgetful habits by recognizing the behaviours that exemplify passion; and the self-awareness arising from ascetic practice properly understood reminds us of the deeper truth of our own nature and its possibilities and prepares us for the liberation given by the Spirit – a stage of experience that cannot be guaranteed by any amount of asceticism but that cannot take root without the habits of self-examination and self-control.

This state helps us make sense also of the superficially puzzling language of Isaiah the Solitary about passion that is 'according to nature' (*On Guarding the Intellect* #1, and cf. 18, 19, 25; I, pp. 22, 25–7). Anger at the intrusion into the intelligence of alien habit is a precondition for the 're-naturalizing' of the intelligence – by way of releasing the proper use of *epithumia*, desire, towards God (ibid., p. 25) – and so is itself in a sense natural. The general point is found in Evagrios (*On Discrimination* #15, 16, I, pp. 47–8) and Cassian (*On the Eight Vices*, I, p. 83), who uses the same language as Isaiah about anger 'according to nature': 'natural' anger is the repudiating of what is unnatural in the intelligence, i.e., self-serving habits of mind. It is a theme that has quite a long ancestry in Platonic and Stoic discussion and in, for example, the spiritual theology of the Cappadocians,[12] but it is here given a more specific analysis. Diadochos (*On Spiritual Knowledge* #6, I, p. 254) attempts a useful terminological refinement by speaking of an 'incensive' response (*thumos*) that is free from anger (*aorgatos*). When this response is engaged in the battle against irrational passions, the believer must be silent; only when calm is restored can words of praise again be uttered (#10, p. 255). The example of Jesus is cited (#62, p. 272), as he is three times said in John's Gospel to have been moved and troubled (John 11.33, 12.27 and 13.21): he chooses to let his spirit be disturbed by anger against evil and death, even though he does not need his will reinforced by this reaction. The implication is that he makes his spirit vulnerable in this way to remind us that there

---

[12]For a good recent study covering some of this territory, see Paul M. Blowers, 'Envy's Narrative Scripts: Cyprian, Basil, and the Monastic Sages on the Anatomy and Cure of the Invidious Emotions', *Modern Theology* 25.1 (2009), pp. 21–43.

is a proper use of anger directed against the unnatural effects of evil. A pity, Diadochos adds, that Eve did not use anger against the serpent's temptation. The essential point is simply that anger used against any other person is unnatural – not least because it implies that the source of our problems or failures is in someone else's acts and dispositions (cf. the brief and crystal-clear enunciation of this idea by Peter of Damascus, *Spiritual Reading*, III, p. 156). But it is not even that we are encouraged to be angry with ourselves in the ordinary sense. Just as we are told to love our nature and the nature of all people, our anger rightly used is an anger about the devastation of nature overall: it is something like a cry of protest against the freedom we have all lost. This also illuminates why compassion is said to be the best specific against anger (e.g., Evagrios, *On Discrimination* #3, I, p. 40; cf. Maximos, *Third Century on Love*, #90, II, p. 97): the 'incensive power' rightly used is in effect compassion, an intense protest against another's suffering or slavery. To be 'natural' in this connection is to recognize that our restoration to liberty is not purely a matter of reasoning: the positive effect of the divided self is that the debased and forgetful caricature of humanity to which we have become so accustomed can be an object of both reflection and emotion to the convalescent soul as its self-awareness is deepened and clarified. The process of becoming natural is energized by thought and feeling alike, and the passionate or instinctual dimensions of the inner life can be deployed in an unselfish way to push us further towards proper dispassion, which is the gateway to love, in the well-known phrase of Evagrios.[13]

One final point is worth underlining about the restoration of nature, a point already touched on in various ways. Restored nature draws together the scattered powers of perception and re-establishes simplicity; and this means that the body as well as the intelligence is involved. Isaiah the Solitary speaks of a new and inseparable union between body, soul, and spirit brought

---

[13] 'Love is the daughter of *apatheia*'; Evagrios, *Praktikos*, Prologue 8 and ch. 81.

about by the Holy Spirit (#18, I, p. 26); and Diadochos sees the 'single and simple perceptive faculty' bestowed by the Spirit as allowing the intelligence to share its joy with the body (*On Spiritual Knowledge* #25, I, p. 259). In other words, although we generally think of what might be called a renewed or restored 'attitude' towards what is seen and sensed, the philokalic vision is of bodily senses themselves working in a somewhat different way. What this might mean is not clear – though there are other traditions of meditation, notably certain Buddhist disciplines, that would echo the idea and might offer some lines for investigation. The point is clearly connected with the teachings of Symeon the New Theologian and the fourteenth-century hesychasts about the physical sensing of uncreated light, but this is not, I think, the only thing in mind here.

However, the mention of this quietly recurrent theme in the *Philokalia*, the renewal of the body in the restored simplicity of the life of the Holy Spirit (the theosis of the body in Maximos's terms (*Second Century on Theology* #88, II, p. 160)), provides a helpful focus for grasping one of the controlling ideas in the anthropology of the *Philokalia*. We are not yet natural. Instead of envisaging 'nature' as a basic condition that can straightforwardly be recovered or released, the texts present a more nuanced and psychologically complex picture. Created with certain capacities, we have in one sense irretrievably lost our starting point. We have known division and cannot behave as if the divided intelligence could be ignored or overcome by wishing it so. We are as a consequence living in some degree of unreality; we are not really here. The body's habitual response to stimuli has become either defence or absorption (anger or lust), so that we are chronically unable to exist as part of an interdependent created order. To learn to do so requires us to be educated in how we identify destructive behaviour (keeping the commandments) and so to check these habitual responses. In the process, something begins to happen to the instinctive life of aggression and desire, which reconstitutes it as a positive discontent with the present state of slavery. We recognize that we actively and profoundly want something other than the life of passion and fantasy. And that uncovered or reconstituted wanting is our opening up to the life for which we were made and that is made accessible to us once again in baptism, in the identification of ourselves with the self-giving Word of God incarnate. Beyond this, it is the Spirit who acts for the transformation of our awareness, physical and mental, so that the simplicity for which we were designed may pervade our intelligence. Throughout that lifetime's labour, the awareness of the gulf between what we may be and what we have made of ourselves continues to act as a goad to preserve the habit of self-questioning and penitence. We do not simply stop being divided; we learn to use our very dividedness to cast into a stronger light the possibility of a proper presence in and to the world and its maker.

The intelligence that has not yet remembered itself is not yet truly embodied. Our problem, if this reading of the *Philokalia* is correct, is not that we are embodied spirits, but that we are *incompletely* embodied spirits – that is, that we are as yet unable to live in this material and mutable world without clinging to our impressions, distorting our impressions, or compulsively marking out our territory. The things of the world – and our human neighbours in the world – appear either as food or as threat to the ego. Unless we become able to receive the truth of what is before us as it stands in relation to God, not to us, we are failing to be embodied in the sense of being properly part of creation: we are caught in an implicit idolatry, the effort to separate ourselves from the order of which we are a part.

Numerous scholars of early and medieval Christianity, such as Peter Brown, Margaret Miles and Caroline Walker Bynum,[14] have in recent years challenged the cliché that patristic theology

[14] See, among a large literature by these and other writers, Peter Brown, *The Body and Society: Men, Women and Sexual Renunciation in Early Christianity* (New York and London, Faber 1988); Margaret Miles, *Fullness of Life: Historical Foundations for a New Asceticism* (Philadelphia, Westminster Press 1981); *Carnal Knowing: Female Nakedness and Religious Meaning* (Boston, Beacon Press 1989); Caroline Walker Bynum, *Holy Feast and Holy Fast: The Religious Significance of Food to Mediaeval Women*, Berkeley (Los Angeles and London, University of California Press 1987).

and ascetic practice simply internalized a radical opposition between body and soul borrowed from Platonism. We have been reminded that the body is understood as that which connects us to the world, as that which speaks and symbolizes the truth that is being realized in the spirit, and so on. Schmemann, in a memorable passage in his Journals,[15] insists that proper instruction in Christianity 'should start with the body. In the body, everything is given for communication, knowledge, communion'. The intriguing recent work of David Jasper[16] argues that the body in early monastic spirituality is above all the sign of a 'kenotic' abandonment of pretensions to spiritual power, so that bodily ascesis becomes a way of 'reducing' the self to the limitations of the body, not an effort to transcend them. But what lies behind all of this is the belief, articulated in some of the earliest of the philokalic writings, that what needs to be overcome in human consciousness is the alliance of 'perception', whether bodily or mental, with self-interest. The body's needs, sensations and impressions are capable of being freed from the compulsion either to devour on the one hand or to expel or repulse on the other. Ascetic practice and contemplation alike are the means by which this freedom is sustained, though, as we have seen, we cannot achieve our own liberation by our own efforts; we are always responding to the gift of renewal offered us in Christ and the Spirit.

And it is significant that when Hesychios spells out what watchfulness or mindfulness practically entails, he turns to the Jesus Prayer as the activity that above all brings together action and contemplation. It is an action, an ascetical practice, in one sense; but it is also the means of sustaining contemplative self-awareness. 'Letters cannot be written on air; they have to be inscribed in some material if they are to have any permanence' (*On Watchfulness and Holiness*, #183, I, p. 195): the Jesus Prayer

---

[15] *Journals*, p. 157.
[16] *The Sacred Body: Asceticism in Religion, Literature, Art and Culture* (Waco, TX, Baylor University Press 2009), esp. ch. 1.

27

is an 'inscription' of watchfulness in the rhythm of the human body. It invokes the presence that makes it ultimately impossible to live in a divided state, the presence that cannot coexist with demonic fantasies: 'He does not allow them to project in the mind's mirror even the first hint of their infiltration' (ibid., #174, p. 193). As Diadochos further explains (On *Spiritual Knowledge*, #59. I, pp. 270–1), the invocation of the Name is the activity through which the intelligence is held and stabilized when all images and concepts of God have been laid aside. Evagrios's teaching that the contemplative comes to see the light of his or her own intelligence (as in On *Discrimination* #18 and #52, for example, I, p. 49) is here linked to the practice of the Jesus Prayer: what we come to see in our hearts as a result of consistent practice is the fire of Christ's presence burning away 'the filth which covers the surface of the soul'. And when passion has distracted us afresh, we can recover the freedom of our intelligence by simply beginning the action again, saying over the words until the intelligence 'catches up' with their meaning (Diadochos, ibid., #61, p. 271); something of the same underlies the advice in the *Discourse on Abba Philimon*, II, pp. 344–57, esp. pp. 347–9, and it becomes the foundation of later teaching on the practice of the Prayer – as, famously, in the narrative of the nineteenth-century Russian 'Pilgrim'.[17] Like children repeating words they do not understand, we say the words, waiting for the Spirit to help us in our weakness (Diadochos refers to Romans 8.26).

Thus, if we ask what the natural life is for human beings, one very straightforward answer is that, in practice, it is a life in which the intelligence is anchored in the constant invocation of the Name of Jesus. This practice, to pick up Hesychios's image, keeps the mind's mirror clear. And to understand this is to open up a further dimension of the theology of the *Philokalia*, which is simply the centrality of the belief that the essential

[17] See *The Pilgrim's Tale*, ed. and introduced by Aleksei Pentkovsky, trans. T. Allan Smith (New York and Mahwah, NJ, Paulist Press 1999).

activity of the intelligence is always and already grounded in the indwelling Word of God, so that what baptism does is to set free the indwelling Word to shape as it ought the life of the human agent. It is this process that also allows, in some of the medieval material (notably in Nikitas Stithatos and Gregory of Sinai; see, e.g., IV, pp. 144, 213, 220, 237), the analogy between contemplative practice and the Eucharist: the mature intelligence both offers and receives the Lamb of God and 'becomes an image of the Lamb as he is in the age to come' (Gregory of Sinai, *On Commandments and Doctrines*, #112, IV, p. 237). Granted that an explicit eucharistic theology is not an obvious major theme in the *Philokalia*, there are connections here that need drawing out as regards the 'eucharistic' character of the invocation of the Name of Jesus and of the assumption that the prayer of the specific contemplative is the prayer of Christ in his Body.

In the next section of this chapter, we shall look at how the themes we have so far examined point towards the underlying trinitarian theology of the *Philokalia*. So far, we have seen how the teaching of the *Philokalia* presupposes a many-layered analysis of human consciousness at the centre of which lies a very particular reading of the meaning of the image of God in us. It is an anthropology that goes far deeper than the conventional assumptions so often made by Christians and non-Christians alike about the division of body and soul or intellect and emotion; and in positing a fundamental unity of perception of what is lost in the Fall, it challenges all fragmented accounts of human knowing and sensing and insists that a restored humanity must be one in which bodily experience is given meaning. Doing this involves both the capacity to see the material world as 'symbolic', as communicating the intelligence and generosity of the creator, and the transformation of the body itself in its capacity to receive and manifest divine life. Restored humanity is humanity properly embodied, and this embodiment includes the freedom to relate to the things and the persons of the world as they are in relation to God. It is in this connection that the spirituality of the philokalic tradition may rightly be seen as the foundation for a social and environmental ethic capable of addressing the major public crises of our own time.[18]

The anthropology of the *Philokalia* has some obvious resonances with certain currents in both modern and postmodern philosophy. Its avoidance of a fixed account of human nature in terms of a static content sounds initially very congenial to an intellectual culture suspicious of metaphysical models of 'humanity-as-such'; and the idea of embodiment as a project rather than a given is also potentially intriguing for the contemporary theorist eager to deconstruct simplistic and uncritical views of the body. But a degree of caution is in order. The relative indeterminacy of the human intelligence and its embodied expression implies no scepticism about truth. What is often difficult for the contemporary intellect is to see that the contemplative tradition, in relativizing conceptual mastery and finality, is laying claim to another level of truthfulness. The world really is as it is; there is an 'objective' state of affairs in the universe, and it is truly related in every aspect to its maker. But our own truthfulness is more a matter of learning how to exist as a conscious but dependent part of that real or true order than it is of achieving a comprehensive and accurate picture of it, let alone of its maker. Truthfulness is a habit of receptivity, and it entails what I have been calling, in the wake of Evagrios, the ability to read the world symbolically – which does not mean reading it, in full-blown medieval style, as a collection of allegories, but understanding how to receive its diversity as the gift of a freely self-bestowing divine agency. This is where it is crucial for understanding the *Philokalia* to see how the ideal works of a renewed simplicity or singleness of apprehension, free from the anxious question of how I am to exercise power and impose meaning in my environment, human or otherwise.

---

[18]I have in mind here especially the work of a theologian like Christos Yannaras: among many works, see particularly his *Ontologia tis schesis* (Athens, Ikaros Press 2004).

The echoes of this approach in the Augustinian distinction between *scientia* and *sapientia* merit more exploration, insofar as Augustine is trying to identify a knowing that is not function-bound, not dictated by the question of how an object can usefully relate to me. But the philokalic texts establish this in closer connection with the practices of self-awareness, *nepsis*, which teach us to ask of every impression or sensation how far I am turning it into something other than itself by applying its significance to my needs and projections. Very much at the centre of the philokalic vision is the conviction that the ideal and purposed state of being for the human intelligence, its 'natural' life, is a welcoming receptivity to the other, without the violence that seeks either to possess or exclude. To quote Schmemann once more, for the baptized person in Christ, 'The world is again his life, not his death, for he knows what to do with it';[19] everything is now 'given to us as full of meaning and beauty' (ibid., p. 142). It is as we think through the implications of this as the natural, God-reflecting state of human intelligence that we may begin to see how this entire picture requires in turn a particular understanding of the divine nature and persons. To this we shall now turn in more detail.

III

For the created intelligence to become natural is for it to be anchored in the life of the Holy Spirit, which is also the life of the Word, the eternal divine intelligence that is the ground of all created intelligence. Thus Mark (*On Those Who Think … #225*, I, p. 145) describes the ascetic as called to keep on knocking at the door of *Christ's* internal dwelling – the natural intelligence within us that is being restored by the Spirit's grace. To be adopted children in and through the eternal Son is the essence of what baptism confers, a theme prominent in Mark

---

[19] *The World as Sacrament*, p. 91.

31

and Diadochos and richly developed in Maximos: what we aim at is not the perfect keeping of the commandments as some sort of human achievement, but the freedom to receive the gift of Christ being formed in us and to guard it by means of our watchfulness (see, for example, Mark, *On Those Who Think* ... #2, 64ff.; Diadochos, *On Spiritual Knowledge*, ##26, 61, 97–8, pp. 260, 271–2, 293–4). The implication is that our adoptive relation to the Father is a matter essentially of doing what Christ eternally does. Evagrios had said that in sharing the death of Christ through our death to self-oriented passion, we come to share Christ's contemplation of the Father (*On Discrimination*, #17, I, p. 49, echoed by Neilos, *Ascetic Discourse*, p. 201), and Diadochos, (*On Spiritual Knowledge* #61, I, pp. 271–2,) as we have noted, specifically connects the Spirit-aided repetition of the Name of Jesus (understood in terms of the promise in Romans 8.26 that the Spirit will express to God what we cannot express in words through our own prayers) with the cry of 'Abba', which characterizes the Spirit's indwelling (Romans 8.15; Galatians 4.6).

In other words, what the early philokalic authors are assuming is that the natural state of the intelligence is one in which the divine Word is free to live and act within the created subject: noetic prayer is the prayer that Christ offers in us. Thus, also, the sense in which the intelligence in us is the image of God cannot properly be abstracted from the recognition that the noetic image is a created mode of sharing in eternal contemplation; the image is not a static correspondence but an active participation in eternal love.

Maximos picks up this idea and develops it at various points in his *Centuries on Theology*, linking it to the Paschal theme that has been adumbrated in Evagrios and elsewhere. Christ is 'buried' in us as we bury all that has crucified him – our passions and even our intellectual conceptions – so that it is Christ alone who rises in us, marking the dawning of the 'eighth day' of creation, the mystical fulfilment of the process of God's work in us (*First Century on Theology* ##63–7, II, pp. 126–7). He is constantly dying and rising in us, crucified in our weakness, raised in our purification (*Second Century on Theology* #27, II, p. 144). The eternal Word is the 'mustard seed' of the gospel text (Matthew 13.31-2), containing all things in potentiality; it is sown in the human heart and when that heart is purified by the Spirit, the 'energies' of all things are awakened (*Second Century on Theology* ##10–11, II, pp. 140–1). Because all fullness is eternally in Christ, that fullness becomes ours when we open ourselves completely to his gift (ibid. #21, II, p. 142). Thus our failure to grow spiritually is a sort of imprisonment of Christ in ourselves, a crippling of his freedom (ibid., #30, II, p. 145). He seeks to be incarnate in our virtues, and, in our contemplation, to return to his original and eternal state (ibid., #37, II, pp. 146–7); we ascend with him to the Father, while also constantly being ready not to despise following him in 'incarnating' what we are through communicating the mystery to others (ibid., ##46–9, 55, II, pp. 148–9, 150). At the end of the second of the *Centuries on Theology*, Maximos explains Paul's language about having the *nous*, the 'mind' or 'discerning intelligence', of Christ (1 Corinthians 2.16) in terms of perfect alignment with and sharing in the eternal act of noetic contemplation that is Christ's. It is not that we acquire something 'extra' to our humanity or that something in our humanity is supplanted by grace, let alone that we somehow reproduce the unique union in Christ of divinity and humanity; simply that we are taken into the fullness of Christ's eternal life, just as we are taken into Christ's Body in our life within the baptized community (##83–4, II, pp. 158–9). In this way, we inherit the kingdom of God or of heaven, since this is nothing other than the life of Christ within us (ibid, #91ff., II, pp. 161–2), and body and soul are brought into final harmony through this indwelling (ibid., #100, II, p. 163).

So, to return briefly to the themes already outlined in the first two sections of this chapter, our proper and natural openness to all things, the free, renewed, non-possessive vision of the world that is given in the life of grace, is ultimately the contemplative energy of the second person of the Trinity within us, directed towards the Father and the world inseparably. The divine image may be spoken of in terms that seem remote from Christology, static or dualistic,[20] but the governing theological theme is clear. The journey towards the natural condition of the intelligence is a journey towards the uncovering of the act of Christ at the centre or ground of created intelligence. Hesychios's language about keeping the interior mirror clear is taken up and refined further by Philotheos of Sinai (Forty Texts on Watchfulness #23, III, p. 25): the mirror of the intelligence is meant to reflect 'Jesus Christ, the wisdom and power of God the Father'; when it is clear, we can see all things in the intelligence, since we can see that the kingdom is within us – clear echoes of Maximos here. In the same vein, Philotheos can say that, for the mature contemplative, there is 'another activity' going on within, the energeia of Christ (ibid., #37, III, p. 30). And Peter of Damascus stresses the fact that when we do the will of the Father we are assimilated to the Son (A Treasury of Divine Knowledge, III, p. 84), though he is less strong in his language than some others as to the actual embrace of created activity within the action of the Son.

In defining the action of the Son in this way, as the eternal contemplation of the Father, shared in the Spirit with the created intelligences that mirror this eternal life, the philokalic writers are setting out a very clear and distinctive approach to how the unity and plurality of divine life may be thought (however imperfectly). The relation of the eternal Logos to the Father begins to be understood – insofar as it ever can be – as we grasp the character of the selfless receptivity that is given us in the life of grace, the universal and dispassionate love (love that is neither defensive nor possessive) that allows us to be indwelt by the sheer reality

---

[20] It is a pity that the index to volume IV of the English translation has an entry (p. 442): 'divine image in man does not involve the body'; there is a difference between saying that the image is not a matter of bodily correspondence or does not primarily relate to any bodily characteristic and denying that the image includes bodily life in some way, as the texts cited under this heading will show.

of what is before us. Freed from the distortions of anger and possessive desire, we embrace in love and thanksgiving a world and a divine reality that are literally nothing but gratuitous gift or bestowal. And in entering such a state, or at least, as we might say, becoming able to imagine it as possible for us, we come to see something of what the exchange of life and goodness might be in that divine life that necessarily and eternally knows nothing of self-possession or self-withholding, nothing of the fear of loss or of absorption, but is the loving and joyful apprehension of sheer otherness.

IV

Maximos speaks of the contemplative's prayer as characterized by *eros* (*Second Century on Charity*, #6, II, p. 65); and the implication – given what has just been said about the alignment of human contemplation with the eternal contemplation of the Father by the Son – seems to be that we could in some way speak about perfect mutual *eros* as the mark of the trinitarian life. There is another passage, not in the *Philokalia*, where Maximos affirms that God in some sense participates in the *eros* towards himself that he has planted in human hearts (Amb. 48, PG 91, 1361B). But it is not until relatively late in the Byzantine period that there are signs of this implication being drawn out. It is Gregory Palamas who takes up these leads and pursues them in the direction of a systematic theology of intra-divine *eros*. And, although there are later writers who echo the hints of Maximos on the divine origin of human *eros* towards God (as, for example, in the chapters *On Prayer* of Patriarch Kallistos, ##21–2, pp. 327–9 of the Greek edition, as yet untranslated), Palamas's schema does not seem to have been developed – perhaps not surprisingly, given that it is both complex and tantalizingly briefly spelled out.

Much has been written about various aspects of the theology of Palamas's *Capita* ('Topics of Natural and Theological Science and on the Moral and Ascetical Life', as the title is rendered in the English translation of the *Philokalia*); and recent scholarship, especially the distinguished work of Reinhard Flogaus,[21] has opened up the complex question of the degree of dependence on Augustine's *De trinitate* in sections of this work. But this particular focus alone does not exhaust the unique interest of Palamas's treatment of the Trinity here. In sections 34–40 (IV, pp. 359–64), we have a model for the threefold divine life and for the image of that life in the created human subject that does not simply correspond either to an Augustinian pattern or to earlier Eastern ideas, but is, arguably, a creative fusion of these very diverse elements. And what is significant for our present purposes is that it is a model recognizably developing some of the leading themes of earlier philokalic material in respect of clarifying the theological basis of contemplative or hesychastic practice.

The basic structure is this. God is supremely and eternally *nous*, intelligence, and essentially or by definition 'goodness': this intelligence is, or has within it, wisdom and life, which are inseparable from goodness. They are conceptually but not in reality distinguishable, united in divine simplicity. If we speak of divine intelligence generating divine wisdom, a *logos* or object of intelligence coextensive with intelligence itself, we speak of that which is indistinguishable in its goodness from its source but distinguished simply by its relation as derived from the act of intelligence. Logos, it appears, is the 'content' of eternal intelligence expressed as what intelligence itself understands – intelligence producing that which mirrors itself. Eternal Logos is eternal self-knowledge. Palamas appeals (#35, IV, pp. 360–1) to the analogy of our own internal *logos* in a way that strongly evokes Augustine's interior *verbum*. But he goes on to say that we cannot conceive of an intelligent self-awareness such as we have just sketched as deprived of 'life' or 'spirit'; and these terms seem

---

[21] Quoted above, n. 9; see also his contribution to *Orthodox Readings of Augustine*, ed. Aristotle Papanikolaou and George E. Demacopoulos (Crestwood, NY, St Vladimir's Seminary Press 2008), 'Inspiration – Exploitation – Distortion: The Use of St. Augustine in the Hesychast Controversy', pp. 63–80.

to mean what we might call conscious mutual involvement, an eternal flow of life between the two terms that is not exhausted by talking about the basic relation of derivation.

> The Spirit of the supreme Logos is a kind of ineffable yet intense longing or eros experienced by the Begetter for the Logos born ineffably from Him, a longing experienced also by the beloved Logos and Son of the Father for His Begetter; but the Logos possesses this love by virtue of the fact that it comes from the Father in the very act through which He comes from the Father, and it resides co-naturally in Him. (#36, IV, p. 361)

St Gregory is clear about the single procession of the Spirit (ibid., IV, p. 362), but equally clear that the Spirit is the mutual joy or bliss of Father and Son, turned in love to each other.

Thus he can go on (#37, IV, p. 362) to explain how this concept shapes our understanding of the divine image in ourselves. Our created intelligence yearns for the content of what it spiritually understands; just as *logos* is born from the intelligence, so is *eros*, and the latter is present even when the former is inchoate or obscured. What is more, this erotic impulse is what sets us apart from the angelic orders and constitutes us more in the image of God than they are (#38–9, pp. 362–3): our *eros* generates and sustains life in the body and, despite its 'intellectual' character, cleaves in love to the body, which it does not want to abandon. And it is this body-related *eros* that becomes so dangerous for fallen humanity, when the intellective and the erotic energy are not properly directed towards the eternal prototype. The human subject is always at some level aware of its *eros* towards God, but unless the erotic identification with the body is rooted in the desire for God, it degenerates into a self-love that fragments the 'inner world' of the subject as trinitarian image (#40, IV, p. 364) and dooms the body to death – so that the fact that the body does not at once decay when the spirit has rebelled is the result of the providence of a just God who chooses, so to speak, to honour his own intention of giving life and to postpone the punishment that ought to follow in the course of nature (#46–8, pp. 367–9, #51, pp. 370–1).

Unmistakably, there are echoes of Augustine throughout these chapters, but what is most significant is the way in which the vocabulary of *eros* is deployed. Palamas implies that there is in the divine life an analogical foundation for the awareness of the incompleteness of the self in finite experience. Our intelligence is not simply *satisfied* with its self-awareness; it acknowledges the unfinished character of this awareness and longs for completion through relationship with its infinite source and archetype. And, in an idiom that is undoubtedly very bold in theological terms, Palamas posits, not an 'incompleteness' within God, which would be wholly untenable for him as for the entire Orthodox tradition of belief, but what we might call an eternal desire to exist *in* the other that is at the same time never consummated by any collapse into an undifferentiated identity. The 'desire' of the Father to be in the Son, to bestow all that is his as Father upon the Son, is never completed in the sense of pouring himself out without remainder or relation into the life of this divine Other. He is eternally confronted with the sheer otherness of the Son whom he generates. Likewise, the response of the Son to the Father is not a simple abjection and self-cancelling: it is again a desire to give life 'into' the other that is never exhausted. The otherness of the persons of the Trinity to each other is irreducible, and for that very reason their relation may be imagined as *eros*, as 'yearning' rather than consummation, since no amount of self-abnegating love can abolish the eternal difference – which would in fact be to abolish love itself.

But in what sense can we then, with Palamas, see this *eros* as 'hypostatic', as actually a divine person? The role of the Spirit as conceived in this model could be said to be the excess of excessive love itself. The Father begets the Son as that which is wholly other to him as Father and thus cannot ever 'absorb' the Son or be absorbed *by* the Son in his love, since that love is itself the ground of this absolute otherness, an otherness constituted not by any essential difference, any distinctness in predicates or qualities, but by the sheer self-giving of 'goodness'. But this means that when goodness has, so to speak, taken cognizance of its self-giving character in the generation of the otherness of the Logos, this does not exhaust the self-giving act of goodness: generative love does not merely see itself in the mirror of the Logos, a love going out and returning to its source in a way that closes a circle; it returns to itself from the other in a way that displays the inexhaustibility of its own generative or 'productive' agency. It is reflected back to itself as, precisely, the love that cannot ever be absorbed in the other, thus the love that can never be expressed simply as gift and return. For the Father to generate the Son, Palamas says, is for the Father to give to the Son the life that is already in him as Source, the life that is not capable of being absorbed in the other. The excess of love that generates the Son begets in the Son the same excessive love, a love that is not contained in the binary relation of giving and responding but 'overflows' eternally.

This is the 'life' that is designated by the name of 'Spirit'. Eternal intelligence sees itself in the Logos and because it sees *itself*, it sees its own uncontainable excess, already overflowing as the reality of *eros* and *zoe* that cannot be reduced to either the begetting or the begotten agency but is an equally eternal dimension of God's reality (it does not seem right to speak of a 'residue' here, which sounds much too passive, yet one might defend the word as indicating what is *not* spoken of just by speaking of the Father's begetting of the Son).

These are matters – we hardly need reminding – that strain the limits of what we can say. But it is essential to try to follow them through in this connection insofar as they frame what Palamas wants to say about our own spiritual *eros*. We carry the image of the trinitarian life: that is, we are not only intelligent and self-aware, we are carried out from ourselves in excess. The Logos exists in us only as that which moves us to excess, 'self-transcendence', if you want a rather stale technicality – that is, the Logos exists in us only as animated by *eros*, by the spirit that urges us to give to and live in the other. This is supremely about giving to and living in the divine Other, living in communion with the Father through Christ in the Spirit; but the tantalizing reference to the relation of all this to the body suggests that the Logos within us exists in a state of self-giving love towards that which is radically 'other' to the life of intelligence or spirit – towards the bodily world that it is called to make significant, to transform into a living sign of the trinitarian mystery of love. Our own *eros* towards what our divinely gifted intelligence can receive, our *eros* towards the harmony and meaningfulness of the universal Logos, is never restricted to simply being drawn into the Son's response to the Father, since that response in eternity is always overflowing into another 'otherness'.

In relation to Maximos's language about divine and human *eros*, what Palamas in effect adds is that for the human subject to 'mirror' the divine is not simply for human *logos* to participate in the eternal Logos, but for that human *logos* to be activated by *eros*, the dynamic of the Holy Spirit, in its unending urge to immerse itself in the foundational mystery *of nous* itself, which images and participates in the eternal self-giving intelligence that is the divine Source, the Father. Or in other words, for humanity to bear the image of the Son, to have the Son's life at the heart of finite human awareness, is what it means for it to bear the image of the Trinity; we cannot make sense of a humanity that is in the image of one divine person in isolation. We know that by the eleventh century the convention had developed of describing the divine image in humanity as threefold – *psuche noera, nous* and *logos* (Nikitas Stithatos, *On Spiritual Knowledge* #8, IV, p. 141), or *nous, logos* and *pneuma* (Gregory of Sinai, *On Commandments and Doctrines*, #31–2, IV, p. 218), which is closer to Palamas. But Palamas's originality is in doing very much what Augustine does in the *De trinitate*: moving from a discourse about the divine image that is essentially about correspondence (Gregory of Sinai's assimilation of the three persons to the three aspects of human subjectivity might risk that if left without supplement) to a discourse that places at the centre the *relation* of image to prototype as the crucial and irreducible element in a fully theological account of the divine image in us.[22]

---

[22] David Bentley Hart's essay in *Orthodox Readings of Augustine* ('The Hidden and the Manifest: Metaphysics After Nicaea', pp. 191–226, esp. pp. 221–5) has some illuminating perspectives on parallels between Augustine and Gregory of Nyssa that would bear on the present discussion.

'A fully theological account'; to put it like this is to be reminded of that sense of *theologia* that is familiar to us from Evagrios's much-cited dictum (*On Prayer* #45, I, p. 62) that 'If you are a theologian, you will pray truly. And if you pray truly, you are a theologian.' A 'theological' account of the divine image has, in such a light, to be one that begins and ends in the attempt to put into words the relationship that exists between God and the created *eros* of the human self, the relationship that is renewed by the gift of baptism and the practice of watchfulness and *hesychia*. And what the *Philokalia* overall presumes is that this relationship is grounded in an eternal contemplative reality – the contemplation of the Father by the Son, the contemplation of the Son's radical 'otherness' by the Father, which together define the shape of creation's relation to the creator and more specifically the relation of the finite *nous* to the infinite intelligence of God. Human nature – in the sense traced in the earlier sections of this study – is as it is because it has at its centre an impulsion towards union-in-otherness; it has the Logos at its heart. The liberation and purification of this impulsion, this 'erotic' drawing towards the source without which it is incomplete and imprisoned in unreality, allow the Logos to exist freely and transformingly within the created subject, and thus to shape the relation of that created subject not only to God but also to the rest of the universe, human and non-human. But we do not adequately grasp what it means to speak of the divine image in us unless, with Palamas, we see that the presence of the image of the Logos in us implies the image of the Trinity as a whole. Our inner life is both an energy directed by the Spirit through the Logos towards the Father *and* a mirroring in its own workings of the interplay of *eros* between intelligence in its deepest and most comprehensive sense and *logos*, the awareness of intelligence's content. The mind loves God and also loves itself loving God; in so doing, it loves the love of God for the world and thus (an advance here on the Augustinian model) loves its own embodied life, which it seeks in turn to shape into the likeness of divine love. So the focal encounter with God in hesychastic prayer gradually 'unfolds' into a remarkably wide-ranging agenda for anthropology and ethics. The doctrine of the image is very far from being a bald statement of some supposed correspondence between human and divine and is seen to be inseparable from the practical – you could even say 'evangelical' – question of how we are freed from the passions, freed for that openness to the other that is stifled by craving and aggression.

And it is this rootedness in the 'erotic' mutuality of the Trinity that helps us make sense of the fact that hesychastic prayer is not a static gazing into a static void but a steady expansion of desire beyond any thought of satisfaction or ultimate identification or absorption. If the life of the Trinity is an unending openness to the inexhaustible other, then this, 'stretched out' in the conditions of our temporal existence, is the constant growing towards the imageless depths of God's otherness, with all that this implies about the abandonment of any imagined world in which the individual's desires are the arbiter of meaning, and the satisfying of those (uncriticized) desires is the arbiter of what is to be said about 'natural' fulfilment. If – to borrow a phrase I have used elsewhere in discussing some parallel themes in the work of St John of the Cross[23] – the *eros* of the contemplative is a 'desire for the desire of the Word', it is a desire for what can, axiomatically, never be gained or contained, a desire for its own frustration, you would say if you were beginning from the distorted picture of desire we habitually resort to.

In a recent essay by Christoph Schneider on 'The Transformation of Eros: Reflections on Desire in Jacques Lacan', which seeks to bring some contemporary psychoanalytic theory into conversation with Maximos the Confessor,[24] the point is made that the liturgical and ascetical idiom of the Christian East has

[23] See Rowan Williams, 'The deflections of desire: negative theology in Trinitarian disclosure', in Oliver Davies and Denys Turner, eds, *Silence and the Word: Negative Theology and Incarnation* (Cambridge, Cambridge University Press 2002), pp. 115–35.
[24] In Adrian Pabst and Christoph Schneider, eds, *Encounter Between Eastern Orthodoxy and Radical Orthodoxy: Transfiguring the World Through the Word* (London, Ashgate 2009), pp. 271–89.

the resources to break through the highly problematic accounts of the relation of self to other that are offered by Lacanian analysis. If the only alternatives for human maturation and liberation are being subordinated to the 'Law' of the Other (with the consequent erotization of transgressing the Law) or redrawing the map of desire so that the subject can find satisfaction in a detached and limited version of what the Other desires, there is never in fact a properly developed relation with the genuinely Other as it is. Schneider suggests that the classical Orthodox account of relation with God posits a divine desire that, because it is identical with the inmost structure and directedness of the subject, may be 'appropriated' by the subject for mimesis without subjugation (and its attendant resentment and drift to the desire of transgression); yet at the same time, the infinite otherness of the divine act and divine 'desire' means that this appropriation is never a collapse into uninterrupted or unchallenged identity, a static interior life. 'The loving Other unceasingly plays [sic; perhaps an error for "places"] highly specific and highly personalized possibilities in the subject's way, which, if they are actively received and actualized, contribute to its flourishing and spiritual well-being.'[25] Other Orthodox writers have made a similar point, among them Nikolaos Loudovikos, who has stressed the significance in Eastern theology of separating *eros* from the idea of 'self-fulfilment' and the will to power and insisting on its association with *ekstasis* and thus *kenosis*[26] – an association much discussed in modern Orthodox theology, from Lossky to Zizioulas. But the roots of this idea are firmly in the philokalic vision, which sees the fundamental pattern behind the entire universe as that of loving presence-in-the-other, a contemplative immersion in the other that never turns into identity yet is wholly devoid of defence and

[25] Schneider, op. cit., pp. 285–6.
[26] See Loudovikos's essay in Pabst and Schneider, op. cit., pp. 141–55, 'Ontology Celebrated: Remarks of an Orthodox on Radical Orthodoxy', esp. p. 146; also his book, *Eucharistic Ontology: Maximus the Confessor's Eschatological Ontology of Being as Dialogical Reciprocity* (Brookline, MA, Holy Cross Orthodox Press 2010).

aggression. All that can be said about the Trinity pivots around this pattern; and the philokalic connection between the eternal contemplation that is the act of the Logos and the essential or natural orientation of the created self means that we can without absurdity speak of the created self living out the adoptive grace of baptism as the place where the trinitarian life locates itself within the world – and also speak of the awareness of the baptized person as located within the divine vision of things.

So Nikitas Stithatos can say at the end of his 'Century' (the title normally given to collections of a hundred brief texts from a spiritual teacher) *On Spiritual Knowledge* (#100, IV, p. 174) that the hesychast 'standing outside all things … will dwell within all things', having been united with the Father through the Logos and led into this union by the work of the Spirit. Watchfulness or mindfulness of who and what we are, and of what is the nature of the various delusions that make us misuse the world we inhabit, preserves us from slipping back into 'impassioned' perspectives on our environment and our neighbours, and also warns against associating our relation to God with specific images or sensations. If what we are is beings created for the limitless enlargement of desire without possession, we are most 'natural' when most free from manageable images of the divine. Yet – in the central paradox of Christian teaching – this affirmation of the imageless character of God is bound up inseparably with a doctrine that seems to many to make extravagant claims for the positive knowledge of the divine: the doctrine of the Trinity. It is only when that doctrine is firmly located within the attempt to articulate what happens in contemplation that the apparent contradiction disappears: it is this doctrine of God that alone sets out why the self-emptying involved in something analogous to *eros* is the grain or contour of reality itself, why the abandoning of possession or control as an ideal is the fundamentally *truthful* response to the world we inhabit. *Hesychia* and mindfulness dissolve the fiction that the world is constituted by a solidly boundaried self confronting solidly boundaried objects that must be catalogued and filed. They insist that we see the self as never outside relation, never the source of life and meaning as an individual, separable entity. They prescribe a new way of seeing that is the proper outworking of the baptized identity, when the *eros* of the Spirit is bestowed to shape our lives in union with the Logos. Living this identity more and more radically shows us what we cannot help saying about the God who makes this possible: that his life is the defining source and archetype for all the loving contemplation of otherness that is realized in the world by finite intelligences.

The theological world of the *Philokalia*, the indwelling of the created mind in the God whose own identity is mutual indwelling and so makes possible the indwelling of the mind in the world and the world in the mind, is encapsulated – unsurprisingly – by Maximos, one of the most exceptionally creative minds represented in the collection, and it is appropriate to conclude this opening chapter with his words.

God, who created all nature with wisdom and secretly planted in each intelligent being knowledge of himself as its first power, like a munificent Lord gave also to us men a natural desire (*pothos*) and longing (*eros*) for Him, combining it in a natural way with the power of our intelligence (*logos*). Using our intelligence, we struggle so as to learn with tranquillity and without going astray how to realize this natural desire. Impelled by it we are led to search out the truth, wisdom and order manifest harmoniously in all creation, aspiring through them to attain Him by whose grace we received the desire. (Maximos, *Fifth Century of Various Texts*, #100, II, p. 284)

PART TWO

ANALOGUE

2

NATURE, PASSION AND DESIRE: THE EXCESSIVENESS OF BEING

At the end of the last chapter, we touched on the way in which recent analyses of Maximos the Confessor by theologians such as Nikolaos Loudovikos and Christoph Schneider had mapped out pretty clearly an ontology in which *eros* plays a key role. God creates a diverse world, doing so in a way that is conditioned by nothing except God's own self. It is a world that is realized as an immeasurable plurality of particular reflections of and participations in the single eternal Logos; and created *eros* is understood as the energy that drives us to our proper place in the relationships that constitute this universe, an energy that is consistently 'self-relativizing', self-displacing. We can call it 'ekstatic', in the strict sense of the term: it steps out of the closed definitions we instinctively work with, opening the life of any subject, any individual substance, to the life of the other, both the finite and the infinite other. The human subject, on earth the uniquely *conscious* bearer of *eros*, models what is in fact going on at every level of the universe's life. Once we have left behind the myth of a fixed and protected self-sufficiency or self-identity, we can perceive how the conscious and intelligent agent, the finite *nous*, now comes to move in the mode for which it was created, moves in alignment with the purpose of God, habitually echoing in finite form the infinite 'desire' of God for God, of love for love. What makes this possible in our world of distorted desire is the crucial coincidence in the incarnate Logos of a free human 'habit', the 'gnomic will' by which we deliberately shape the *tropos*, the mode, of our existence, with the divine and unchangeable will, which is the exercise, *en energeiai*, 'in actuality', of the essence of the trinitarian Godhead. As Loudovikos has spelled out with such impressive detail in his work on *Eucharistic Ontology*,[1] this coincidence of created and uncreated action is not only celebrated but *communicated* and actualized in the Church's focal self-identifying practice, the Eucharist. And as Schneider argues in his essay on Maximos and Lacan,[2] it is clear that any foundational opposition between desire and *logos* cannot be sustained in Maximos's framework. If this is so, then neither can we defend an opposition between nature as something essentially opaque to consciousness and the constructions of culture and language.[3] The Lacanian paradox, which insists on the notion that the sense of boundless libidinal energy and movement is both generated and checked by the authority of the symbolic order, will, on this 'Maximian' account, come dangerously near to simply rehearsing a particular kind of sub-Platonic pathos in which innocence is set against history, speech and particularity. Lacan himself is quite consciously working with this mythology, in which an immortal oneness and integrity is interrupted by speech – though he of course does not treat the state of immortal oneness as 'an' actuality in the world; it is 'the real', that which surrounds the 'reality' we habitually utter and imagine. But the Maximian world assumes that particularity stands at the very beginning of finite life, substance and agency, and looks forward to an eschatological 'rest' – to what we might call a fully harmonious 'culture' in which

---

[1] Loudovikos, *Eucharistic Ontology: Maximus the Confessor's Eschatological Ontology of Being as Dialogical Reciprocity* (Brookline, MA, Holy Cross Orthodox Press 2010), ch. 1 in particular. See also his more recent study, *Analogical Identities: The Creation of the Christian Self* (Turnhout, Brepols 2019), esp. pp. 79–88, and the further discussion of Symeon the New Theologian in ch. 2, esp. pp. 107–25.

[2] Schneider, 'The Transformation of Eros', pp. 272–6, 285–6. See also Nikolaos Loudovikos, 'Analogical Ecstasis: Maximus the Confessor, Plotinus, Heidegger and Lacan', in Sotiris Mitralexis, Georgios Steiris, Marcin Podbielski and Sebastian Lalla, eds, *Maximus the Confessor as a European Philosopher* (Eugene, OR, Wipf and Stock 2017), pp. 241–54, esp. pp. 243–4, 251–2.

[3] Schneider, op. cit., p. 276.

nature has attained its purpose of universal mutuality and (to borrow John Donne's delightful coinage) 'interinanimation'. It assumes a model of peaceful but active diversity.[4]

To put this another way: a Lacanian opposition between undifferentiated libidinal desire and the realm of culture, language and authority proposes that the central ontological difference is between the formless and the spoken (the immortal and the mortal) within the realm of speech and experience. The symbolic order (language and particularity) necessarily generates its own frustration by invoking the Other of indeterminate (and thus always frustrated) desire. The Maximian ontology, in contrast, affirms that the significant difference is between what moves as an *eros*-driven mode of existence towards its proper place within a finite universe of mutuality and the infinite act of God, which generates finite *eros* as an echo of its own love for itself in the mutual inexhaustibility of trinitarian life. What is finite is always already propelled towards its inherent destiny in language and mutuality; there is nothing that is unreasonably natural, natural in its dissonance with other subjects and substances, or indifferent to the promise of a universal eschatological 'culture'. And what is preconscious is not a privileged or uncompromised selfhood or desire but simply 'human powers insofar as they are not actualized in accordance with their natural principle'.[5]

This may help us to make sense of one specific set of Maximian ideas clearly of great importance in the *Centuries on Charity* and rather open to misunderstanding in the contemporary intellectual context. *Cent.* I.17 and 25 touch on a theme that will recur several times in the text: the imperative to love all human beings equally, as God does. God loves human beings because of their nature: as we read later on,[6] 'Perfect love does not split up the single human

---

[4] Cf. Loudovikos, *Analogical Identities*, pp. 99ff.

[5] Schneider, op. cit., p. 276.

[6] *Centuries on Charity* I.71; translation from *The Philokalia: The Complete Text*, vol. II, trans. G. E. H. Palmer, Philip Sherrard and Kallistos Ware (London, Faber & Faber, 1981), p. 60.

nature, common to all, according to the diverse characters of individuals.' At first sight, this may look like a recommendation to what we might think of as an impersonal sort of love, indifferent to the need of specific persons and reducible to benevolence towards humanity as a whole. This is in fact completely contrary to what Maximos argues: to love human beings in their nature is to be awake to the very particular things that make each of them more or less in tune with that nature and to respond accordingly. What matters is that we should not begin by assessing the claims of human beings to be loved on the basis of individual characteristics; love is not a reward if we understand it in the light of God's love. And if we put this together with the repeated emphasis in the Centuries on what 'dispassionate' love means, the point becomes still clearer. Nothing is by nature evil or unlovable, because all things come from the loving will of God, embodying particular reflections of the one Logos in their diverse *logoi*, and thus have the potential for mutuality or reconciliation; but when we view them through the lens of passion, self-serving self-referential desire, we do not see things as they are, in their nature. The basic theme is familiar from Evagrios's treatise *On Thoughts* 8[7] with its seminal distinction between angelic, human and diabolical awareness of things, where the angelic consciousness knows things in their essences and the initially 'neutral' human consciousness has to beware of slipping into the diabolical knowledge that sees things only in terms of their use to another self. Love must be grounded in the recognition that all things are what they are by nature in virtue of their participation in the Logos: nothing can take away their 'entitlement' to love, because they are all capable of growing through the exercise of their proper *eros* towards their destiny. All are struggling towards mutuality, the fullest possible action of reciprocally sustaining each other's lives by the gift of their own. Our own love for any other person or indeed any other finite

---

[7]Evagrios, *peri logismon* 8, and cf. 4; text in *Sur les pensées*, ed. and trans. Paul Gehin, Claire Guillaumont and Antoine Guillaumont, Sources Chrétiennes 438 (Paris, Les Éditions du Cerf 1998), pp. 176/7–178/9 and 164/5.

substance is rooted in our own longing to become 'natural', to be in perfect mutuality. My *eros* aligns itself with theirs.

Passion-free *eros* is the desire that the other be itself – but not in quite the Levinasian sense of abjection before the other because this is rooted in an ontology for which there is no being-for-the-other abstracted from the pattern of *mutual* life-giving. Passion is thus what is fundamentally anti-natural, what seeks, consciously or not, to frustrate the natural desirous movement of all finite substances in concert. Maximos can put it even more vividly in the *Centuries on Theology* II.30, where he speaks of how my failure to grow as I should into my nature is a diminishing of *Christ*. And in defining passion as a moment of frustration or stasis, we are reminded of the crucial point that at no moment *in time* is any finite substance or agent yet fully natural. To love their nature is to love both what they already are as *logos*-bearing and to love the unknown future into which their *eros* is moving them – to love the 'excess' of their being, what Loudovikos would see as their 'eucharistic' future as perfected gift.[8] All things are en route towards this future, and thus en route towards – as we put it earlier – a universal culture; and, to go rather beyond what Maximos himself says in so many words, this is to say that all things are always already on the way to language, to being understood and spoken, being present in the 'priestly' discourse of human beings who make connecting sense of the *logoi* of what they encounter.

Loving what is true or real, free from the distortions of passion, is loving what is grounded in the Logos; hence the paradox asserted in *Centuries on Charity* III.37 – 'he who loves nothing merely human loves all men'.[9] To love what is 'merely human' must here mean loving simply what is contingent in this or that

---

[8]Loudovikos, *Ontology*, e.g. pp. 36–41, 152–3.
[9]Translation from *The Philokalia*, p. 89. Lars Thunberg in *Microcosm and Mediator: The Theological Anthropology of Maximus the Confessor* (Lund, Håkan Ohlssons Boktryckeri 1965), p. 333, seems to take 'loving nothing human' as implying that we need first to devote our love entirely to God rather than creatures. This is correct only in a limited sense: it risks missing the point that we love humanity properly by never loving humanity in its isolation from its maker.

individual, what does not belong to their nature as related to God. Universal love is love for the individual as related to the infinite act that sustains it through its particular logos, its specific reflection of the one divine Logos. Proper Christian love thus 'dispossesses' itself of its object in more than one sense. Not only does it seek to see and know the object without passion (without self-referential desire), it recognizes that the true being of the object is always in relation to something other than the beholder prior to the seeing or registering of this particular other by the beholder. Thus there is always some dimension of what is encountered that is in no way accessible to or at the mercy of this particular beholder. It is in acknowledging this relatedness to a third that a relation of love involving two finite subjects becomes authentic and potentially open to the universal. What is in relation to the 'third' is precisely what exists in and by the action of that 'third', which is the nature of the subject in question, the project defined by infinite act that is now working through by its own particular mode of *eros* towards its ultimate purpose. If our love is conditioned by the specific point currently reached by the other subject, it will not be universalizable; it will not be love for the whole project, nature realizing itself through *eros*. It will be love for a fiction, for the unreal object that is just another finite substance or ensemble of finite substances conceived in abstraction from God and *logos*. We cannot *properly* love an *unrelated* object; if we start from that particular fiction, we rapidly come to regard the other as available for our possession because it is cut off from its ground in God/*logos*/nature. Our relation to it is no longer truly *eros*, because we have isolated it in our thoughts from its own desirous movement towards its natural place in the universal network of mutual gift. It cannot be gift to us any longer, and we cannot relate to it in gift-like mode. But if the relation is one of my *eros* communing with the *eros* of what I love – desiring the desire of the other, but not in competitive and exclusive mode – the possibility of that 'eucharistic' interrelation noted already is opened up to us.

Summarizing Maximos's ontology in the light of all this, we could say that his chief contribution to a strictly metaphysical discussion (bracketing the purely theological for a moment) lies in the twofold characterization of finite being as always moving 'erotically' towards its optimal position of mutual relatedness and thus always manifestly related to more than now appears – to the God who has freely uttered the creative *logos* of each element in the world, and so to a future that is necessarily involved with other subjects. As I have suggested, this means that finite being tends towards being spoken, being apprehended, represented, regenerated in human response and engagement. The healed world is one in which human beings have learned to speak truly about the environment in which they live – the Eucharist being the foretaste of that speech, in that the divine Logos actually transforms the stuff of the world by Word and Spirit in the sacrament. Maximos's scheme lays the foundation for an aesthetic as well as an ethic, and allows us to think of human creativity itself as an attempt to align the *eros* of the artist with the *eros* of the material around: the artist is far from being a creator *ex nihilo* because s/he is always feeling for the 'impulse' in this or that aspect of the world that is moving towards a new and more nourishing relatedness, to the rest of the material order as well as to the human understanding. Those artists who insist that their work is nothing to do with the will as we normally understand it are echoing in different terms the Maximian concern for dispassionate seeing. And in epistemological terms, we should have to define comprehensive knowing as something other than grasping the internal workings of an object; knowing would have to be an awareness of the relations in which something could stand, the meanings it could bear. More than that, it would be bound up with an actual sharing in what I have been calling the 'project' of nature, a mutual process of shaping towards eschatological mutuality. Here – returning again to Schneider's essay and developing its argument a little further[10] – we can see in a particularly concentrated way

[10] Schneider, 'The Transformation of Eros', pp. 277–80, 285–9.

55

the tension between a Lacanian account of how 'desire for the desire of the Other' works in the psyche and what a theological account informed by Maximos might say. The Lacanian subject is endlessly frustrated by the desire of the Other, which cannot be formulated, thematized or assimilated and so cannot ever be satisfied. Language is the frontier between the speaking subject and the limitless libidinal realm: it is only in language that the desire of the Other is available for imagining, yet it is precisely available for imagining *as* other and thus as always escaping. The subject is confronted by the baffling aporia that libidinal freedom can only be thought of in terms of a dissolution of language. In contrast, the Maximian subject is drawn by a no less unassimilable desire in the other, but drawn in the hope of a fulfilment that the individual subject's own account of what is desired can never produce. The other, the infinite and the finite other, is not an obstacle to the subject's desire, an alien demand to be either submitted to or resisted. Language cannot be an alienating thing, because it mediates a desire of the other that is a promise or an offer to my desire, not an empty source of frustration. As we read in *Centuries on Theology* II.60, the Logos is incarnate in what he says as well as what he is and does: we attain to the ultimate harmony with and in him for which we are made only through language, even if we know quite well that words alone will not bring us to him (cf. *Centuries on Theology* II.73–4). If otherness is inscribed in the finite world from the beginning in the diversity of the *logoi*, there is no necessary binary rivalry between finite subjects, and the infinite other is not a competitor for what is desired. Indeed, I can say, on the basis of the doctrine of the *logoi*, that *I am* the desire of the infinite other, in the sense that my existence is a fact only because of an act of loving freedom in which God unconditionally desires the joy of a finite other (as he eternally desires the joy of an infinite other in the life of the Trinity).

Such an ontology makes sense of both art and asceticism; it suggests a high doctrine of finite creativity (and in this respect Maximos stands close to some aspects of Bulgakov's doctrine of Sophia as the *eros* of created things towards their optimal interrelatedness, in art and liturgy alike[11]), but it also prescribes a formidable exercise of 'mindfulness' in respect of human perception of the world and its distortions through the working of 'passion'. It is why Maximos's ontology cannot be properly thought about in separation from his analyses of faulty and misdirected desire. But perhaps the most important aspect of his metaphysical vision, the aspect that has stimulated most constructive reflection among contemporary theologians, is his refusal to define nature as an ensemble of static properties. The *logos* upon which each being is established is, of course, stable; but it has no reality except as the moving principle of the history of its *tropos*, the development in time of its own particular and unique journey towards itself. Not the least of the Confessor's originalities is to make the Christological distinction of *logos* and *tropos* work as a general key to ontology. But that is entirely in keeping with a theological scheme in which it is the Incarnation of the Logos that is the gateway to understanding anything that matters about the universe.

In the next chapter, we shall look in more detail at the interweaving of *logos* and embodied, particularized agency within a finite world. A fuller exploration of this helps us see how and why the central vision of divine *logos* enacting its unifying and healing function in the limitations – and indeed the catastrophes – of finite material life can become the linchpin of a theological account of being itself, grounded in the self-forgetting relatedness of the trinitarian life. But to begin with, we need to turn back

---

[11]See the discussion of some of these themes in Rowan Williams, *Sergii Bulgakov: Towards a Russian Political Theology* (Edinburgh, T&T Clark 1999), pp. 127–31, 155–9. Cf. John Milbank, 'Sophiology and Theurgy: The New Theological Horizon' in Pabst and Schneider, pp. 45–85, and also his 'Christianity and Platonism East and West', in Daniel Haynes, ed., *A Saint for East and West: Maximus the Confessor's Contribution to Eastern and Western Christian Theology* (Eugene, OR, Wipf and Stock 2019), pp. 149–203; and cf., in the same volume (pp. 204–22), Nikolaos Loudovikos, 'Theurgic Attunement as Eucharistic Gnosiology: Divine *Logoi* and Energies in Maximus the Confessor and Thomas Aquinas'.

to the way in which the tradition before Maximos thinks about *logos* and the nature of its dysfunctions, concentrating especially on the analyses offered by Evagrios, which we have already briefly touched on, and seeking to trace the line of argument and insight that leads from these analyses to a vision of participation in the eternal Word's relation to the Father.

3

THE EMBODIED LOGOS: REASON, KNOWLEDGE AND RELATION

I

The fourth chapter of Evagrios's *Gnostikos* summarizes the difference between *gnosis* from outside and knowledge that comes from God.[1] The former allows us to engage with the reality of material things and represent them to ourselves by way of *logoi*; the latter, by the grace of God, brings realities into direct contact with our intellective capacity so that this capacity receives the *logoi* themselves, the 'inner life' of what confronts us. Thus, to quote the text, 'What stands in opposition to the former is error; what stands in opposition to the latter is anger and the spirit of aggression' (*thumos*). There is a crucial difference between simply being in error about the material shapes that surround us, the sort of error that ignorance or inattention or incapacity might lead us into, and the failure truly to know that shows itself in reactions that display a stance rigidly 'over against' what is there. The chapter that follows develops this a little further, comparing

---

[1]Evagrios, *Le Gnostique, ou à celui qui est devenu digne de la science*, ed. Antoine Guillaumont and Claire Guillaumont, Sources Chrétiennes 356 (Paris, Les Éditions du Cerf 1989), pp. 92–3. For a good introduction to Evagrios with some representative texts, see Augustine M. Casiday, *Evagrius Ponticus* (London, Routledge 2006). On the use of his work in the *Philokalia*, see Julia Konstantinovsky, 'Evagrius in the *Philokalia* of Sts Macarius and Nicodemus', in Brock Bingman and Bradley Nassif, ed., *The Philokalia: A Classic Text of Orthodox Spirituality* (Oxford, Oxford University Press 2012), pp. 175–92.

the indulgence of aggressive passion with stabbing yourself in the eye (an image that recurs in other writings by Evagrios). The aggressive instinct – in other words, the passion that prompts us to push away what menaces us – is what prevents the *logos* of any object encountered from entering into the intelligent spirit, *nous*; so that the problem is not that we have *made a mistake* about the world (as we might with the outer forms of things) but that in one crucial sense we have *mistaken what the world itself is*. We have acted or reacted as though the world were a separate agent or set of agencies, with an interest or agenda standing in rivalry to our own individual interest; and so, by misconstruing the very nature of our environment – as the metaphor in chapter 5 graphically puts it – we pierce our eyes with an iron stylus (surely not an accidental image in its evocation of the world of learned writing).

This distinction between error and the effect of *thumos* is a useful point to begin from in thinking about what the anthropology of the Greek Christian tradition has to say about mind, sense and embodiment. Evagrios is, it seems, offering a way of distinguishing between a direct and an indirect encounter with *logos*. Knowledge 'from outside' is the process of making sense of the objects around us; whereas the *gnosis* given by God is a 'receiving' of the *logoi*, not a process in which the rational structures of things are deployed by the human knower in constructing a coherent representation of the world. In the knowledge that comes from God, the *logoi* as activated by God act upon us, not the other way around. And if we put this brief passage alongside a couple of others later in the treatise, we can see emerging a clear picture of how passion distorts the gnostic's calling.[2] Chapter 42 asserts that the characteristic trial or temptation of the gnostic is the kind of false apprehension

---

[2] Evagrios's use of 'gnostic' is eccentric to the modern reader, suggesting as it does the dissenting Christian and para-Christian sects of the second century, but there is no obvious alternative translation of *gnostikos* as a term for someone encountering and embracing the inner energy of what is to be known.

that presents what is existing as if it were non-existent, or the non-existent as real, or the real as existing otherwise than it actually does. The chapter immediately following ascribes such 'false *gnosis*' to either the presence of passion or the fact that the origins of some enquiry are to be found in something other than the quest for the good – which amounts to much the same thing.[3] A little more elaborately, the treatise *peri diaphoron logismon*, *On Thoughts*, spells out in chapter 8[4] the differences between angelic, human and diabolical *logismoi* in a way evidently connected with the model presupposed in the *Gnostikos*. Angelic thought searches for the spiritual *logoi* within what is perceived; diabolical thought proposes to the perceiving self the *acquisition* of what is perceived; and human thought simply registers the *morphe psile*, the simple form, that is there to be perceived. As such, it is neither acquisitive nor contemplative. Where angelic knowledge grasps the symbolic significance of things and how all external phenomena have something to convey from God to the *nous*, and where diabolical knowledge seeks to use the things perceived for gratification, human *logismos* is primitively just the receiving of an intelligible form. Evagrios is primarily concerned with how this works as an exegetical tool, shaping the way we make sense of passages in Scripture and saving us from literalism; but the distinction is clearly of wider pertinence. If we render *logismos* as 'a process of reflecting', we can see Evagrios as, in effect, teasing apart two kinds of *non*-egocentric thinking and one kind of thinking that is directed to the self's ambitions (as spelled out in more detail in chapter 1 of *On Thoughts*,[5] where the basic passions are named as gluttony, avarice and vainglory). True knowledge, so this implies, is the receptivity of human *logismos* instructed and enlarged by angelic.

---

[3] Ibid., pp. 170–1.
[4] Evagrios, *Sur les pensées*, ed. Paul Gehin, Claire Guillaumont and Antoine Guillaumont, Sources Chrétiennes 438 (Paris, Les Éditions du Cerf 1998), pp. 176/7–178/9. ET in Casiday, op. cit., pp. 91–116.
[5] Ibid., pp. 148–9, 150–1.

It is not, then, that 'passion' causes us to make mistakes – as if we were simply being recommended to keep a cool head in our deliberations and our analyses of the world and ourselves. Evagrios is stating more than a prudential commonplace. And the exercise of ordinary human *logismos* is already an activity that requires grace for it to avoid the lure of diabolical selfishness. If we are genuinely able to see 'humanly', to allow the simple contact of the knowing subject and the 'simple form', we may also be free to see 'angelically'; but the fragility of our capacity to know truly is there from the start, so that the innate freedom to grow from human to angelic perception is in no way automatic; we may be lured into a thinking that is 'sub-human'. The defensive/aggressive spirit in us will always be present, pushing us towards the refusal of the simple *logoi* in themselves that prevents genuine *gnosis*. Or, as in *On Thoughts*, it may equally be the acquisitive spirit that distorts and diabolizes our relation with what we encounter: Evagrios is not creating a single consistent system in these works, but offering diagnoses of the various sources of our failure to arrive at authentic knowledge. But what these diagnoses have in common is the conviction that passion creates a particular kind of *gap* between the knowing subject and the world that is known; and the implication of this is that the renewal of mind and spirit must involve a closing of that gap. As Evagrios's language makes plain, this does not mean that the distinctive agency of the *nous* in any one of us is somehow cancelled or swallowed up in something alien to it: what is given/acquired in the state of 'graced' knowledge, 'angelic' thinking, is a habit of perceiving the world that is irreducibly linked with ethical practice. The *praktike*, the ethical discernment, that has already been learned by the would-be gnostic remains fundamental, and the gnostic has to be faithful in generosity, material and spiritual,[6] so that there remains a clear sense of a conscious subject adopting and maintaining

[6] *Gnostikos* 7, ed. cit., pp. 98–9.

policies of behaviour – at this stage at least with a measure of deliberateness, even if in higher states such policies become second nature. The key capacity for the gnostic is the consistent refusal to treat the world as pure object, ontologically alien (and thus as either desirable for the ego or threatening to the ego). And this is, as chapter 4 of the *Gnostikos* says, a matter of the *nous receiving* the *logoi*.

To pick up the language of another tradition, this presupposes a 'non-dual' basis for epistemology. Raimon Panikkar, in a dense and suggestive discussion in his book on *Mysticism and Spirituality*,[7] considers this question in the light of the way our intellect constructs a 'mythos', a comprehensive stance towards reality that does not lend itself to any translation into 'logos'. This latter term is used here in a rather different sense from the way Evagrios deploys it, as denoting some kind of systematic knowledge. Panikkar's 'mythos' is a pervasive perspective acknowledging that we as knowing subjects are part of a net of related agencies making up the finite world, and as such it is close in meaning to Evagrian *gnosis*. 'The participative knowledge we refer to is not the knowledge of one part of reality, but the consciousness of all reality from a concrete perspective. An a-dualistic [Panikkar prefers this term to "non-dualistic"] consciousness is needed that *relates* us at the same time as it keeps us at a distance. It is the consciousness of relation as such and not that of entities that relate to each other.'[8] The phrase 'from a concrete perspective' is important here as clarifying that a non-dual approach is not equivalent to any view that denies the reality of finite substance in any sense; nor is the phrase 'at a distance' meant to suggest that there is some priority of separated identities. Each subject begins from a distinct location; and this entails a recognition and acceptance also of beginning from a *bodily* location; we do not have any other means of specifying what makes a perspective

---

[7] Raimon Panikkar, *Mysticism and Spirituality: Part One: Mysticism, Fullness of Life* (Maryknoll, NY, Orbis Books 2014), pp. 142ff.
[8] Ibid., p. 144.

'concrete' or distinctive. And in this light, Evagrios's phrasing about *logos* and matter needs some careful parsing. It is easy to take it as most have done simply as another version of the recurrent temptation of 'Platonized' Christianity to try and shrug off the material as such; and this may well be a strong element in his thinking and that of his disciples. But it is important to understand what proper theological and metaphysical concerns might underlie this, and how those concerns may be salvaged from a distorted spiritualism. The 'from outside' knowledge he describes is a knowledge of material substances, organized into a coherent system by the application of the idea of *logoi* as potential tools for making intelligible connections between phenomena and representing them accordingly. This much the human knowing subject can manage in principle without too much risk of distortion. But it is not to be identified with the action of divine grace in granting a genuine participation in the *active* intelligible structures of the material things of the world: this level of relatedness is something that, while not abolishing the particularity of our base of orientation, denies us the illusion of existing in a self-contained 'elsewhere' from what we are encountering, or of somehow being 'ungenerated', self-starting beings with no intricate webs of dependence shaping what we are.[9]

In other words, it is not that the *gnosis* that comes by grace allows us access to a world of *logoi* somehow *independent* of the material, a 'realm of ideas' existing 'somewhere' else. To recover an awareness of a place in the order of things, a position within a connected web, is necessarily to acknowledge the body. Ironically, an epistemology that knows only the operation of 'from outside' knowledge applied to a material universe is in danger of occluding the reality of the body in its *specific*

---

[9] The significance in the spiritual life of accepting that one is 'generated' has been developed recently in the work of Luigi Giussani; on this, see, for example, Julian Carron, *Disarming Beauty: Essays on Faith, Truth and Freedom* (Notre Dame, IN, University of Notre Dame Press 2017), pp. 45–6.

location and embeddedness in a pattern of interdependence, and of nurturing the fantasy that knowing is essentially the action of a disembodied subject working on embodied data – the default position of a good deal of post-medieval Western thinking about knowledge, as if the object is always somewhere and the subject is nowhere. The Evagrian perspective takes seriously – on the one hand – detached and accurate seeing, unclouded by aggression or acquisition (the human style of *logismos* understood independently of its distortion by passion), and – on the other – the difference between the flawed vision that comes from simple error and that which comes from passion. And this points us back – perhaps unexpectedly, and almost certainly in tension with Evagrios's conscious intents – to the possibility of a new account of *sense*, understood as first and foremost the reality of bodily connection, resonance and responsiveness, the capacity to move and adjust and improvise within a world of stimuli reaching beyond what can be grasped at any given moment and involving the actuality of the knowing subject. In the striking phrase used by Orion Edgar in his study of the theological implications of Merleau-Ponty's philosophy,[10] '*nature* lies on both sides of perception'. For the *gnosis* that is given by God, sense (material stimulus) and intellection at the deepest level (awareness of the interconnection of reality) are inseparably bound up together. The renewal of mind and the transformation of sense go hand in hand.

It is obvious that this condition of *gnosis* is something quite other than a simple capacity for acquiring information. Evagrios approaches it as a spiritual gift because it is not a capacity that can be defined in terms of its *function* alone: it is intrinsic to a habit and quality of life as a whole that is to do with growing into adequate relation with the rest of finite reality rather than gaining tools for technical mastery. This does not mean that 'technical mastery' is by definition an evil, let alone that the

---

[10] Orion Edgar, *Things Seen and Unseen: The Logic of Incarnation in Merleau-Ponty's Metaphysics of Flesh* (Eugene, OR, Cascade Books 2016), p. 187; itals in original.

task of representing the world with some degree of success is to be deplored. Evidently, Evagrios believed that knowledge 'from outside', a competent practice of representation, with the practically useful consequences that this entails, was a given element in human life. What is more important is what disciplines are in place to check the 'diabolization' of such practices when they serve nothing but the passions that Evagrios outlines at the beginning of *On Thoughts*. Passion, in this scheme of understanding, is essentially what seeks to de-realize the material world by reducing it to whatever functions we are determined it should perform for our benefit; it is not too difficult a step from 'successful representation' to this reductive picture, though there is no *necessary* trajectory. But unless our practices of organized representation are seen in the context of a prior and larger question, the question of how we attune ourselves to the rest of the finite world's energies, we yield to a model that reduces both object and subject. It reduces the object by encouraging us to 'see' only in terms of our wants, and the subject by ignoring the already given dependence of our material identity on the pre-existing web of agency that forms and situates our specific reality. This is why 'impassioned' knowledge is more than a mistake, why it must be understood as a misapprehension of the very nature of a 'world'. Knowledge that is substantially determined by aggression or acquisitiveness is dangerous to the extent that it encourages a perilously inadequate recognition of the limits within which we live our lives. The 'diabolical' consciousness works on the tacit assumption that my will and my interest are primordial, undefined affairs, unrelated to my history and my body, un-'worldly'. Hannah Arendt famously reproached classical Christian – especially Augustinian – anthropology with creating a 'worldless' ideal of love;[11] but the truth is almost diametrically opposite. It is the reduction of the world to an ensemble of passive objects to be desired or avoided

---

[11] See Hannah Arendt, *Love and Saint Augustine*, ed. and tr. Joanna Vecchiarelli Scott and Judith Chelius Stark (Chicago, Chicago University Press 1996).

by an individual appetite that most lethally dissolves the sense of a world. The critique of a desire directed towards 'the world' in the Augustinian (or indeed Johannine) sense is a critique of a very specific model of reality. The 'world' in this context is the environment understood simply as a reservoir of objects whose significance is in their utility in satisfying an indeterminate series of desirous reactions in us, producing an indeterminate series of particular gratifications. An engagement with the actual created world that is in some measure free from passion is one that recognizes both the dependence of the knowing subject and the 'excess' in the object that makes it more than simply *my* object, oriented towards my desires. What sustains my awareness in this framework is the complex of connections I have not chosen and do not wholly see; and this is how we might render in somewhat different terms the Evagrian language of receiving the *logoi* of what we encounter, rather than understanding them *only* as useful tools for assembling perceptions into a coherent representational system.

Full 'gnostic' awareness, then, entails the knowing subject's sense that it is located in a world exceeding any account of its life that is solely focused on the functional matching of objects to desires. The renewed mind is free to share in a network of embodied interaction, which it attends to, learns from and takes time with; the mind is not driven by the need to use its environment to find answers to its questions or satisfaction of its wants. Hence the appropriateness of calling this sort of awareness 'contemplative'. Contemplation might be understood as the discipline of opening the mind to a 'world' in the full sense we have been discussing – a complex within which the particular subject stands but which is not to be mastered or exploited by the subject as if that subject stood 'somewhere else' or, worse, 'nowhere in particular', in the fictive world of ego and gratification. It is a discipline that inhabits limit, location, time and constraint, seeking above all to allow the interaction of the 'network' to happen in *this* place and time; and this in turn entails learning physical habits and disciplines that are appropriate to a life lived in accordance with *logos*. There are things we 'know' in and only in physical attunement to the world. Finally, in its freedom to welcome and acknowledge this kind of engagement in the world, the mind is opened to the unifying source of every *logos*, the self-communication of God. In the classical language of the Greek contemplative tradition, this is where 'natural contemplating', *phusike theoria*, becomes *theologia*, attunement with the divine Logos.

II

The transformation of knowledge, mental and material, is thus bound up with the education of the mind in inhabiting its location in time and space – learning to be a *creaturely* mind, we might say. To be hospitable to *logos* at any level is to encounter and acknowledge a boundary – but precisely *not* a boundary between self and world, rather the boundary of existing as an embodied subject in *this* location as related to *that*, in interaction with *that*. Transformed *sense* is what happens as we become more seriously aware of the interface between my physicality and the physicality around me; when I begin to see and sense what is there, stripped of my passionate intention towards it. When Pope Francis and Patriarch Bartholomew speak of our environmental crisis as a 'sin against ourselves' and of the interconnectedness of environmental disorder with other sorts of disorder and imbalance,[12] we are reminded that the effect of 'passionate intention' is a state of *irrationality*. A definition of reason only in instrumental terms produces, it seems, the corporate insanity that is the prevailing human attitude to both the material order we are part of and the societies we create. Irrationality at this level is humanity at war with itself, and this is inexorably our destination if we become incapable of asking about how we might become receptive and attentive to the *logos*-level of our universe.

[12] See, for example, sections 16, 34 and 56 of Pope Francis's 2015 encyclical, *Laudato si'*.

To quote Evagrios once again, the *gnostikos*, in being attuned to *logos*, is also attuned to the diverse levels of capacity in his/her audience, and is thus able to communicate with 'justice', giving each what is proper for them: direct and simple teaching for some; *ainigmata*, significant riddles, for others.[13] So the person who has received the life of *logos* into the mind (and body) becomes the perfect communicator of what has been received because she/he understands what can be heard and received in the process of teaching in the case of each person. Attunement to the world's harmonics brings attunement to the diversity of the human world also; and this is hardly surprising since what is needed for both is freedom from passionate intention, from aggression and acquisitiveness. A world whose sanity is restored would be one in which 'reason' had been rediscovered as a condition not of instrumental control and conceptual precision but of *appropriate responsiveness*, to the human and the non-human order alike. The key insight of the theological perspective offered by the Pope and the Patriarch is to do with this: with the recovery of the idea of an 'apt' or fitting relation that is not simply translatable into comprehensively conceptual terms; absent this recovery, we remain at war with our humanity, as with our planet.

If, then, we are to talk about spiritual transformation, it must be a way of talking about how we learn to inhabit our place within a connected environment, within a world of limit and mutuality. This is not an eccentric innovation for our theology of the 'spiritual': what I have so far been stressing is that the heart of the Greek Christian tradition involves a doctrine of what *logos* means and a practical diagnostic of the damage done by passion to our knowing at the most comprehensive and truthful level. And to understand this is also to open the door to a fresh understanding of the notion of *theosis* in the Greek Christian tradition, a topic to which we shall be

---

[13] *Gnostikos* 44 (ed. cit., pp. 174, 175).

coming back later in this book. At first sight, it seems that the aspiration to deification is an aspiration to be freed from the limiting perspectives of materiality and passion alike. In chapter 22 of *On Thoughts* (referring also to the texts on the subject in the treatise *On Prayer*), *apatheia* entails being freed from 'worldly desire' and from the concepts or representations of sense objects (*aistheta pragmata*);[14] advance in the life of the spirit towards its fullness apparently has as its condition the abandonment of any awareness of the particular, the 'located'. But there are two basic points that should qualify this reading of the texts and of the model derived from them. Early in *On Thoughts* (ch. 3),[15] Evagrios notes how the aggressive passion is tamed by practical charity ('almsgiving'), the *nous* is purified in prayer and desire is disciplined by fasting. The passion-free spirit is then able to look at the human world without making distinctions: Paul's language about there being neither male nor female (Galatians 3.28), neither Greek nor Jew, slave nor free (Colossians 3.11) is quoted. And the point seems to be *not* that freedom from passion abolishes the particular but that it liberates us to love without reference to our own preference or affinity – in a way that reflects the indiscriminate love of God. *Apatheia* is the liberty of the mind to see and respond without what we would call an 'agenda' of its own. Similarly the critical comments about sense-based concepts are specifically linked to what happens in prayer: what is going to be most destructive is the confusion of an awareness of God with the awareness of any thing in the perceptual field. Such confusion is one form – the most damaging – of precisely the sort of *misidentification of what is real* that Evagrios is diagnosing in chapter 42 of the *Gnostikos*: to see the other whom I must love primarily in terms of the identities that I can successfully categorize (as familiar or unfamiliar, as like or unlike myself) is precisely that 'reduction of the real' that passion invariably generates; and

[14] *On Thoughts* 22 (ed. cit., pp. 230–1, 232–3).
[15] Ibid., pp. 160–1, 162–3.

the 'seeing' of God as something like an item in the field of my routine material/intellectual perception is the most extreme case of such reduction.

So what this does *not* mean is that the spirit on its way to unity with the divine, to *theosis* (which is in fact not a common Evagrian word), *itself* becomes in some way 'limitless', simply identified with or absorbed in what it encounters, undetermined and unlocated.[16] Such a picture of the self or spirit would in fact be another product of 'passionate' thinking, seeking to remove from the world anything that I as an individual mind or spirit cannot contain. Non-passionate engagement with the world is invariably *responsive*: its dispassionate character is shown in its freedom to receive what is there to be understood and loved without asking about its use. It is a freedom to see what God gives to be seen. Growing into what God intends for us is growing into undistorted vision (to echo the original title of Fr Sophrony's famous study of St Silouan of Mount Athos, *The Undistorted Image*[17]) – but it is also the prosaic business of sustaining that vision by fasting and almsgiving, by the daily business of engaging rightly or justly with what is in fact in front of our eyes. But this reminder that the Evagrian account of spiritual maturity depends on a fundamentally 'responsive' dimension in our humanity opens the door to a still more important theological point, one that will take us beyond much of what Evagrios explicitly says and closer to the world of Maximos the Confessor and the tradition flowing from him. Briefly: our divinization is not the (impossible) acquisition of impersonal divine attributes, but our assimilation to the eternal Logos in the Logos's *filial* relation to the Source of Godhead. We are to become 'divine' only after the pattern of the Son. The entire direction of classical Christian theology is defined by the basic conviction that we are adopted into the relation that Jesus enjoys

---

[16] Nikolaos Loudovikos, *Analogical Identities*, pp. 264–70, is helpful here.
[17] Archimandrite Sophrony (Sakharov), *The Undistorted Image: Staretz Silouan 1866–1938* (London, Faith Press 1958).

with the Father and that we are enabled to pray with his prayer (as in the two classical Pauline texts, Romans 8.15 and Galatians 4.6, and in the Farewell Discourses of the Fourth Gospel). When this is translated into the more abstract language of patristic and Byzantine trinitarianism, it evolves into a complex but closely interconnected theological vision of how the structures of all finite agencies and substances realize aspects of the fullness that is eternally in the divine Logos; the Incarnation of the Logos is the means by which the diversity of finite life – a diversity that, because of sin, has become fragmentation and rivalry – is once again made coherent, mutually life-giving instead of mutually destructive.[18] And that making-coherent is realized as finite reality opens itself more fully to the creative act that sustains it; as finite reality becomes receptive and responsive, as it comes to actualize the image of the eternal Logos.

For finite *intelligence* this means the acquiring of what we could call the 'filial' mind. The reality of the eternal Logos is simultaneously wholly dependent and wholly creative: it is not 'receptive' in any sense that could mean simply that it was passive, yet it is not 'independent' in any sense that would imply that it could be itself without receiving all that it is from an other. All created agency thus has to be seen in this context: to be created is to derive from an act that is not ours, but it is also to be the conduit of generative gift to the rest of the finite order, each finite agent giving in its own unique way the life that it has itself been given. For the human creation, characterized by love and intelligence, to actualize the life of *logos* is to exercise at whatever level and in whatever mode the human capacity for self-representation and world-representation *in such a way* that how we represent ourselves to ourselves and the world to ourselves is permeated

[18]For further discussion, see chs 3 and 4 below. See also Antoine Levy, OP, *Le créé et l'incréé: Maxime le confesseur et Thomas d'Aquin* (Paris, Vrin 2006), especially chs 2 and 3, which is the most comprehensive and insightful of recent discussions of Maximos's Christocentric metaphysics. Lars Thunberg's older *Microcosm and Mediator: The Theological Anthropology of Maximus the Confessor* (Lund, Håkan Ohlssons Boktryckeri, 1965), remains a dependable guide.

by response to eternal gift. And the fundamental problem with the life of 'passion' is that it drives us to representations that are detached from the awareness of gift, gift received and gift transmitted. As we put it earlier, the passionate mind lacks *hospitality*, the readiness to give habitation to both the finite and the infinite other in their sheer non-negotiable difference from the knowing self. This is why Evagrios and the tradition stemming from him see the opposite of significant knowledge not as error but as anger or acquisitive desire. In contrast, the hospitable mind is remade in the image of eternal Logos, eternal filiation, insofar as it receives what it encounters at the level of *logos* – that is, at the level where what is 'sensed', apprehended, understood is the relation of what we encounter to its maker. Our own 'hospitality' to the world unites with the 'hospitality' to the act of the creator that lies at the heart of the reality of this world's objects, and ultimately to the 'hospitality' of the eternal Word to the gift of the eternal Father. And my own conscious and linguistic welcome to the *logoi* as a finite knowing subject – my active/contemplative knowledge of the world – becomes a means for the interactive life of the creator within creation to reach a deeper intensity and communicability; hence the familiar language about humanity as exercising a 'priestly' role in creation, though the exploration of that would take us into a still wider discussion.

The balance in the 'rational' creation of receptivity or dependence and generative, innovative liberty is uniquely complex and significant in the human subject – which is why a theological perspective should both welcome *and* qualify the language of Simone Weil in her retrieval of a Platonic and Christian account of our human presence in the world. 'God', she writes, 'has created a finite being, which says "I", which is unable to love God. Through the action of grace the "I" little by little disappears, and God loves himself by way of the creature, which empties itself, becomes nothing.'[19] Well, yes and no: if the

[19] *The Notebooks of Simone Weil*, vol. 1, tr. Arthur Wills (London, Routledge & Kegan Paul 1956), p. 331.

process were *only* the repetition of finite subjects learning to cancel their individual agendas, this might serve as a summary. But it does not really do justice to the supplementary idea that the act by which the individual ego gradually comes to see itself in a 'converted' way, as an element in the interactive world of *logos*, is itself life-giving, and is so in a unique mode. 'We have got to renounce being something', writes Weil in her notebooks:[20] we must imitate God's refusal to be an identity over against an other. Creation is the act by which God refuses to be 'everything'.[21] But there is a conceptual tangle here. To be a finite substance – and more particularly a finite spirit/*nous* – is to be *located*, to be placed here and not elsewhere in the network of finite interrelation and to have a perspective that is neither universal nor freed from specificity. The life that is lived in and from that location, seeking to see truthfully and to engage dispassionately, is, in its ascetical struggle to move away from acquisition and aggression, becoming a gift to the life of other finite substances, mediating to them the liberating presence of the creator in new ways, ways that are inextricably bound up with the particularity of who and where each subject is. The creature does not *become nothing*, as if its particularity were essentially an obstacle to God being God: that would reintroduce the perennially seductive error of treating God's reality and the world's as competitors. On the contrary, a theology and metaphysic of *logos* insists that the creature – and supremely the 'rational', *logikos*, subject that is the human *nous* – becomes the bearer of an irreplaceable grace within the exchange of finite life. And Weil's language also risks giving house-room to precisely that fiction of a 'limitless' selfhood that we have seen to be alien to the central thrust of the ascetical tradition. The corrosive effect of passion is not – as Weil often seems to suggest – that it ties the subject to the sheer fact of finite individuality; it is the consistent refusal to understand

[20] Ibid., p. 193.
[21] Compare the formulation of Jacques Pohier in *God – in Fragments* (London, SCM 1985): 'God is God, so God is not everything' (the title of the book's third section).

and inhabit that individuality in the awareness of being a means of gift, the bearer of a needed or desired element in the total of finite interaction.

Orion Edgar's work on Merleau-Ponty, already referred to above, draws this out in a somewhat different but recognizably convergent idiom. Seeing an 'environment' is, he notes, necessarily an enterprise that is not to be completed or mastered in a single moment and angle of perception. 'The "incarnational" logic that we have been arguing for ... takes account of the location of the perceiver in the world, it understands Being as given in limited aspects and not as a reality that could be best seen and ideally known from the perspectivelesss position of an absolute observer or a purely transcendent God, or described in terms of a pure geometry.'[22] A fuller grasp of what the Evagrian and Maximian tradition implies allows us to map this with some clarity, in that it allows us to understand the interconnection of finite agency, arising as it does from the measureless plurality of possible finite perspectives, 'points of orientation', as the *mimesis* in time and space of the infinite divine Logos. As such, it cannot be something whose sole purpose is self-cancellation; but at the same time, its imitation of the divine Logos entails a radical dissolution of the image of a solid selfhood with self-defined and autonomous interests; or, to use the traditional and evocative theological term, it entails a kenotic element. Passion-free perception and reception of what is real is at the heart of what we might call a 'filial' mode of awareness: a Christomorphic mind (cf. Romans 12.2; 1 Corinthians 2.16; Philippians 2.5) is one that understands itself as receiving and communicating the one Logos in a uniquely located mode, from where it actually sits as a material system of energy. The divine Logos is 'embodied' in the entire scheme of finite 'rationality' and its unique and definitive embodiment in the person of the incarnate Word is, above all,

[22] Orion Edgar, op. cit., p. 135.

that which restores to finite substances the capacity to function as vehicles of gift and mutuality rather than being warring elements in a fundamentally violent cosmic system.

III

We have learned, rightly, to be wary of appeals to 'rationality'; the characteristic modern usage of the term is instrumental and focused on the reasoning skills of individuals; it normally stands at a fastidious distance from any kind of metaphysical, let alone spiritual, concern. And in standing at that distance, it continues to compound the increasingly deadly problem of our era, the persistent myth of our essential disembodiedness – in the sense of a belief in our capacity to determine our goals and our fate independently of any alignment with the facts of our always prior belonging in the material world. The characteristic twin distortions of much contemporary semi-popular scientism are, on the one hand, a strict mechanical model of *all* material interaction, including our own brain activity, to the extent that some can toy with the oddly self-subverting notion that consciousness is purely epiphenomenal, and, on the other, a 'trans-humanist' or 'post-humanist' aspiration to reduce our human experience to non-organic systems of information exchange, invulnerable to time and decay. Both assume a gulf between mind and matter, both see 'reason' as a process of solving mental problems. It is incidentally worth asking about the impact of this on some kinds of philosophical anthropology for which a particular model of 'reasoning' capacity becomes what we appeal to in settling the normal conditions for recognizing an agent as 'personal' and deserving of the rights of a person; it is essential for us to think about the 'rationality' of those we stigmatize, patronize, ignore and exclude whose mental capacity is not what we define as 'normal'. The response of gratitude, affection, human sensitivity, ability to relate and cooperate that is visible, for example, in members of the L'Arche communities, where people with significant learning challenges live alongside those who do not have such challenges, should make us hesitate about defining the limits of 'rationality' without reference to such relational qualities. We may begin to see 'reasoning' as a richly analogical term, with an application to any form of consistent and life-sustaining adjustment to the environment, human and non-human.

It is an insight expressed with characteristic clarity by one of the twentieth century's greatest Christian writers. Flannery O'Connor, meditating on Aquinas's definition of art as 'reason in making', laments the way in which 'reason' has 'lost ground' in modernity: 'As grace and nature have been separated, so imagination and reason have been separated, and this always means an end to art. The artist uses his [*sic*] reason to discover an answering reason in everything he sees. For him, *to be reasonable is to find in the object, in the situation, in the sequence, the spirit which makes it itself.*'[23] Which is perhaps as good a definition of *logos* as modern Christian reflection has to offer.

Speaking of *logos* in this connection is therefore a way of challenging the hegemony of a profoundly inadequate account of what we mean by reason. The path to *theosis* is a path to rationality, counter-intuitive as this may sound, once we have grasped something both of the diagnostic of passion and the metaphysics of *logos* in the patristic and Byzantine texts with which we started. We have seen in this and in our introductory chapter that the ideal of perception assumed by these and comparable texts (in the Christian West as well as the East) is 'filial' in the sense that it looks to a state in which we are receiving as fully and comprehensively as possible what God gives for our specific mode of finite existence, and freely cooperating in transmitting life to the rest of the created network – thus echoing the eternal identity of dependence and initiative that is the life of the divine Logos. And whether we are thinking of

---

[23] Quoted Greg Wolfe, *Intruding Upon the Timeless: Essays on Art, Faith, and Mystery*, 2nd edn (Baltimore, MD, Square Halo Books 2018), p. 21.

the needs and dignities of human persons who may not embody the rationality we casually treat as normal and normative, or of the disastrous and suicidal folly of our policies towards the environment we inhabit, it is this filial reasoning that will provide the alternative to an increasingly narrow and life-threatening set of models and rhetorical conventions. In sum, and echoing O'Connor: 'reason' is what attunes us to the reality of where we live in a way that makes possible the fullest mutual movement of life and intelligent communication; it is to be understood theologically as the embodiment in time and space of the eternal receiving and communicating/responding that is the life of the second divine hypostasis. To live consistently as human spirits within this *logos*-animated exchange is 'deification' in the sense of growing into the filial identity for which we are made. From beginning to end, this is a narrative of embodied agency (as if there were in the world any other kind), and to apprehend it as such is to be delivered from the tyranny of a fantasized 'elsewhere' that is the true and proper home of a detached spirit; yet it is also to reflect with sharpened intelligence on the complexities of 'representation' – both the representation of the world we inhabit and the representation of the unrepresentable God. It is a commonplace that the Evagrian tradition provides a clear critique of all attempts to represent God as an inhabitant of the universe and so of all unthinking physical imagery; but this is not a scheme that simply asserts the superiority of spirit over matter as if there were two competing realms. God cannot be materially itemized, listed alongside the ensemble of finite substances as some sort of 'extra' unit, simply because God is the context within which any meaningful representation makes any sense at all: God is that which eternally begets *logos* within the divine life, and gratuitously shapes a finite order in which that *logos* is imitated and participated by in limited and particular material systems. But this could be taken further to imply that *truthfully representing the world we inhabit* means seeking representation that does at least some justice to the range of interconnection that surrounds us – which might suggest some reflection about the 'rationality' of metaphor and symbol, and the activity of the artist as a witness to 'reason' in the sense here outlined.

Thus the discussion so far will have left us with some inchoate thoughts about how the seed sown in the Evagrian texts may grow to have bearing on artistic as well as ethical and even political questions such as we wrestle with in this bleak time of the breaking of cultures and the loss of an authentic humanism. But can we press the question a little further and suggest that the very idea of truthful or just representation – and so of truthful and just *reasoning* – is, for Christian theology, grounded in the divine begetting of *logos*?

IV

Fundamental to the trinitarian vision of divine life is the conviction that it belongs to the very grammar of the divine that God's life is *generative*: it is impossible to think of the divine simply as a One beyond relation or reciprocity. When Karl Barth in the twentieth century writes of God's 'self-repetition' in the trinitarian life, he is giving important expression to this basic orientation.[24] God generates God, and in that sense 'repeats' God. Part of the hinterland of trinitarian language is, of course, the Wisdom tradition of the Hebrew Scriptures and the para-canonical texts that elaborate them. Whether we are directed to a Wisdom that is, before creation, 'alongside' God (as in Prov. 8), or a Wisdom that 'emanates' from the divine like a breath, naming herself as God's active and glorious presence (Sirach 24, Wisdom 7) or a mirror of divine agency (Wisdom 7), the underlying insight is one and the same: it is intrinsic to divine action that it 'resonates' with itself, that it lives and acts in a self-generated harmonic. It gives itself to be given back again; its unity is not naked self-identity, but a moment of self-reflexivity that we could clumsily call a

---

[24] Karl Barth, *Church Dogmatics I.1: The Doctrine of the Word of God*, tr. G. W. Bromiley, 2nd edn (Edinburgh, T&T Clark 1975), e.g., pp. 348–55.

sort of eternal 'feedback'. And the elaboration of the language of *logos* in Greek Christian theology is the canonical vehicle in early Christian thought for expressing this belief: eternal reality is productive of its own reflection, inseparably moving into otherness and returning in what I have elsewhere called[25] (in a different, Christological, context) a non-dual non-identity. God is God in acting so as to be God *to* God; God is God as generating God's perfect reflection *and* God is God in the generativity of that reflection itself as it returns to its source – as Source and Word and Spirit simultaneously.

The idea of eternal *logos* and *sophia* in the divine implies that we can think of the trinitarian life not simply as God's repetition of God, in Barthian terms, but as God's 'correspondence' with God;[26] or in other words, the ontological basis of *truth* is God's self-relation, God's own identity-in-difference, an identity that can be shown/spoken in what it is not. To grasp what truthfulness means, we look to this fundamental fact of divine self-resonance or – to borrow the characteristic vocabulary of the Fourth Gospel (as in, for example, chapters 5 and 15) – divine self-*testimony*. In the Johannine account of divine action, Father, Son and Spirit testify, bear witness to one another; each realizes and manifests what the other is, each tells the truth about its other, and about its other's relation to what is other to that other. Any language about this shows immediate strain; but the basic point is not a complicated one. If God corresponds to God and so truly reflects God, that reflection is a witness to the truth reflected. It is this self-relation and self-testimony that, for a theologian like Origen, enjoins the conclusion that God is 'rational' and that the eternal Logos incarnate in Christ is witness to this rationality – rationality understood

---

[25] Rowan Williams, *Christ the Heart of Creation* (London, Bloomsbury 2018), esp. the concluding chapter.

[26] The awkwardness of speaking about God's 'self-correspondence' was pointed out in discussion of this chapter on its first delivery as a paper, and I grant the problem; but it is difficult to find another way of articulating the idea that God generates a form of divine life and agency that is a non-identical repetition of its source.

as communicable life, life that can represent itself to itself in a non-identical fashion, as a 'true and faithful'[27] repetition of divine life. And if rationality is so understood, as communicable life, non-identically repeated, we can see more readily why, for the Greek Christian tradition, *logos* in the created order is a dimension of finite reality that shares in the eternal Logos: the very idea of intelligibility is grounded in the character of infinite act as self-giving and self-correspondence. Hence the notion we explored earlier in this chapter, a theme central in Eastern Christian thought from Evagrios to Maximos and beyond:[28] mature knowledge is a union of the *logos* in the knower and the *logos* in what is known, so that the paradigm of knowledge is resonance and participation.

This is not a theme without echoes in Western Christian metaphysics, however different the idiom. The Aquinas of the *de veritate*[29] treats the eternal *verbum cordis* within the divine life as the model and source of intellection in finite minds: God's 'word' is God 'imaging' God, 'manifesting' God to God, expressing (in a phrasing that Aquinas takes from Richard of St Victor) the *sensus Patris*, the Father's 'meaning', in and through the immeasurable diversity of finite particulars considered as it were abstractly – as the modes in which divine life is imitable and participable even independently of the actual existence of finite substances. The eternal Word as the Father's infinite other is the ground of the relation of all otherness – finite otherness – to the Father. It is the ground of finite reality's sharing in divine act; it is what holds the diversity of finite existence within the otherness of God to God; it is the way in which the one God is active in the multiplicity of finite reality – not as an external agency alongside finite act, but as infinite act 'corresponding' to itself through the medium of

---

[27] See, for example, Origen's *Commentary on John* I.42, II.4 (GCS *Origenes Werke* 4, Leipzig 1903; ET in *The Anti-Nicene Fathers*, vol. X (Grand Rapids, MI, Eerdmans 1974).
[28] Above, pp. 63–5, 69, 72–3.
[29] See especially *de veritate* IV.1.

finite diversity, just as divine life corresponds to itself eternally and necessarily in the purely relational otherness of the divine persons. So the *verbum* in the finite subject is the subject in harmony with itself in and through its relation with what is other – as it is also the object 'repeating itself' in the knowing subject. Because in finite intellects knowing and existing are *not* the same reality (whereas in God they are the one identical eternal act that is divine life), our 'word' does not *constitute* the otherness in which it is repeated. Our speech does not literally bring into being a radically other reality but 'finds' itself in a reality already spoken to and for it. In God, the Father eternally generates the Word that is the self-correspondence of the Father's hypostatic being in another hypostasis, and also freely repeats that self-correspondence in the 'uttering' of the finite world in which intelligible form is apprehended through the reception by finite intellect of forms grounded in the ultimate structure of intelligibility, the divine Word. Those who have argued that Thomas Aquinas is primarily interested in the *theological* grounding of true knowledge in the *de veritate* are not wrong, though it is somewhat misleading to suggest that his explorations here are therefore not intended to be 'philosophical'.[30] We could more accurately say that Aquinas is arguing that certain convictions about God are basic for making sense of truth-telling, if truth-telling does indeed presuppose a genuine modification of the intellect by what is known (rather than being a simply self-generated activity with no connection to what is other)[31] – and this is a philosophical point as far as it goes; but the convictions about God that are relevant here are convictions about the trinitarian life, not about deity in general, and this should dispose us to take

---

[30]For some helpful discussions of this debate, see *Mental Representation*, vol. 4 of the Proceedings of the Society for Medieval Logic and Metaphysics (Newcastle, Cambridge Scholars Publishing 2011), especially the papers by Gyula Klima and Joshua Hochschild.
[31]See above, pp. 65–6, 68–9.

seriously the claim that Aquinas is advancing a consciously theological, and specifically trinitarian, epistemology.

We could sum up what has been said so far as the argument that God's truthful or faithful correspondence with God's own divine life or act is the condition for all that we call intelligence or rationality; and since that self-resonance or self-correspondence is built in to the doctrine of the Trinity, we have a clear connection between a trinitarian ontology and the particular epistemology – centred upon the idea of knowledge as resonance with *logos*, the range of behaviours expressing and enacting attunement to the communicative and intelligible energy of what is known – that we have traced earlier in this chapter. I have used the phrase, a '*range* of behaviours': as I have argued elsewhere,[32] one of the deepest cultural problems of our day is the assumption that a certain limited range of linguistic and representational behaviours, concentrating on causal analysis, repeatable manipulation and the search for some 'fundamental' level of causality, is what constitutes truthful knowing. In fact, to pick up a theme developed by some phenomenologists in the tradition of Merleau-Ponty, knowing an object in our habitual and unreflective understanding may well include a diversity of sense experience and habitual physical response – the clues and prompts given by taste or touch or smell, all part of our capacity to recognize and map an environment in which we are finding our way as material agents. There is here no substitute for the time it takes to learn such habits of recognition, no timeless compact digest of criteria to be marshalled in the concept-forming mind: ask yourself, for example, what would substitute for the way the sense of smell works in identifying decayed or infected food, or incipient

---

[32] In a forthcoming paper, 'Understanding Our Knowing: The Culture of Representation', presented at the second colloquium of the After Science and Religion' project in Cambridge, July 2019. See also 'Appendix: On Representation', in Rowan Williams, *The Edge of Words: God and the Habits of Language* (London, Bloomsbury 2014), pp. 186–97.

fire.[33] A 'rational' connectedness with the material environment is one that would include appropriate awareness – even if not a conceptually refined translation – of such habits of 'educated' response. To understand human knowing, we need to imagine what we might call an educated *body*. How does this relate to the picture so far sketched?

Educated sense/sensuality implies a physical, ultimately neural, capacity to connect diverse experiences and make of them a coherent pattern; it is a kind of intelligence in the sense that intelligence identifies connectable *form*, consistent patterning in diverse phenomena. Bodies gradually accumulating 'reasonable' habits do just this. And this in turn means that intelligence is naturally working with a spectrum of different kinds of difference – a spectrum of ways in which one substance may be active in another, one set of coherent actions moulding the shape of the act and identity of another. The point is that the way in which a material substance 'repeats' itself is precisely this spectrum of impacts and transactions through bodily engagement that produce in the knowing subject a set of 'apt' or congruent behaviours whose success and sustainability through changing and challenging circumstances demonstrate the reality of the contact with a real otherness. 'Correspondence' to reality as a definition of truthfulness means *the range of sustainable response* activated in a knower in contact with a known object, not simply a set of checkable statements about an object.

Put this in the light of what has been discussed earlier about the trinitarian life, and what comes into focus is this: the universe that we know is a system in which coherent and durable patterns of energy (intelligible forms) characteristically generate in other levels of organized energy a version of their own pattern of life (form gives intelligibility to matter, in more conventional language); and in the case of intelligent,

---

[33] Cf. Orion Edgar, op. cit., ch. 2 on eating as a form of perception/knowledge.

language-using subjects, this generated version of a received form may exist across a range of activities from physical habit to mental representation of various sorts (picturing, mathematical modelling, verbal symbolization and so on). This is how in the finite world a substance 'corresponds' to itself, repeats itself; this is how it is 'truly' received. In rethinking our epistemology to escape from the tyranny of a representation confined to one limited, 'canonical' mode (say mathematical modelling), claimed as the fundamental form of true knowledge, we need not only a participatory model of knowledge (as an increasing number of thinkers seem to agree), but more specifically a model that understands the shape of finite reality itself as non-identical repetition – grounded in the truth that the source of finite reality is the non-identical repetition that is the divine life. To speak of what is actual is always to speak of this: 'what is' is always necessarily action that generates its reflection in difference. As we noted earlier, difference within God can be thought only in terms of relation, since there can be no intelligible way of ascribing temporal dilation, physical distance, oppositional or exclusive confrontation to the ultimate generative act that is God's life. But, as Aquinas argues, echoing Richard of St Victor, God expresses the *sensus* of what God is in the begetting of the eternal Word; God 'acts upon' God, the Father acts in begetting the Word, in something we can only represent as analogous to our self-reflection, the process by which we continuously *own* what is already the content of our identity, but in so doing augment and differentiate that content. We cannot *in divinis* speak of 'augmentation', of course, but we can perhaps use the language as a springboard for imagining how the non-identical repetition that is the eternal Word is also the condition of that divine dimension of action that we call Spirit, that which is irreducible to either 'Father' or 'Son'. Divine life is not an emergence into duality and a collapse back into identity; if we pursue the 'feedback' analogy mentioned earlier, we can dimly see how the primordial repetition that is the Word, in reflecting the Source's reality truthfully to the Source, posits that the Source *as* self-giving and self-corresponding is not now 'caught' in a sterile self-repetition, a mere second identity, but is established as generative in a different mode.[34]

V

To say that these are ambitious (over-ambitious?) and speculative ideas is obvious. But it is important to try and set out how a trinitarian ontology mandates a particular approach to epistemology, so as to clarify a central and pivotal concern for any theologically inflected philosophy – the need to challenge reductive models of knowing that assume the normative status of non-relational, descriptive and external modes of understanding the environment and fail to deal with the mutual 'implication' of knower and known. If the foundational rhythm of reality is – so to speak – utterance and resonance and enhanced utterance, then it is not merely the case that language 'represents' reality: reality itself is linguistic, in the sense that intelligible communication, the giving and receiving of intelligible form, is ultimately *what there is*. And this in turn is not just to say that fundamental reality communicates what it is: mutual communication, the life of reality in what it is not and the simultaneous return of that 'what it is not' to what it repeats, is the most basic characterization of 'being' that we can offer. It is not a theme that has found many modern theological explorers, but the not very well-known work of Sergii Bulgakov, *Chapters on the Trinity*, sketches such a 'linguistic' account of trinitarian life, seeing the relation of subject, predicate and copula as a reflection of the grammar of divinity.[35] What *is* is not exhausted in its bare self-identity; it is capable of being

---

[34] This is the force of John Milbank's seminal essay, 'The Second Difference', in his collection, *The Word Made Strange: Theology, Language, Culture* (Oxford, Blackwell 1997), pp. 171–93.

[35] Sergii Bulgakov, '*Glavy o troichnosti*' part 1, in the journal *Pravoslavnaya Mysl*, 1928, pp. 31–88.

'named', and so establishes itself as generating a kind of 'tension' (in a non-pejorative sense) between its sheer exercise of being and the interwoven actuality of that being as gift and response. If all language is not to fall back into tautology ('x is what it is'), it must reflect the truth that x's being what it is involves its being in or for what it generates in action and 'feeds back' into itself as part of its definition. 'x is y' states that x cannot be itself without an active exercise of being in which it is not self-identical; and, for Bulgakov, this is grounded in the ultimate 'antinomy' of being that is the simultaneous absoluteness of God, God's 'no-thing-ness', and God's self-differentiation or self-relation.[36] Recognizing this antinomy saves us from two basic errors in theology: making the 'absoluteness' of God a sort of exclusive conceptual definition that would render the trinitarian life (and so ultimately the engagement of God with creation) unthinkable; and reducing the divine life to a contingent plurality of instances of 'divine nature' – with the implication that the foundational structure of the world is likewise a series of instances of nature, existing primitively in mutual isolation, and subsequently coming into relation. What Bulgakov is seeking, in common with many more recent theologians, is a way of affirming the irreducibility of relation; his originality is in linking this to the working of language itself, seeing language as a key to the inescapability of non-identical correspondence and being-in-the other for our understanding of the real.

I have suggested above that truthful representation is a notion that should include all forms of appropriate and sustainable responses to the environment in which intelligence is at work.[37] In this sense, a certain kind of habit may constitute for some purposes a 'truthful representation': the exercise of a skill like wood-carving or violin-playing involves the body in *showing* how an instrument is constructed and how it can effectively operate. The skill *tells* us something. Its successful exercise is the meeting place of identities

[36] Cf. Bulgakov's *Icons and the Name of God* (Grand Rapids, MI, Eerdmans 2012).
[37] Cf. the essay referred to above, n. 30.

realized in each other – the tool or instrument is meaningless independently of its activation in this particular mode, and the craftsman or performer is 'in-formed' by the possibilities of the tool or instrument, acquires new definition through this formative relation and in so doing exhibits both their own identity and that of the object used. But this in turn moves into a 'telling' about the material worked on, whether the literally material stuff of wood being carved or the 'matter' of musical relations and frequencies; another definitive frontier between identity and otherness opens up. Truth-telling comes into focus as something involving a whole history of convergence between identities, centred on what could be called a sustainable habit of engagement, an 'apt' response that is effective and generative because it is fitted to the *act* of what it responds to/represents. As Klaus Hemmerle observes in his celebrated *Theses on Trinitarian Ontology*,[38] things are only what they are in action, 'And this action is a constitution, a communication, a delimitation and an adaptation to an overarching context.'

The present discussion has attempted, as Hemmerle himself does, to move a little further. The contention is that knowledge is like this, intelligence is like this, because of the basic character of reality as shown in the trinitarian life of God. Logos, as we all know, is more than 'word'; but what theologians came to say about the eternal Logos, and then about the role of *logos* in the processes of human cognition and conscious agency, allows us to say that – as Aquinas seems to assume – our speech, in the broadest sense, is both a clue to thinking about the triune God and a reality comprehensively illuminated by that God. The act of naming, representing, acknowledges the way in which identities 'call out' for vehicles that will manifest their non-identity, that will repeat them in a correspondence that is not just static 'reproduction'. This is why – to borrow Hemmerle's phrasing again[39] – human beings discover that they are 'present

[38] Klaus Hemmerle, *Thesen zu einer trinitarischen Ontologie* (Einsiedeln, Johannes Verlag 1992), #20. ET *Theses Towards a Trinitarian Ontology* (New York, Angelico Press 2021).
[39] Ibid., #11.

in everything which [their] questioning and thinking encounter'. And at the heart of this aspect of our intelligence – which is both verbal in the straightforward sense and also pre-verbal and para-verbal and post-verbal – is the trinitarian source of finite being, which *is* only in differentiated harmony with itself. Because it corresponds to or coincides with itself in non-identical fashion, we can understand that there is no context in which mere self-identity is the final stopping-point of ontological analysis. What is, is communicable, repeatable, generative of representation. All our own intelligent life is in one way or another bound up in 'cultures of representation', the search for sustainable relatedness within the complex of the finite world. But because the divine is not in any way a further or supreme instance of 'being', God in 'telling the truth' about the divine life through the generation of the Word simultaneously tells the truth about all finite reality, establishing that it is in relation to God that each finite identity ultimately has its ground, and so also grounding the irreducibility of mutual relation between finite identities in virtue of their common relatedness to God. If all *logoi* exist in the one eternal Logos, each distinct finite *logos* has at its root a relation it shares with every other; and thus each has a relation with an eternal Logos that is simultaneously the root and rationale of every other, so that the *multiform* relatedness of the eternal Logos is what each is related to – and thereby related to each other.

The Wisdom celebrated in Hebrew Scripture is therefore not just a mechanism for diffusing divine agency to an inferior level (arguably this is the position associated with Arius in the debates of the fourth Christian century). The significance of words like 'mirror' and 'emanation' (*katoptron* and *aporroia* or *apaugasma*) for the Origenian tradition makes a larger claim about a God whose life is intrinsically communicative – not in any sense that would 'require' creation as a recipient of communication but in virtue of its own reality as intelligent and loving. We assume that God's generative life cannot be *less* than intelligent and loving, even if we cannot say what the inseparable exercise of infinite intelligence and love is *like*. That God is in correspondence with God is, for the Nicene theology of the fourth century, the condition of the reality of divine communication with the finite, both in the ongoing self-giving of creation itself and in the specific moments we identify as revelation. Karl Barth's fundamental theological insight about trinitarian theology was that the Trinity illuminated how and why God could speak to us; God is able to speak in revelation because God is primordially the God who utters God's self to God's self. In the grammar of our talk about God's eternity, this is not – as it is in God's relation with the finite and in the relation of one finite substance to another – any kind of supplement, making up what is lacking, initiating a process of enhancement or (to use the word used here earlier) 'augmentation'. God does not 'inform' God, activate a potentiality in God and so forth. The challenge of a thoroughgoing trinitarian scheme is to imagine a being-in-the other that is purely and simply a matter of simultaneous self-constitution in relation; and for this we have no adequate analogy. To return to Bulgakov's treatment of his 'antinomies', this is where the real absoluteness of God imposes an apophatic humility. It is not that we are unable to discover an essential/conceptual definition of God; we have no tools that could finally clarify what it means to say that the Father is not Father except as Father of the Son and breather of the Spirit – that God is not God except in giving and bringing back the divine life to itself and so establishing itself as intelligent and loving.

The point about apophasis is important. None of this discussion should be taken as an attempt to anatomize the divine life 'in itself'. Its purpose is simply to clarify what is entailed by the claim that our own intelligence and love 'image' their divine origin. What Hemmerle calls the discovery of my knowing self in all that I know is the finite echo of the truth that infinite agency is a self-differentiation, an identity in otherness. This is shown to us in the event of Jesus, the human life in which the internal reciprocity of God with God and the overflow or excess of that reciprocity is spelled out in temporal sequence – as the gift of the Father to the incarnate Son by the bestowal of the Spirit, the gift of the Son to the Father in obedient love and the gift of the Spirit to the Church, a process in which each divine agent bears truthful witness to the other(s), as the Farewell Discourses in John's Gospel explain. We are able to understand this idea of divine witness in the context of historical narrative; but we have no resource that will enable us to conceptualize what this 'witness' means in eternity, except to say that it is the way in which God exercises indivisibly the love and intelligence of which we are the created shadows. And if the whole structure of this argument is correct, then our knowing of the triune God is in any case not the construction of a conceptual framework but the 'aptness' of a life that fits with the constraining and defining reality of God's being – a knowing that is first the relation of self-forgetfulness in the face of the divine, the carrying of the cross, and the filial prayer of *Abba*. This is what a theologian like Vladimir Lossky meant by insisting that 'negative theology' could not be understood as simply a moment in the verbal negotiation of what could and could not be said of God, a phase in the to and fro of definitional ventures; it had, rather, to be grasped as a habit of faithful living (once again, an 'apt' response to divine agency).[40]

Rethinking *logos* – infinite and finite – for our times is thus a matter of thinking together God's self-correspondence, God's truthfulness to God, with our own self-discovery in what we know and our attempts not only to create truthful formulation of what we encounter but to develop a sustainable lived response to it. The more we elucidate what is meant by God's self-correspondence in the trinitarian life, the meaning of terms like Word and Wisdom and image, the more we understand how language – generously defined – is ontologically basic. The more we clarify what our own knowledge as finite intelligences involves, the more we see that intelligence and speech – again, generously defined, and including symbolic and communicative

---

[40] E.g. Vladimir Lossky, 'Apophasis and Trinitarian Theology' in *In the Image and Likeness of God* (Crestwood, NY, St Vladimir's Seminary Press 1974), pp. 13–29; cf. 'Lossky, the *via negative* and the Foundation of Theology' in Rowan Williams, *Wrestling With Angels: Conversations in Modern Theology*, ed. Mike Higton (London, SCM Press 2007), pp. 1–24.

gesture – are not inexplicable or gratuitous outgrowths on the body of solidly atomistic material realities. Bringing these two intellectual exercises together is a complex business, but it is, so I have argued, a necessary task in a climate of debased accounts of human intellect and a nervousness about religiously moulded metaphysics. I have tried to suggest that it is ultimately scriptural talk of God that prompts the particular metaphysical trajectory we have been considering, and that the emerging metaphysic and epistemology, so far from making our discourse more abstract, in fact reinforces the centrality of practice and of material location and temporality. Appropriately perhaps, it is a metaphysic that proposes incarnation and kenosis to finite subjects as the ground of truthfulness – just as they are the form taken by divine truthfulness, 'self-correspondence', in God's enfleshed speech to us.

4

PARTICIPATING DIVINITY, ENTERING EMPTINESS: THE SHAPE OF TRANSFORMATION

I

The preceding chapter began to look at the ways in which we might seek to understand the classical Christian language about 'deification', participation in the life of God, *theosis*, as the goal of God's saving and restoring work in human beings – language that continues to puzzle and even alienate some, though the number of careful and wide-ranging studies of the subject in the last couple of decades has made such alienation rather more rare, at least among those with any claim to serious familiarity with Christian intellectual history.[1] Part of the difficulty lies in the hybrid conceptual origins of the idea; part lies in an uncertainty about where and how it fits with both fundamental teaching about prayer and its disciplines and central doctrinal themes.

---

[1] The work of Norman Russell deserves special mention here, from his magisterial monograph on *The Doctrine of Deification in the Greek Patristic Tradition*, 2nd edn (Oxford, Oxford University Press 2006), to his overview of more recent theology in *Fellow-Workers With God: Orthodox Thinking on Theosis* (Crestwood, NY, St Vladimir's Seminary Press, 2009). See also Panayiotis Nellas, *Deification in Christ: The Nature of the Human Person* (Crestwood, NY, St Vladimir's Seminary Press 1987), for an attempt to integrate the theme into a comprehensive Christian anthropology, and Emil Bartos, *Deification in Eastern Orthodox Theology: An Evaluation and Critique of the Theology of Dumitru Staniloae* (Carlisle, Paternoster Press 1999), for a wide-ranging comparative discussion of a number of twentieth-century Orthodox writers (though not including Fr Sophrony).

This chapter will attempt both to clarify these origins a little and to tease out why the diverse elements need each other and combine to produce what is not only a coherent doctrinal stance but one that illuminates other areas of theology – and practice – in unexpected ways. And to elucidate this, we shall be making use especially of the distinctive perspective of one modern Orthodox spiritual teacher, whose analysis of what deification means succeeds in holding the elements of the tradition in an unusually cohesive scheme.

The 'hybridity' mentioned can be briefly categorized in these terms: on the one hand, Christian teaching from the very first has taken for granted that the fundamental *novum* in Christian identity is the gift of being able to address God as Jesus did, as 'Abba, Father' (Romans 8.15, Galatians 4.6; and cf. Ephesians 2.18, as well as the Johannine development of the idea, as in John 14.3, 6-7, 20; 16.23-4; 17.24; 20.17; 1 John 3.1-2, etc.); on the other, Christian practice took for granted a disciplining of the passions that was oriented towards a state of freedom from compulsion by instinct, a state that could be described as godlike, a *mimesis* of divine life involving a share in divine wisdom (e.g. 1 Corinthians 2.13-16; 2 Corinthians 4.4-6; Ephesians 2.4-7, 3.19, 4.24, 5.1-2; Colossians 2.9-10; and, most famously, 2 Peter 1.4). In the context of the New Testament, any disjunction between the two approaches is pretty artificial, since sharing in Christ's relation to the Father is manifestly and explicitly the ground of transformed behaviour and a new mind. However, as Christian reflection developed, the idea of reflecting the *kind* of life lived by God, immortal, stable and free of passion, drew more and more deeply on available models of such transformation in the intellectual world of late antiquity,[2] and the

---

[2] Apart from Russell, *The Doctrine of Deification*, see, for example, D. L. Balas, *Metousia Theou: Man's Participation in God's Perfections* (Rome, Studia Anselmiana 55 1966); and Richard Sorabji, *Emotion and Peace of Mind: From Stoic Agitation to Christian Temptation* (Oxford, Oxford University Press 2000), on models of stability and passion-free mental existence. More recently, Andrew Davison, *Participation in God: A Study in Christian Doctrine and Metaphysics* (Cambridge, Cambridge University Press 2019), offers a wide-ranging and sophisticated discussion of the relevant language.

connection with the basic theme of filiation is sometimes hard to discern. The undeniable difference in focus between emphasizing relation to the Father and emphasizing our accession to a certain 'interior' or 'spiritual' state becomes ever more marked. And so in Christian history these two emphases, which we might call 'filiation' and 'purification', constantly drift apart, recombine, are redefined and reworked; it is the positive tension between them that gives the doctrine its significance, as we shall see, but that positive tension needs to be repeatedly refreshed by new theological strategies. Such refreshment is part of what this chapter aims at.

The more the Church clarifies its belief in Jesus Christ as the unique incarnation of the eternal Word, the more an understanding of filiation moves away from the simple 'imitation' of a paradigm of spiritual practice (calling God what Jesus called God) into a comprehensive re-framing or reconfiguring of a finite life in relation to God. Paul's language in Romans 8 already understands the 'Abba' prayer as an act that is not our own but the activity within us of the Spirit: our prayer is immersed in eternal activity, specifically the divine 'repetition' in us by the Spirit of the movement of the Word towards the Father. This prayerful immersion in eternal act, with its expression in the word of address to God the Father, is the manifestation of a comprehensive transformation, since it expresses what we have actually become – adopted children. And while the language is inevitably rooted in and connected in certain ways with our habitual ways of speaking about relations between specific finite agents, the increasing refinement of Nicene theology in East and West makes it clear that we cannot characterize the relation of Father and Word as a *case* of interpersonal intimacy of the sort usually designated by this language of familial intimacy. Various theologies have found various ways of reinforcing the point, from Dionysius's insistence that the Trinity is not either one or three in the sense we are used to,[3] up to Nicolas of Cusa's use of

---

[3] Dionysius, *de divinis nominibus* XIII.3 (PG 3, 981A).

non aliud – non-otherness, distinguished from simple identity –
to describe the divine relations and the relations between God
and the creation.[4] To speak of filiation in the context of a fully
developed trinitarian schema is to speak of induction into a
relation with the divine Source which is, crucially, *non-dualistic* –
neither an undifferentiated identity nor a confrontation of distinct
self-subsisting subjects. And so to pursue an understanding of
filiation becomes something that challenges certain models of
relation between finite and infinite. It means that we cannot
ultimately conceive of our relation to God as that of individual
to individual; and our prayer is invited to move out of a simple
model of *address* in the direction of what we could call an
'inhabiting', difficult (appropriately) to define within the usual
terms of finite interrelation, subject to subject, subject to object,
substance to substance.

Filiation thus understood implies the dissolution of our familiar
models of the religious subject – a human individual having
'religious experiences' or enjoying 'personal relation' with God
(in the conventional sense of those words). If our encounter with
God the Father is encounter with the trinitarian *non aliud*, then
the otherness between myself and God is – to offer a hopelessly
but unavoidably clumsy formulation – 'other' to all other forms
of otherness. And to assimilate this and live from it thus requires
me to strip away in my relation to God all habits and images that
potentially reduce God to 'other forms of otherness'. But this – as
we saw in the last chapter – is in turn to pose a radical challenge
to the entire gamut of human 'passion': to all the defensive and
aggressive patterns of relating to what is other to my ego or my
will that dominate our humanity and secure its unredeemed
state of slavery. To reconceive encounter with God as something
beyond a confrontation of 'selves' relativizes what I say, sense or
believe about my 'self' and its supposed needs and well-being.
And this relativizes all the strategies by which I seek to sustain

---

[4] See his treatise, *de non aliud*, of 1462; ET by Jasper Hopkins 3rd edn (Minneapolis, MN,
Arthur J. Banning Press 1987).

or protect the self I am familiar with; in this context, it should be possible to see how those forms of discipline that steadily erode such habits are aimed not at some detached condition of ideal spiritual independence but at filiation in its fullest meaning. The trinitarian grounding of filiation pushes us to a deeper grasp of purification; the work of purification helps us avoid a model of filiation that leaves the protective/protected self intact. We should expect a certain movement back and forth between the two poles at different points in theological development; but what is important is that they continue to illuminate one another. An orientation towards filiation in simple terms will risk making relation to God a *case* of relation to others – here am I and there is the God I call 'Father' – leaving the self's habits intact and untransformed. An orientation towards purification alone may focus our attention on the condition of our 'interior' life in a way that could tempt us to forget that this 'inner' life, if it is life in Christ, is a process of coming to inhabit divine relatedness. It may indeed issue in what is finally no more than a vastly refined individualism, potentially worse than the unreconstructed individualism of 'naive' filiation.

The category that holds all this together, as several writers of the last century argued,[5] is *kenosis*. The eternal existence of God the Word is 'kenotic' in that it is wholly defined not by any individual intrinsic property located in some autonomous divine subject but by its derivation from and orientation to the Father: what it is to be the Word *is* to be that which is poured out from the eternal Source (which is thus itself kenotically actualized, in being entirely that which 'spends itself in bestowing life in the

---

[5] Vladimir Lossky, *The Mystical Theology of the Eastern Church* (Cambridge, James Clarke 1957), especially pp. 144–9; for the theme in Sergii Bulgakov, see, for example, Rowan Williams, *Sergii Bulgakov: Towards a Russian Political Theology* (Edinburgh, T&T Clark, 1999), pp. 177, 193–6, and Aidan Nichols, *Wisdom from Above: A Primer in the Theology of Father Sergei Bulgakov* (Leominster, Gracewing 2005), especially ch. 6, an excellent summary of Bulgakov's handling of this subject. See also Christos Yannaras, *Person and Eros* (Brookline, MA, Holy Cross Orthodox Press 2007), for a developed anthropology in which this theme is of focal importance.

Word and Spirit'), and that which responsively flows back to the Source. To attempt to put it in the most basic terms, there is nothing for the Word to be or do except to *be from* the Father and towards the Father (the *pros ton theon* of the first chapter of John's Gospel); the Word has no action or subsistence that is not wholly characterized by relatedness to the Source. The life of God is entirely the *communication* of life; so what we mean by speaking of the divine *hypostaseis* – the three 'persons' or 'subsistent realities' that constitute the life of God – is simply the moment or point from which life is being communicated: the point of the eternal Source, the point of the eternal derived and responsive Word, the point of the inexhaustible 'witness' to the Source and the Word that preserves their relation as open and generative and is nothing but what the Father gives and what the Son gives back, yet is not identical with either or both. To inhabit this reality is to be assimilated to this 'hypostatic' world, where there is nothing that is *possessed*, no solid self that owns, accumulates, gives or holds back according to will: in this sense, 'deification' is the process of becoming hypostatic, personal in the strictest theological sense. Archimandrite Sophrony (Sakharov 1896–1993), whose writings set this out more explicitly than any other twentieth-century teacher, speaks of the human potential given by God in creation to be not simply a 'created hypostasis', a centre of communication and intercommunication within the world, but a 'universal centre',[6] a place where the boundaryless action of God *occurs*; the eternal 'I Am' is now uttered in the creaturely 'I'.[7] When the created subject receives the revelation of divine hypostatic being through relation with Christ in the Spirit, that subject is radically altered: our existence begins to become hypostatic in the divine mode, that is, to be structured by, defined by, kenosis, the dissolution of the ego's defence and individual

---

[6] Archimandrite Sophrony (Sakharov), *We Shall See Him As He Is* (Maldon, Stavropegic Monastery of St John the Baptist 1988), p. 201.
[7] Ibid., 199, 204–5; cf. Coleridge's often-cited remark about the repetition in time of the eternal 'I AM'.

interest. This is not, as Fr Sophrony makes plain, a reduction to 'impersonal' life but exactly the contrary: our distinctness becomes not a solid identity but a unique 'point', to use the image again, from which the communication of life radiates. But to become personal in this mode is indeed antithetical to most of what we typically think of as personal, which is in fact to do with the fantasy of the substantive individual over against God and other subjects. The discipline of realizing the gift of deification/ hypostatization is precisely that purification from passion that has figured so largely in traditional accounts of deification, but has to be contextualized within the frame of filiation.

Fr Sophrony's perspective becomes still clearer (and more challenging) as he interprets this particularly through the lens of the prayer of Jesus in Gethsemane and in connection with the experience of 'God-forsakenness' – a nexus of insights explored with great precision and perception by Nicholas Sakharov in his monograph on Fr Sophrony.[8] Gethsemane is for Christ the moment when the human realization of his final self-emptying on the cross becomes most immediate, and the abyss of human need and pain opens up with unprecedented clarity. Hence his prayer of 'Abba, Father' in Gethsemane is a kind of summation of 'hypostatic' prayer, a summation of the kenotic intensity of identification with all. As Sakharov brings out in his chapter on Fr Sophrony's teaching on God-forsakenness, the focus here on deification as a participation in the hypostatic life of God allows for the *effect* of kenotic identification to be experienced in a way that is not so obviously intelligible within the more traditional framework that associates deification with the divine energies; or rather, Fr Sophrony's model insists that the life of God *en energeiai* can never be other than hypostatically actualized, and thus kenotic.[9] When God permits the believer to feel the full weight of the world's anguish, without any sustaining awareness

---

[8]Nicholas V. Sakharov, *I Love, Therefore I Am: The Theological Legacy of Archimandrite Sophrony* (Crestwood, NY, St Vladimir's Seminary Press 2002).
[9]Ibid., pp. 175–6.

(at the affective level) of God's presence, this is, according to Fr Sophrony, in order that we may rediscover that we are not so *dominated* by the grace of God that we are no longer free. The sense of being forsaken and at the mercy of the diabolic is an aspect of our growth in 'hypostatic' maturity: we are confronted with the intrinsic emptiness of our 'selfhood' in isolation, and so are redirected to our need to renew our openness to the reality of the threefold God. But to be confronted with that emptiness is to see both in ourselves and in the world the intensity of evil, 'the "curse" of our inheritance.'[10] Hence Fr Sophrony's charting of spiritual growth as a movement of three stages:[11] an initial radical opening to the hypostatic reality of God; a 'descent into hell', in which we are faced with the vacuity of what is not God, in and beyond our own selves, provoking revulsion, a hatred of the illusory self; and finally a realized awareness, a spiritual 'settling' in which God's truth is transparent, not as a content of the intellect but as an unmistakeable climate for the life being lived. Fr Sophrony describes[12] the transition from second to third stage as a transformation from anguish over one's own suffering to anguish over the world's suffering: 'My sense of being doomed caused me great agony and this agony cracked the walls of my stony heart. As I was accustomed to apply my experiences to all mankind, I felt pity for all who, like me, were distanced from God. Thus humanity's sufferings became mine, and in the solitude of the desert prayer would come to me for the whole world as for myself.'[13] What is being described, it seems, is the process whereby my sense of desolation is transformed into a Gethsemane-like prayer that takes on the burden of suffering, seeking to 'align' it with the relational life of the threefold God; and in that process the anguish of acknowledging Godlessness

---

[10] *We Shall See Him As He Is*, p. 123.
[11] Nicholas Sakharov, op. cit., pp. 177ff., cf. *We Shall See Him As He Is*, pp. 223–32.
[12] *We Shall See Him As He Is*, pp. 229–30.
[13] Ibid.

within my own soul and in the world becomes a compassion that is aware of its eternal rootedness.

Thus what is distinctive in Fr Sophrony's presentation of deification is that the state of fully inhabiting the divine interaction or interdependence is connected at every level with the personal/ hypostatic: deification is 'hypostatization' in its fullest possible sense – growth into a mode of life that is continuous with that of the Word's relation with the Father and as such is radically exposed both to the mystery of divine self-bestowal and to the need and suffering of the world. The 'divinized' subject is the undefended subject; the narrative of deification as outlined by Fr Sophrony is the narrative of losing protection – first through the sheer impact of revelation, then through the consequent exposure to inner and outer meaninglessness and the assaults of the negative and destructive agencies that will afflict a self with its defences down, then through the habitual recognition of alignment with a limitless relatedness that comes to light in the process of desolation or forsakenness. Nicholas Sakharov has a very illuminating discussion of where this scheme does and does not overlap with that of St John of the Cross, noting that in Fr Sophrony and other Eastern authors the equivalent of the 'passive night of the spirit', the most intense phase of desolation, is associated directly with diabolical assault rather than, as in John, with the increasingly consuming pressure on the soul of divine reality itself, the blinding effect of too much light.[14] It might also be noted that John of the Cross does not specifically associate the intensity of desolation with a breakthrough into solidarity with the suffering of others, though a case could well be made that this is an implication of his language about the purification of love involved in the process. As Sakharov rightly notes,[15] there is a nineteenth- and twentieth-century Russian background to Sophrony's stress on Gethsemane, from Metropolitan Filaret of Moscow through Antonii Khrapovitskii to Sergii Bulgakov.

[14] Nicholas Sakharov, op. cit., pp. 181–6, 187ff.
[15] Ibid., pp. 186–7.

Gethsemane exhibits Christ's sharing in human fear and abandonment, but it thus also exhibits the character of God's personal being as free from defence against the world's otherness in its most malign manifestations. This is both a theological insight about *kenosis* and (especially for Khrapovitskii) a model for pastoral engagement;[16] but none of the earlier Russians connect it explicitly with the development of the life of prayer in the way Sophrony does. For him, Gethsemane represents a specific stage in spiritual growth, when divine personal being breaks through in a new way as a result of an awareness of apparently inexhaustible suffering outside and humiliation, failure and emptiness within.

As Sakharov stresses, this inscription of God-forsakenness at the heart of the narrative of deification is in marked tension with the approach of some other Orthodox writers, especially Vladimir Lossky,[17] but it is not wholly without patristic support. What matters, though, is that the connections opened up by this all show an understanding of deification that links it far more deeply and intrinsically to practice as well as to other areas of doctrine. First of all: the fundamental challenge to any picturing of our relation to God as that of finite individual to infinite individual is obviously of a piece with all those elements of the ascetical tradition that insist on the abandonment of images at certain points in the spirit's growth. The Father who is *non aliud* to the Son is likewise not an object or item among others in the mental world of the baptized believer, the person praying in Christ; not 'an' other, yet in no way identical to the self's contents. This 'otherness to all other kinds of otherness', as we called it earlier, requires a complex and self-aware deployment of images and ideas to do with the divine – not a plain rejection (because our notions of what constitutes an absence of images will be as

---

[16] See, for example, Antonii Khrapovitskii, *L'idée morale des dogmes de la Trés Sainte Trinité, de la divinité de Jésus-Christ et de la rédemption* (Paris, Welter 1910), pp. 33 to end.

[17] Nicholas Sakharov, ch. 7, *passim*; cf., for example, Lossky, *Mystical Theology*, pp. 226–7.

laden with presuppositions as the rest of our imaginative life), but a consistent habit of 'reading' images so as to allow their own tensions and tendings to break open various fixed assumptions about or pictures of the divine. The cross of the incarnate Word is, of course, the primary instance of an image that breaks images and opens a path. But, as we have seen, the challenge to images of the divine entails a challenge also to images of the self, involves a questioning of the solid autonomous or self-subsistent subject. And thus the *askesis* of denying images of the divine is inseparable from the denial of an illusory selfhood; it is an opening up of the idea of the subject simply as 'place' or 'moment', that from which divine life is communicated in one unrepeatably distinctive mode. The entire ascetical endeavour is thus configured as a dissolution of what is *not yet personal* in the full and theologically determined sense. And connecting this to the discussion of earlier chapters, we could thus say that encounter with and union with *logos* in the created order and ultimately with the divine Logos in which/ whom all *logoi* are unified and grounded is a breakthrough into *personal*, 'hypostatic' existence.

Deification understood as 'hypostatization' in Fr Sophrony's sense is the culmination of baptismal identification with and incorporation in Christ: it denotes the change in how we apprehend the self that results from being opened up to the divine agency. Because this divine agency is always irreducibly and fundamentally a kenotic movement, the way in which it modifies our habitual self-image and self-experience is in a kenotic direction; and in the light of the gospel narrative, especially the account of Christ's agony in Gethsemane, we grasp that the act of kenosis in respect of the world we live in is not simply a pouring-out of the self but an opening of the self to the anguish and need of others. Deification is an intensified vulnerability, not some movement into a secure isolation; though at the same time it is important not to see this as some sort of enhanced emotional sensibility, an indulging of 'passion' through the suffering of others (a complex issue that would require longer treatment). Sophrony's analysis of the stages of growth suggests that what happens in the second level of maturation is that my own awareness of my inner emptiness, my utter failure to embody by my own will and strength the self-bestowing love that is God's agency, brings me into solidarity with any and every human situation where the non-appearance of divine love creates pain and fear: not, therefore, a matter of identification with the emotional state of another but the awareness of a *shared* condition of suffering and insecurity, bearable, if at all, through the acknowledgement of what is being broken and remade in this process, that is, the acknowledgement of this as that by which we become 'personal'.[18] Twentieth-century Orthodox theology – Lossky especially but others too[19] – has laid great stress on the interplay between the one unchanging form of sanctified life, which is the self-emptying of God the Word, and the infinite diversity of particular lives of faith shaped by the indwelling of Christ's Spirit. From the point of view of Fr Sophrony's account, this duality means simply that each particular human 'location', each site in which the hypostatic life of God will be actualized, will *receive* in an unrepeatable mode that gift of personalization and live it out in the way it also receives the will, need, pressure of the human other: Nicholas Sakharov traces how this shapes Sophrony's understanding of obedience in the believer's life as a realization of divine *perichoresis*, interpenetration: but he also notes that it is grounded in the ascetic practice of first 'taking into oneself' the will and reality of the other through formation in obedience to a spiritual elder:[20] the basic practice of attentive openness to the authority of the elder equips us to enter and be entered by the suffering of the other. In other words, the point of asserting the uniqueness of each particular finite image of God as he or

---

[18] For a modern testimony to the faithful and hopeful handling of extreme spiritual dereliction as intrinsic to sanctification and 'personalization' by means of an unprotected identification with the God-forsaken, we might look to Mother Teresa of Calcutta's letters and journals: *Come Be My Light: The Private Writings of the "Saint of Calcutta"*, ed. Brian Kolodiejchuk (New York and London, Doubleday 2007).

[19] See, for example, John Zizioulas, *Communion and Otherness; Further Studies in Personhood and the Church* (London, T&T Clark 2006).

[20] Nicholas Sakharov, op. cit., pp. 213–16.

she is deified is not to make what could be a rather routine point about how grace does not extinguish natural human diversity; it is more to say that we are constantly becoming, in the life of deifying grace, ever more uniquely 'personal' precisely in our opening to the otherness of God and our neighbour. Or, put more simply perhaps, it is not that grace simply affirms our existing diversity but that it creates a *deeper* diversity, a spiritual uniqueness, through the reconstruction of our selfhood in kenosis.[21]

Summing up the areas of theological discourse that are thus illuminated by such a view of deification, we may point to:

i. The theology of creation: understanding God's agency
    as always kenotic means that the difference between
    God and creation – and most specifically between God
    and the human subject – is unlike any other difference.
    It is not a distance between two coordinate realities, it
    is not in any conceivable way a rivalry requiring one
    to flourish at the other's expense. This is an otherness
    grounded in the simple freedom of divine agency,
    the will that there be an other to God; but because
    it is grounded in this will, it cannot be other as finite
    realities are other to each other. Such finite otherness is
    supremely the embodiment of our limitedness, while the
    otherness between God and the world is the actualizing
    of God's unlimited freedom.

ii. The theology of the Trinity: God's unlimited freedom is
    not the supreme instance of *individual* self-determining –
    the fantasy that we create out of our misunderstanding
    or lack of understanding of the personal. It is the
    freedom of self-bestowal or self-sharing without limit.
    Nothing constrains the giving of God's agency. The life

[21] See the brilliant essay by Verna Harrison, 'Human Uniqueness and Human Unity', in John Behr, Andrew Louth and Dimitri Conomos, eds, *Abba: The Tradition of Orthodoxy in the West. Festschrift for Bishop Kallistos Ware* (Crestwood, NY, St Vladimir's Seminary Press 2003), pp. 207–20.

of God as revealed in the events of the life and death
and resurrection of Jesus is neither the story of a divine
individual nor the story of a transaction between distinct
agents, but the manifestation of the *non aliud* relation
of interdependent moments or points from which divine
giving occurs – neither assimilation nor separation.

iii. The theology of the person of Christ: in the life of Jesus,
there is a unique and unconditional coincidence of the
eternal 'point' of divine agency that we call the Word or
Son and a point within human history. Thus from this
point in human history, divine life is communicated in its
fullness; but this also means that the form or 'site' of divine
life in the world is radically exposed to suffering, since the
divine gift or communication can mount no finite defence
of itself (John 18.36). Gethsemane as the manifesting of this
exposure in or to the finite awareness of the incarnate Word
takes on a particular theological weight in this context.

iv. The theology of the Church: to be associated with or
incorporated into the identity of Jesus through baptism is
to be committed to the process whereby Christ's radical
exposure takes place in us through the mediating action
of the Spirit. This is an exposure both to the non-dual
otherness of the God and Father of Jesus and to the
otherness of the human neighbour. Our formation in the
life of Christ's Body takes place through the variety of ways
in which our will is challenged and reconstructed, from the
practice of monastic obedience to the elder through to the
ordinary pressure of the will and need of any finite other.
And Fr Sophrony also insists that the liturgy itself is the
recapitulation of the divine act of kenosis, the place where
Christ descends again to receive into himself the needs of
creation and our prayer moves outwards, away from selfish
limits, to expose ourselves to his act and his offering.[22]

[22]Nicholas Sakharov, op. cit., pp. 112–15.

In the most immediate and practical terms, all of this means that deification is the vehicle of our *solidarity* with all – a theme that we shall be revisiting in general terms in the next chapter, and, in chapter 9, in specific relation to the thought and witness of another great twentieth-century Russian monastic, Maria Skobtsova. Rather than being in any way a privilege that divides believers from non-believers or the ascetically proficient from 'beginners', *theosis* is the emptying-out of separateness and worldly security. It is also a challenge to models of solidarity that depend on the simple assimilation of the feelings of others to my own. Fr Sophrony, as we have noted, speaks of being 'accustomed to apply my experiences to all mankind'; but we should not read this as meaning a projection of individual subjective states on to others, but as referring to the conviction that what is most deeply true of my spiritual condition apart from God reveals what is true for all creatures – that they are poised over emptiness. What makes the difference is this awareness of how my particular suffering and desolation genuinely reveals something, so that my own desolation does not become an interesting psychological phenomenon to be explored with fascinated self-absorption. It is the occasion of a sober recognition of the radical groundlessness of any and every inner condition. To see myself as having no intrinsic worth or achievement *as an individual* is precisely the precondition for breaking down barriers between myself and others, so that what I *as an individual* am experiencing (positive or negative) is in some important sense irrelevant to the process going forward in me of becoming 'hypostatic'. This alone makes room for new being to unfold.[23] Our deepest human solidarity, in this perspective, is in our ineradicable need for relatedness to God, in which alone we become personal, and thus distinct in a way that is not exclusive, self-asserting and self-protecting. What I see when I contemplate the suffering of another is not simply another complex of individual suffering like mine but a unique

[23] E.g. *We Shall See Him As He Is*, pp. 130, 146, 169.

manifestation of the reality we share as creatures who *live* only in communion. Sophrony's sharply expressed language about self-loathing, difficult for most contemporary readers, has to be read as having to do with the call to reject an existence cut off from trinitarian communion – that existence which our individual suffering shows us and which we have to endure and interpret as God's showing to us of what the divine purpose ultimately is in deification. The communion or community that is born out of this solidarity is one in which compassion, the accompaniment of the other in the isolation that characterizes hell, is beyond sentimental fellow-feeling; compassion is simply how the divine solidarity with suffering and failing human beings takes flesh and form in this place that is 'me'.

Despite the various ways in which Sophrony's theological scheme departs from that of Lossky, there is one respect in which he echoes Lossky quite closely. Both see Orthodox Christianity as refusing the crude polarization between supposedly personal and supposedly impersonal aspirations in the life of Christian prayer, between a simplistic focus on a 'personal God' (basically a divine *individual*) and a 'mystical' fusion with divine life. On the one hand, it is possible to see the spiritual and ascetical task as a matter of acquiring particular kinds of experience, a particular kind of sensed interiority that can be perceived and in some degree measured as an aspect of individual awareness. On the other, it is possible to see this task as the shedding of all specificity, of difference itself, and the negating of the particular. Lossky wrote[24] of 'two monotheisms': on the one hand, a

[24] *Orthodox Theology: An Introduction* (Crestwood, NY, St Vladimir's Seminary Press 1989), ch. 1. This book is a digest of unpublished lectures given in Paris by Lossky in the last years of his life, in which the theme of Christian theology as a *via media* between mythology and monist abstraction became a dominant and shaping motif, applied at one level to Christianity in the context of world religions, and at another to the 'mediating' position of Orthodoxy within Christian thought, between what he saw as the individualism of Protestant theology and the repressive collectivism of the Catholic Church. Ironically, some of the closest parallels to this, as many have noted, are with the thinking of French Catholic writers such as Henri de Lubac.

rather mythological ultra-personalist scheme, and on the other, a focus on monistic absolute unity; Fr Sophrony, recalling[25] his own youthful fascination with the idea of 'the Supra-personal Absolute' and his absorption in styles of transcendentalist mysticism, identifies his problem as failing to grasp the distinction between the individual and the hypostatic. It is *true* that the imagined individual self is an obstacle, a restriction of fullness; what is *not* true, dangerously not true, is that this must entail a rejection of the 'personal', because this would mean a rejection of two fundamental realities: the eternal interdependence in giving that constitutes the trinitarian life, and the dependence on eternal gift that constitutes the finite world. We need here something like the Buddhist language, which denies both the affirmation and the denial of 'self'.[26] But – to extrapolate from Fr Sophrony's own presentation a little – making such an observation in the abstract is going to be no more than point-scoring; the definition of a practice that is not reducible to either of the 'two monotheisms' is indeed simply that – the definition of a practice *by* practice, of the kind that Fr Sophrony describes.

Nonetheless, this chapter has attempted to show how the implications of the practice as expounded by Sophrony make it clear why deification in the sense of adoption into the relatedness of the Word to the Father and to the creation is a theme that has the capacity to draw together the widest imaginable range of Christian reflection and – in its reconfiguring of what the call to solidarity might mean – also to direct us to a new imagining of Christian ethics. Our world is, for Fr Sophrony, irreducibly a world in which the gift of a life lived in joy and reconciliation is bestowed from multiple points or in multiple

---

[25] *We Shall See Him As He Is*, pp. 195–6; cf. Nicholas Sakharov, pp. 17–18.

[26] Buddhist meditation requires a passage beyond the dualism of any theory that tries to decide whether there is in the world such a thing as a self. Quite clearly there is no thing that corresponds to this word; equally clearly, the denial that there is such a thing is spiritually vacuous if it leaves in position a catalogue of other fixed things that confront an individual knowing subject as objects. What matters is the practice of 'emptying' and the full appropriation of one's absolute relatedness.

moments; being itself is relational – a familiar enough theme in modern Orthodox dogmatics.[27] But this entails understanding our own created being as – in God's purposes – on the way to a mutual transparency that deeply relativizes and problematizes all we might want to say in our habitual modes of speech about selfhood. We are left with the uncompromising repudiation of the myth of *individual* autonomy – but not in the name of some elevation of collective dignities over the particularity of human agencies. The profound theological affirmation of the uniqueness and dignity of the person, so characteristic of many Orthodox theologies, is given by Fr Sophrony a further critical edge by being linked with the conviction that a theologically significant personal distinctness or uniqueness is the fruit of ascetical practice rather than some sort of given. It is arrived at when and only when our uniqueness, *our singularity as irreducibly distinct images of God*, is understood as radical receptivity – as something that can transform our occupation of a unique place in the complex of created interaction into a single and unrepeatable 'site' for God's relation-making liberty to occur. It is of course equally important to stress that, in the context of the spiritual discipline Fr Sophrony and others advocate, this receptivity and obedience (in the sense Sophrony gives to this concept) is not passive or uncritical, a rejection of the call to act and to make a difference: our action in the world is properly and lastingly transforming to the degree that it is united with the hypostatic act of God, the mutual self-giving of Father, Son and Spirit in which we are 'immersed' and which alone liberates us decisively from the protective individualism that blocks relation with God and creation alike. So long as we assume the individualist stance, we are in fact preventing ourselves from genuinely *acting*: we remain in the realm of passion, and so of reactive behaviour. To become 'personal' is to become a point from which transforming

---

[27] Classically articulated in John Zizioulas, *Being as Communion* (Crestwood, NY, St Vladimir's Seminary Press 1985); new edition (London, Darton, Longman and Todd 2004).

communication acts – a created reflection of what it is to be 'hypostatic' in the life of the Trinity.

Deification understood simply – as it sometimes is in the Fathers – as the acquisition in some degree of divine *attributes* is a concept that does less than justice to the genesis of the notion in the belief that, in Christ, believers are given a new form of relation to the divine Source, the relation we call that of adopted children. Equally, a stress on this relatedness that refuses to ask about ontological and qualitative transformation in the finite subject will do less than justice to the mature trinitarian understanding of Christ's relation to the Father. The argument of this chapter has been that the kind of approach outlined by Fr Sophrony, building on much of the 'personalist' concern of other modern Eastern theologians, and by clarifying and deepening what it means to become 'personal' in Christ, gives us the elements of a theology of deification that not only avoids the risks noted but provides significant resources for a deeper apprehension of both theology and ethics – suggesting indeed that a theology or ethics that ignores this theme is likely to be seriously impoverished.

5

HUMANITY IN CHRIST

What emerges from all our discussions so far is that the doctrine of human nature developed and explored in the tradition stemming from early Greek spiritual writing and practice is one that is grounded in affirmations about Jesus Christ and in turn generates an increasing clarity about what needs to be said concerning his identity and role. The tradition builds upon a comprehensive set of convictions about humanity when it is in its proper 'rational' condition – a condition that is not that of disembodied observation and external analysis but a constantly adapting harmony with the complex interactive life of a universe woven together in *logos*. The restoration of that condition is brought about by the action of the divine Logos itself acting out of the centre of human identity, re-creating our rational freedom by enacting a life of self-forgetting, reconciled response both to the world and to its divine Source – which is the direct Source of the eternal Logos itself, the Father of the eternal Son. Thus an anthropology, a doctrine of the human, that is informed by the contemplative tradition will necessarily be a Christologically focused enterprise – even if the Christological content is not instantly patent in some of the literature about spiritual struggle and growth. As noted more than once in this book, it is important to hold together language about spiritual practice and development with the location of 'spiritual' life within the historical and sacramental Body of Christ; in this chapter we shall be looking at some of the themes that connect the earliest Christian reflections on the renewal of human identity in Christ with the perspectives already noted in the contemplative tradition and in contemporary Eastern appropriations of it – the understanding of the divine image as realized in the unique 'hypostatized' agency we call the person, the recognition of *kenosis*, self-emptying and self-forgetting, as constitutive of renewed and authentic personal existence, and the grounding of all this in the character of Christ's relation to the Father. As we shall see, much of this unfolds from what seems to be a very early acknowledgement that Christ's saving and transforming work begins in the fact of radical solidarity with human experience in its fullness; and we shall attempt to trace how this opens into the wider theological perspective of the restoration of the divine image in the form of self-giving filial maturity.

I SOLIDARITY

At the heart of the earliest Christian language in Scripture about salvation is the simple statement that the humanity once defined by Adam's rebellion is now defined by Christ's obedience. Paul's painstaking exploration of this in chapters 5 and 6 of his Letter to the Romans – and, in a slightly different register, in the fifteenth chapter of 1 Corinthians – sets out something of how this is to be understood. Our natural kinship with Adam means that we are inheritors of the destructive impulse that turns Adam away from God and leads to isolation and death. The biblical narrative is a record of how God's action steadily shifts humanity towards a different kind of kinship – initially the kinship of God's people united by the fact of the covenant, living under a law that judges and condemns the imbalance and injustice of Adamic life, and ultimately the freely bestowed kinship with Jesus that makes us inheritors of Jesus' own relation with God – a relation that death cannot touch. Where Adam seeks to create a human destiny independently of relation with God, Jesus lives out a humanity whose identity and integrity are inseparable from God; he lives in obedience to God, not in the sense that he offers an example of unbroken adherence to a set of

113

commands, but that he lives in unbroken alignment with the will and action of divine life – living uninterruptedly what the Law of the First Covenant points to. Adopted into his relation with God by the action of the Spirit, our human lives are gradually brought into the same 'alignment', so that there is living in us something that death cannot touch. 'As all die in Adam, so all will be made alive in Christ' (1 Corinthians 15.22).[1]

Despite some rather literal-minded challenges from modern theologians,[2] nothing here depends on an unreconstructed belief in an historical Adam or a 'Fall' that could in principle be dated: the logic of Paul's argument is to do with different kinds of solidarity in the present – the solidarity of humanity left to itself and the solidarity created by the divine act that affiliates us with Jesus. But this immediately gives us one of the most obvious building blocks for thinking further about what a Christological anthropology entails. We cannot in this context speak of humanity without speaking of an *unlimited* solidarity – that is, of a human community whose character and possibilities are the same across every possible local and contingent frontier. Whether or not we are thinking primarily in terms of a single common ancestor for the human race, the point is that the condition of the human race is ultimately *one*: there is no difference between what makes for the life and well-being of one individual or one group within humanity and what makes for the life and well-being of another. And this in turn means that what wrecks and limits humanity in any one context wrecks and limits every human context: there are no impervious boundaries in time or space that will allow some portion of humanity to secure itself against the inheritance

---

[1] Michael Banner, *The Ethics of Everyday Life: Moral Theology, Social Anthropology, and the Imagination of the Human* (Oxford, Oxford University Press 2014), especially ch. 2, has some very important reflections on the centrality of redefined kinship in Christian ethics, and the scepticism that ought to be shown by an informed Christian theology towards any sacralizing of literal bonds of blood. See also, Rowan Williams, *Christ the Heart of Creation* (London, Bloomsbury 2018), pp. 52–4.

[2] The best-known example is the essay by Maurice Wiles, 'Does Christology Rest on a Mistake?', in his *Working Papers in Doctrine* (London, SCM Press 1976), pp. 122–31.

of death. Indeed, the attempt to do this becomes itself one of the most dramatic illustrations of the seduction of the myth of self-made destiny and so of the sovereignty of death. What rescues us from death cannot be an act that separates us from one another, cannot be an act that seeks any local or limited solution to our shared deprivation; it can only be another kind or level of solidarity. Hence the ultimate simplicity of Paul's worldview: we live in one or the other kind of solidarity, the death inherited from Adam or the living Body of Christ. And this latter can by definition never be something that is attained, earned or owned by any individual or group: it must be given; it must be a matter of invitation, not entitlement.

Thus a Christological anthropology begins in recognizing that our human kinship in all its forms is shot through with a fundamental disorder, which we can describe as the urge to secure who we are in our own self-referential terms, looking for an identity that is clear and open to us, whose limits we can patrol or control, extend or shrink, and which we can defend against rivals. To secure who we are in the contests of human history and society is something we can and must do to avoid losing what we have; and the loss experienced by another is not connected with any loss to – or of – myself. Yet this pattern of refusal to recognize another's loss as mine leads, with a grim paradoxicality, to a more and more deeply entrenched isolation and a less and less secure sense of who we are. In contrast, the restored kinship that is created by our affiliation with Jesus secures who we are at two fundamental levels. It gives us an identity in relation to God – a 'name' bestowed by God, the mark of recognition in another's regard, which is both the unique and hidden heart of every particular human identity and also the name that belongs to the glorified Christ (see, for example, Revelation 2.17, 3.5, 12); and it incorporates us into an exchange of human relatedness in which each radically diverse member is recognizable to every other as the bearer of the same 'Spirit', the same voice in which prayer is made to God as *Abba* (Romans 8.9-30; 1 Corinthians 12.1-13, etc.). To put it concisely, the

115

believer receives the identity of Christ, becoming, so to speak, recognizable to God as an adopted child bearing the designation of Christ and speaking with Christ's voice, and recognizable to others as sharing the same life and thus the same inseparable calling. In place of the flawed and partial kinships we create and defend as children of 'Adam', we live in a mutually nurturing and interdependent environment in which no member's growth and maturation is a threat to any other – but also, therefore, an environment in which the loss, failure and pain of any one member is an injury to all.

As we have noted already, this is something that cannot be understood as a goal to be achieved, something proposed to an individual will as a desirable outcome. Once presented in such terms it becomes immediately a *goal among other goals*, one of the many things that an individual will may seek for itself. So long as this grammar of 'seeking for itself' remains, the basic structure of Adamic kinship is unchanged. Entry into the kinship of Christ is thus death for the individual will as the putative author of its own well-being. 'If it dies, it bears much fruit' (John 12.24): the sheer acceptance of the utterance that names and invites is the task set before the human subject. In the biblical perspective, the new humanity, the kinship of unlimited mutual gift, is inaugurated by an initiative that does not come from a human decision – in Hebrew Scripture, the inauguration of a literal but unconventional kinship in the form of an ethnic group identified as partner to a divine 'treaty' or covenant; in the Christian Scriptures, the creation of a communion without ethnic boundaries. In both cases, it is specific historical events that constitute the new kinship group – the call of Abraham and the exodus from Egypt, the resurrection of Jesus of Nazareth – not any human project or any 'given' state of affairs. A Christologically focused anthropology is thus not only one that imagines human beings as inseparably embedded in systems and protocols of mutual recognition, in the mutual investment of assured identity and life-giving dependence, but also one that sees the human condition as essentially responsive; to be a guest, to be addressed and invited, becomes something basic to any human agent's self-understanding. And accordingly, damaged and disordered models of humanity are those that mute, deny or distort this receptive dimension in human identity, as well as those that nurture the fantasy of independent, self-generating human identities and radically divergent human goods.

In brief, the central elements of Christological anthropology as we might begin to derive it from the basic texts of Christian faith cluster around these models of receptivity and responsiveness, and the reality of a form of human kinship in which the only ultimate good is a good that is shared. Theology across the centuries has spelled this out further in a number of ways – in connection, for example, with the idea of the divine image in humanity, and with reflections on the nature of our adoptive relation with God, and in terms of what the role of human agency is in the entire created order. In what follows, we shall be looking at these themes at greater length. As they unfold, it becomes possible to shape a distinctive understanding of what we mean by terms like 'person' and 'freedom' – commonly regarded as the keywords in any Christian doctrine of the human – and more particularly what these words mean in the context of the era we have come to think of as the 'Anthropocene', in which the capacity of human agency to affect the overall ecology of the planet appears to be unprecedented. Yet this cannot be merely or even primarily an exercise in seeking stronger motivation for ethical intervention: in its biblical context, it is irreducibly a matter of both imaging our entire identity afresh and of discovering how we are to grow in alignment with what is actual, with the creating reality of God, and thus a matter of how we expose ourselves in the fullest possible way to that reality in prayer as much as in thought and act. The early Christian theologians who saw moral discernment as educating us in the truthful perception of the natural order, and that perception opening up to the reality of God, were articulating the belief that contemplative openness to the divine act is the thread that connects prayer, perception and action, and that the life of what they called *nous*, the sheer capacity for receptive and transformative understanding, was where the divine image was to be sought.[3] All that we say theologically about our humanity must be framed by this sense of connection, and of the 'simplification' of our bodily and mental life, its drawing into unity and coherence, in a way that allows us to act from the centre of what we are in the divine gift.[4]

II IMAGE

When early Christian writers identify *nous* as the divine image or the locus of the divine image in humanity, the natural interpretation seems to be that this is the particular 'area' of the human constitution that is marked out as reflecting divine life. God's image is not to be found in any material correspondence, since God is not in a material substance comparable to other material substances; and the life of *nous* is not confined by material circumstances, limited in its exercise by the physicality of what it encounters and interprets.[5] It is the seat of free self-determination, and as such it can be seen as the ground of those actions where the human subject acts in a 'godlike' way. But, as a number of significant studies have shown over more than half a century, this as it stands is a misleading characterization of what the doctrine asserts. Vladimir Lossky, writing in 1957 and commenting on Henri Crouzel's monograph on Origen's doctrine of the divine image,[6] carefully distinguishes the idea of some aspect of humanity that corresponds to the divine from that of a relationship in virtue

[3] On the patristic scheme of advance from 'practical' to 'natural' contemplation and thence to *theologia*, the contemplation of God, see, for example, A. M. Casiday, *Reconstructing the Theology of Evagrius Ponticus: Beyond Heresy* (Cambridge, Cambridge University Press 2013).

[4] Terms related to *haplos*, 'simple', are increasingly used in Greek spiritual writing for the state of the soul in contemplation, especially after Pseudo-Dionysius in the sixth century; see Dionysius, *de caelesti hierarchia* I.1, I.2, etc. (PG3.121A–B).

[5] A classical statement of this can be found in Origen's *de principiis* I. 1.6, ed. P. Koetschau (Leipzig, J. C. Hinricjh 1913), pp. 20–3.

[6] Vladimir Lossky, 'The Theology of the Image', in *In the Image and Likeness of God* (Crestwood, NY, St Vladimir's Seminary Press 1974), pp. 125–39.

of which the divine becomes perceptible. The former, he says, still carries the traces of a pre-Christian doctrine of *suggeneia* (a 'generic' comparability, as of two examples of the same sort of thing) between God and the finite self – the assumption that they are two instances of one kind of life. Such traces remain visible in the theology of otherwise impeccably orthodox Fathers; but their distinctive teaching centres upon the convention of speaking of the eternal Logos or Son as the Father's *eikon*, an idiom very common up to the middle of the fourth century, with its origins in the deuterocanonical Wisdom of Solomon (7.25-6) and the language of Paul in Colossians 1.15. The Logos is (Lossky quotes Gregory Nazianzen) the 'definition' (*horos*) of the Father: the simple reality of the Father (immaterial, unchanging, non-composite) can be shown only in the life of another divine subsistent sharing exactly the same simplicity. God is such that only God can represent God truthfully.[7] But at the same time, this representation of the Father shows us that the Father does not possess divinity in isolation: the *repeatability* of the divine life we call 'Father' manifests the relational character of divine life: it can be shown because it is always already shared.

But, as Lossky stresses, this means that the divine image cannot be thought of as the reproduction of a *part* or aspect of one subject in some part of another. The way in which the Son can be thought of as the Father's image has nothing to do with the enumeration of various respects in which one resembles the other: it is a matter of how the act of the Father is received and re-enacted in its wholeness in the life of the Son – how it is 'repeated' or 'represented' in the Son's correspondence with the life of the Father, to echo the language we used in chapter 2. And the sense in which human beings can be understood as made in God's image is determined by this prior understanding of the image relationship. 'Christ', says Origen, 'is the first principle [*arche*] of

---

[7] Gregory Nazianzen, Or. 30.20 *Discours 27–34*, ed. P. Gallay and M. Jourjon, Sources Chrétiennes 250 (Paris, Les Éditions du Cerf 1978), pp. 268–9.

those who are made according to God's image';[8] we image Christ in the way that Christ images the Father. That is, the human *nous*, the capacity for living in total conscious responsiveness to the gift of God, manifests in the entirety of its action the 'repeatability' of the life of the divine Logos – that is, it manifests the Logos as eternal response to the Father, the Logos in its eternal relation of re-enacting the life of the Father. As Lossky puts it elsewhere,[9] this implies that the image of God in humanity cannot be thought of in 'objective' terms as an aspect of human nature; it is human identity living in alignment with the Logos's own alignment with the ultimate source of divine reality. That alignment is embodied, of course, in the *incarnate* life of the Logos: human responsiveness to the self-gift of God is inescapably a matter of the shape of an embodied life, growing into its maturity in relation with a material world – hence the intrinsic connection between behavioural maturation (the *praktike theoria* of the Greek ascetical writers), perception of order in the world (*physike theoria*) and the intimate contemplation of the divine.[10] What is given or restored or brought to full maturity in Christ (and all these terms are defensible in different contexts as descriptions of what Christ does) is the freedom of responding to what is not the self in a 'truthful' way – i.e. without the distortions of our self-protecting and self-isolating agendas. In slightly more abstract terms, it is the capacity for *knowledge in communion* – awareness of and participation in the agency or energy that surrounds us. To recognize Jesus Christ as the Incarnation of the Logos is to affirm, among other things, that his human identity is the place where unqualified intimacy with or openness to the Father makes possible an unqualified liberty to relate transformingly to every finite situation and every finite subject.

[8] Origen's *Commentary on John* I.XVI (19) ed. E. Preuschen (Leipzig, J. C. Hinrich 1903), p. 22.
[9] Lossky, *Théologie dogmatique*, ed. Olivier Clément and Michel Stavrou (Paris, Les Éditions du Cerf 1978), p. 101; and cf. *In the Image and Likeness of God*, p. 120.
[10] See above, section 1.

To quote Lossky once more – and here he is close to the analysis of Sakharov outlined in the last chapter – this means that identifying the image of God in humanity is never a matter of looking for 'a certain something' in human nature that can be distinguished from other aspects of humanity that lack the divine image.[11] If we say, along with the great mass of the theological tradition, that the image is 'in' the *nous* or, more loosely, the 'soul' rather than the body, this is seriously misleading if what we mean is that one part of human nature is 'more like' God than another. That would take us back to the impossible notion of God and the soul as two comparable instances of free and spiritual substance. The truth of saying that the image is in the *nous* is simply to deny that the language of image here has anything to do with external resemblance, and to state that the core of the doctrine is something about the character of our relation to God and the character of God as *generating and inviting response*, a response that is at its fullest when the whole of our subjectivity is involved. But Lossky, like other modern Orthodox theologians, goes rather further in following through the implications of this: if the life of the *nous* in the extended sense we have given the phrase is where the image of God is identifiable, that image is bound up with the possibility of engagement in, 'investment' in, the other, and a being-engaged or being-invested-in *by* the other; and this, says Lossky,[12] tells us that the human person is never

---

[11] *In the Image and Likeness of God*, p. 138. This is a point of some relevance to modern debates about the legacy of certain discourses about 'the human'. Postcolonial and feminist theorists frequently note the complicity between such discourses as expressed in post-Enlightenment moral philosophy and the actual practice of racial and gendered inequality; the universalizing language conceals a set of normative assumptions about what counts as human that can exclude extensive categories of human categories of human agents (see, for example, the essays on and by the Caribbean novelist and theorist Sylvia Wynter, *On Being Human as Praxis*, ed. Katherine McKittrick (Durham and London, Duke University Press 2015). Lossky's approach and kindred theological understandings of the divine image at least prohibit the idea that any section of the human race can possess and define the dignity of the human in terms of their own characteristics.

[12] *Théologie dogmatique*, pp. 101–2.

properly characterized as an individual instance of a general 'nature'. The image is 'the liberty of the human being in respect of their nature'. It is set over against the realm of necessity, the predictable behaviours that allow us to categorize some substance as an individual of a certain kind. The person is what exceeds the realm of 'nature' in the sense that 'personal' activity is the unpredictable, cumulative and interactive dimension of human engagement – what might be thought of as (in the widest possible sense) the *linguistic*, relation-building element, the construction of a shared world of reference and shared ideas and models of human selfhood or agency. It is *not* (Lossky is clear about this)[13] a transcendent 'portion' of the human constitution; the person is not an extra bit of nature but is how we understand and speak of the way in which exemplars of human nature construct an identity that is thought, spoken and more or less consciously nurtured.

Summing up this approach to the divine image, we can say that (i) the foundational insight is that God's life is 'repeatable', that divine life is communicable and intelligible because always already *given*; (ii) the finite intelligent and creative subject exists as essentially a reflection of this eternal responsiveness; (iii) human fulfilment therefore consists in the activation of a capacity for mutual creative involvement or 'investment' and in exposure to the act of the divine in prayer; and (iv) this lays the foundations for a model of *personal* existence that is set over against the realm of necessity and is realized in the 'excess' of human activity beyond the bare instantiation of natural characteristics. The location of the image in the *nous* is not a sort of territorial restriction but something more like a 'grammatical' point: to speak of the divine image is not to speak of a material object correlating with another 'object', material or spiritual, but a way of thinking about the relation of a complex finite agent to infinite agency. Just as, for the patristic tradition, the soul is not a part of, or present in a

---

[13] *In the Image and Likeness of God*, p. 120.

part of, the body,[14] so the image is a pervasive aspect of human existence; the term designates that aspect of human existence that is involved in a solidarity that entails a mutual 'entanglement', such that no particular agent or subject can be thought without thinking the network of relations that constitute it as an active reality. And our language of the person is the clearest vehicle for this, once we have decisively separated this from concepts of mere individuality.

III PERSON

If we can, as so many Eastern Christian thinkers argue, derive the idea of the personal from a Christologically informed doctrine of the divine image, one implication is that the *unity* we associate with the notion of personal identity is not simply a given internal characterization of the human subject. I am 'one' in virtue not of a primitive atomistic core of my being but because of a coherence or integrity in my relations with my environment and my creator. I receive a consistent call: the word by which God has called out a response in this particular enfleshed reality is not rescinded, it does not return empty to God (Isaiah 55.11) but continues to establish an invitation, a space for this enfleshed reality to occupy in God's presence, and indeed in God's life. What the spiritual writers of the tradition describe as the *haplosis*, the 'simplification', of our human condition in the life of grace is a fixed inhabiting of that divine word of invitation, not seeking to ground our identity anywhere but in that, not in our achievement or standing or in any feature of our natural life, but solely as the recipient of the word. It is a theme that has been developed in Protestant as well as Orthodox theology. Jens Zimmermann, in

---

[14]For a clear statement, see the quotations from Maximos the Confessor's *Ambigua ad Iohannem* in *The Oxford Handbook of Maximus the Confessor*, ed. Pauline Allen and Bronwen Neil (Oxford, Oxford University Press 2015), p. 374.

a valuable recent study of Bonhoeffer,[15] notes the way in which Bonhoeffer maps the tension between the divided self of fallen human subjectivity and the unified reality of life in the divine image: fallen Adam tries to *attain*, even to seize (Philippians 2.6), equality with God, to become *sicut Deus*, 'like God', while the image of God is realized precisely when our being in Christ pulls together the divisions of our selfhood into a single act of all-encompassing faith, liberated from the craving for self-justification. 'This means that from now on I can only find unity with myself by surrendering my ego to God and others.'[16] To be at one as a person is to 'inhabit' the invitation of God, seeing this as the sole foundation for a security that does not depend on what I can do, what I can master, what I can achieve.

'Participation in Christ ensures that Bonhoeffer's Christian humanist self is not beset by this rift between desired meaning and a silent universe, or an infinite ethical demand and an absent ethical norm.'[17] The human person is alive in and only in the reality of Christ's Incarnation, in which the fictitious self-sufficient subject is put to death and the ground of action becomes the sheer act of opening up to the purpose and action of the divine Source – yet without becoming impersonal or overriding finite will by the imposition of infinite will. Christ is the model of personhood because in him the embodied history of a human agent, developing in time, reacting to contingent situations and so on, is completely 'embedded' or grounded in the eternal responsiveness of the Word of God to the Father's self-giving. When we come to share in the life of Christ, we too are embedded in and come to inhabit that unconditional response; the language and culture we create as finite agents working with and answering to each other, developing the

---

[15] Jens Zimmermann, *Dietrich Bonhoeffer's Christian Humanism* (Oxford, Oxford University Press 2019), pp. 131ff.
[16] Ibid., p. 134.
[17] Ibid., p. 143.

criteria and conventions of human recognizability, are, in Christ, the realization of the solidarity for which we were made and which we have lost through the partiality and self-interest of the solidarities we create to defend ourselves. What some have called the foundational error of 'self-creation' gives way to the acceptance of our createdness, in a remote but real analogy to the eternal Word's acceptance of derivation, form and dependence upon the Father. Thus, as Zimmerman says, there is now no pathos of frustration in a meaningless universe to be negotiated, and no drama of self-transcendence by strenuous ethical self-assertion. Bonhoeffer's Lutheran orthodoxy points him towards the rootedness of all good action in the indwelling of Christ, not in the effort to earn grace and mercy. But – although Zimmerman suggests that Bonhoeffer is deliberately modifying the theology of the patristic consensus – this is entirely congruent with the Greek patristic notion of spiritual maturity as aligning the created *logos* with the uncreated, and leaving behind the 'heavy burden' of self-justification.[18] As Bonhoeffer movingly spells out in his prison poem 'Who Am I?', the 'true' self is what God alone sees – neither the individual self-image nor the performance put on for the sake of a human audience, but the bare location of a divine address and welcome.

The person realizes the divine image precisely by abandoning the aspiration to be like God. Just as in Philippians 2, Christ fully restores what we have lost by not attempting to be 'godlike' in his earthly life, by renouncing power and advantage, so, for the believer affiliated with Christ, the image emerges in and only in the embrace of contingency, bodiliness, the lack of any certainty about control of the environment, the processes of growth.

'Person' is in some ways a paradoxical concept. In the light of what we have just been considering, it is crucial that we do not think of person as an item within us that we can *observe*, a 'true self' underlying the artificialities of social and relational identity

---

[18] The phrase comes from *The Sayings of the Desert Fathers: The Alphabetical Collection*, tr. Benedicta Ward (London, Mowbray 1975), p. 77, ascribed to Abba John the Dwarf.

that needs 'liberating' from these accidents; this is one of the most pervasive and problematic of modern myths. Yet at the same time, the personal is what *discloses* and is disclosed in relation. The Greek theologian Christos Yannaras, in his seminal work on *Person and Eros*, writes of *logos* as the principle of disclosure: the *logos* that defines personal being is the act of self-unveiling or self-exposing that occurs in relation; each person/*logos* is unique because each position in the network of relating is unique. Every intelligible reality is 'logical' in the sense that it can be understood and expressed only in relation; but what we call personal being is distinct to the extent that it freely, actively and reflectively shows and communicates what it is. *Logos* is 'a person's power to reveal and express the uniqueness and dissimilarity of its ecstatic reference and its universal relation with other beings or other persons'.[19] Personal life is 'ecstatic' in the sense that it exceeds the mere activation of a set of generic potentialities – doing the sort of thing that this sort of agent does; it is the kind of activity that creates new possibilities of communication because it sets in motion a *history*, a reflective telling of the world's process that is not just a description of *kinds* of action and *kinds* of agent. Personal being is, we have suggested, 'linguistic' being in an extended sense: but so far from this leaving us with a world of atomistic subjects expressing their selfhood, it points to a world in which each point of intersection in the complex of agencies in that world grows into a perceived, located, embodied distinctiveness through declaring itself to and in relation with what it is not. The person is indeed not an item within 'nature' nor a given and deeply buried stratum of sheer naked individuality: but it is that which shapes itself through exposing or declaring itself in relation. The mysteriousness or hiddenness of personal distinctiveness is not the adventitious hiddenness of something that, *as it happens*, we can't see; it is systematically unseeable because it is always coming into being through encounter and

---

[19]Christos Yannaras, *Person and Eros*, tr. Norman Russell (Brookline, MA, Holy Cross Orthodox Press 2007), p. 167.

reworking or redefining its being in those moments of encounter, of giving and receiving.

When we speak theologically of the 'person' of Christ, we do not refer to some element within a mixture, or to the strange bundle of psychological phenomena we call 'personality'. The classical doctrinal definition of Christ's identity as one person in two natures is meant to clarify the conviction that *the mode of response to divine gift* that is eternally real in the life of God, showing what God is and reflecting back what God is, is one and the same in the eternal life of the Word and in the human life of Jesus of Nazareth. No analysis of the human nature of Jesus, the bare material individuality of this member of the human race, will uncover some buried element of divinity; the statement that this human individual is the Word of God in flesh means that this human identity as it unfolds or declares and defines itself in history, as it speaks and is recognized and responded to, is the point at which God declares and defines God's identity and does so not by delivering a message or a system but by creating a form of solidarity, the Body of Christ, in which human beings are free to declare themselves fully in a reconciled pattern of belonging together that has no natural foreordained limits. A Christologically shaped anthropology is thus one that foregrounds the mystery of the 'personal', not as a mystique of fathomless and arbitrary liberty or a sentimentalism about the oddities of human psychology, but as a recognition of the centrality of freely responsive action in any account of the human – action that, in responding to the call or invitation of its divine source, acquires an identity that can be declared or exposed in relation to other created beings.

IV FILIATION

The eternal Word's relation to the divine source is consistently understood as 'filiation', being a son/daughter; and the sense of this is laid out in human terms in the history of Christ's

LOOKING EAST IN WINTER

humanity. If we want to know what the divine relation of begetting and being begotten, Father and Son, looks like in terms that we can to some extent imagine, we have to reflect on this history. It is variously expressed in the Gospel accounts, most fully in John's Gospel. The Son receives all that the Father has and knows the Father uniquely (Matthew 11.27); the Father declares himself to the Son, who does what the Father does, sees what the Father is, and reciprocates the self-giving and self-declaring of the Father (John 5.19-27, 17, *passim*). In other words, what we see as giving consistency or unity to the life of Jesus is the abiding fact of seeing, knowing and reflecting the act that characterizes the Father. Jesus gives life as does the Father, realizing this in acts of absolution and healing; Jesus shows his followers who the Father is and what the Father does in his own intimate declaration of himself to them – and ultimately in his death understood as an offering that connects them with the Father once and for all. His life is unintelligible, formless, without his unbroken conscious dependence on the Father; he 'can do nothing on his own' (John 5.19), but that dependence makes it possible for him to act authoritatively and freely in the Father's name. He has 'authority to execute judgement' (John 5.27) – i.e. he has the right to determine or define the relation of things and persons in the world to what is truly and ultimately the case, he establishes and enacts the 'truth' that displays what in any situation is in accord with reality and what is fictive and self-serving (e.g. John 5.31-47, 12.46-50, 15.26–16.11). Jesus' dependence on the Father is a matter of consistent attention to the pattern of divine act such that the pattern of his own action takes the same form and consequently has the same authority and the same declaratory and illuminating effect. To live humanly as the divine Son is to be a conduit of divine act, to live in uninterrupted continuity with what God is doing in healing and in judgement.

A Christological anthropology is thus a model of humanity that sees the acknowledgement of dependence as fundamental. Living as we now do in a cultural context where dependence is so often seen as problematic, this is not a simple notion to clarify (though the notable essay by James Mumford on *Ethics at the Beginning of Life* includes some very fruitful discussion of the point).[20] However, the narrative and rhetorical shape of the Gospels make it plain that the recognition of dependence – and the way in which (to echo Mumford) dependence is understood as one of the things that makes humans recognizable to each other – is the opposite of a recommendation to passivity or a sanctioning of human systems of unquestioned authority. Openness to the sustaining and pervading reality of divine action, both in prayer and in the attentive and interdependent habits of life in the 'kinship' of Jesus, the Body of Christ, means being established at a critical distance from contingent human power, and also being liberated from the sense of having to succeed in imposing one's own agency at the expense of others. If we think back to Bonhoeffer's concern to overcome the divided self of fallen Adam, obsessed by the unattainable goal of being 'like God', we can see that growth towards Christlike dependence is again a way of securing a unity of personal being that does not depend on either a fixed interior identity or a record of satisfactory achievement. Our being in Christ connects us with the unifying and reconciling purpose of God; the more we are identified in and with this purpose, the more our action in the world is in accord with the truth of the world's need and the world's possibilities. 'Dependence' here is a liberation from private fantasy and egotistic struggle, and signifies not a reduction or weakening of the reality of finite being in its distinctive embodiments, but an establishing of this on the only firm ontological ground it can have, which is the divine invitation.[21] As we noted earlier, the process described in terms of 'simplification' in the spiritual tradition is a process of

[20] James Mumford, *Ethics at the Beginning of Life: A Phenomenological Critique* (Oxford, Oxford University Press, 2013), ch. 3. Note the emphasis here on the idea of kinship as something always prior to any kind of consciously determined 'contract'.
[21] Zimmermann, op. cit., pp. 188–93.

freeing our finite agency from the distracting and fragmenting compulsions, cravings and fictions that paralyze it. When we are able to live out of the reality of divine invitation, we are at one with ourselves and our neighbours and God; we discover personal integrity in our interdependence within the community of belief, and it is centred in and founded upon our freedom to attend to and receive in prayer the action of God towards us. The prayer, 'Abba, Father', mentioned by Paul in Romans 8 and Galatians 4 as the quintessential utterance of the Spirit within us, is the key to understanding where we derive the mode of agency by which the world might be changed – which is why a properly Christological anthropology illuminates the non-contradiction or non-duality between contemplation and action.

What humans have to learn in the newly illuminated world of Christocentric reality is the patience to live in the presence of God's invitation and in the utterance of the prayer *Abba* as they receive the 'inheritance' promised by their new kinship with Jesus, the incarnate Word, their metaphorical 'descent' from him that heals the damage done to Adam's lineage. The reality of filiation is what is articulated both in silent attention to God and in response to an untransformed and imprisoned world. Contemplation and liturgy are inseparable from the imperatives of active love. And this active love will seek – as Maria Skobtsova, like Bonhoeffer a martyr of the Third Reich, argued – to bring others into the state of filiation, to allow them to be liberatingly dependent on God's word.[22] Anthropological vision entails the commitment to recognize and help actualize in others the same realities out of which we ourselves act, so that these categories of solidarity, the divine image, personhood and filial liberty give us not only ways of understanding who and what we are in Christ, but a set of aspirations for the humanity we seek to make real around us.

---

[22] *Mother Maria Skobtsova: Essential Writings*, tr. Richard Pevear and Larissa Volokhonsky (Maryknoll, NY, Orbis Books 2003), pp. 70–5. For a fuller discussion of Mother Maria, see ch. 10 below.

The maxim that 'the Holy Trinity is our social programme'[23] can readily be misunderstood as a naive picture of divine and human 'sociality' assimilated to one another, the persons of the Trinity being thought of as separate subjects brought into harmony; but there is a sense in which it can perhaps be defended. The self-communicating, self-repeating life of God is such that its activity sets up a chain of implication for us, whereby we see that what we desire for our own healing is inseparable from the desire for the healing of others – because the communication of who and what God is entails the sharing of an energy that *cannot but* make for personal communion, and thus cannot but make for a state of affairs in which each agent is involved in bringing alive in every other the reality of self-communicating/self-repeating life – life that gives life and so gives the liberty to give life all over again.

V PRIESTLINESS

The calling both to receive and to give life is very particularly crystallized in the liturgical action that declares the Church's identity. In the eucharistic mystery, the community of Christ-centred solidarity 'declares itself' in the act of taking the material stuff of the world and naming it afresh as the vehicle of God's gift. It repeats and inhabits Christ's word and action at the Last Supper in identifying his mortal and suffering body with the shared matter of a meal. It locates itself within the act that is evoked in the Letter to the Hebrews, the passing of Jesus, like the Jewish High Priest, into the Holy of Holies, offering as sacrifice his material humanity – and implicitly the material world that makes this humanity possible, as well as the whole human kindred with which the human individual Jesus is in solidarity (Hebrews

---

[23]The phrase originates with the nineteenth-century Russian philosopher, Nikolai Fyodorov, but has been much discussed in recent years by contemporary theologians. On some of its strengths and weaknesses, see, for example, Miroslav Volf, *After Our Likeness: Church as the Image of the Trinity* (Grand Rapids, MI, Eerdmans 1998); also the seminal paper by Karen Kilby, 'Perichoresis and Projection: Problems with Social Doctrines of the Trinity' in *New Blackfriars* 81 (2000), pp. 432–45.

4.14–5.10, 7.26–8.7, etc.). The community affiliated with Christ is described as priestly (1 Peter 2.4-5; and cf. Revelation 22.3-4) primarily because it is taken up into the movement of Christ into the heart of divine holiness through his self-offering, included in his act of uniting earth with heaven. And so the sense that can be made of the world's raw material through the culture of food preparation and food sharing is identified with the sense that is made of the whole human environment by the self-offering of Jesus to achieve reconciliation and absolution for the world.

It is undeniably an intricate set of ideas, and in the history of theology different themes within this complex have emerged at different times; but there is a focal cluster of meanings that has remained fairly consistent, a cluster of ideas that has to do with the transformation of the material order as a dimension of what we are called to affirm and realize in worship. In this context, Christian anthropology has explored the notion of the innate 'priestliness' of human existence, at least from the time of Maximos the Confessor. For Maximos, the distinctive role of the human is to be the mediating and uniting agent within creation in virtue of humanity's union with Christ, in whom the divisions and oppositions that characterize creation as we know it are decisively overcome.[24] And adapting Maximos's vision to the argument we have so far been exploring, we can see the human renaming of the elements of the world utilized in the Eucharist as a refusal to treat the material world as 'dead matter': the human being who is united with the eternal Logos becomes fully *logikos*, speaks and acts in accordance with the harmonics of the world as God has made it, and so is able to declare or disclose the *logoi* of the material environment – which means seeing them as vehicles of communion, a world with a common good in which no part can be injured or diminished without hurt to all. The communion of persons in the Body of Christ is, so to speak, extended into a communion with the whole material

---

[24] Maximos, *Ambigua ad Iohannem* 41, and cf. *Mystagogia* 5 and 7; see the *Oxford Handbook*, pp. 425–6.

order, as that order is made to speak of reconciling gift. Nature, we could say, is decisively included in culture, material things become communicative signs without losing their ordinary physicality and distinctiveness.

So the logic of a Christological anthropology is that humanity's self-disclosure must be a disclosing of the 'logic' of the world around – that is, of the world's relation to the self-giving act of God. We have seen the impossibility of thinking of an individual human identity abstracted from the relations that nurture and make possible disclosure; and the same can now be said about the identity of humanity in collective terms. There is no 'true' human identity that is not always already implicated in the material order, living in and from and with it. And this living in, from and with the rest of the material world involves also the exercise of the unique level of communicative freedom that is proper to humans: it involves 'speaking' the material world in harmony, naming it as communicating gift to us. This challenges at the very root the idea that we are free to exercise power over the material world as if it were not already the carrier of grace – existing in relation to God before it exists in relation to us humans. And our capacity to disclose this pre-existing truth and bring it to speech and meaningful action, to bring it to 'culture', is the exercise of our priestly calling. We are most distinctively human when we refuse to think of ourselves in isolation from matter and animality; and thinking of ourselves in solidarity with matter and animality involves, among other things, the thinking of the world around us as shot through with the same life of *logos* that we live from. As Yannaras stresses,[25] the etymological roots of *logos* have to do with 'collecting' or 'assembling', linking together: recognizing that we live in a world united in *logos* is to recognize our implication in that world and our answerability to it. If the unity of each human subject is, as we have seen, grounded in the consistency of a divine invitation to participate

[25] Op. cit., pp. 159–61.

in the interaction that constitutes the world, we need to think of other substances or agencies in the world in similar terms: they are what they are, they have intelligibility and unity, they can be spoken of and understood, ultimately because of the word that has invited them into life. The life they live cannot be at the mercy of human desire, collective or individual; and we live out our own invited nature, our role in the complex whole, by attending to what God invites other substances to be, and by acting towards them in the light of that discernment. We cannot legitimately ignore this dimension and imagine that all things in the world are there to serve the functions we prescribe for them. It is certainly not an implication of this that we should be passive in the face of our environment (which would in any event be impossible); but the interventions we make, the uses to which we put the stuff of the world, need to be undertaken with a view to the need of the whole and the continuing balance of forces and agencies that keep the system functional and life-giving – the balance that makes it a genuine *ecology*. As I have argued elsewhere, this is the essence of learning to see the world as 'sacred', in the sense of being radically other to our designs and supposed needs.[26]

Liturgy, then, is an inescapable dimension of human activity. The culture we create as conscious persons aware of our invitation to live out the filial calling of Christ must be, at its most developed and self-aware, a liturgical culture – one that celebrates and enacts the transition from slavery to liberty or darkness to light. Christian liturgy presents the narrative of Jesus living out his identity as Logos incarnate by refusing violence and retaliation, renewing his call into 'kinship' in the face of the most extreme rejection and betrayal, and (to return to a point noted at the beginning of this chapter) establishing a bond between God and humanity that death cannot cancel. It is the record of a life, death and resurrection in which the Adamic urge to isolation,

[26] Cf. Rowan Williams, *Faith in the Public Square* (London, Bloomsbury 2012), pp. 13–14, 17.

unilateral control and fictive godlikeness is exposed as lethal to humanity and replaced by the gift of a new pattern of relation. Its liturgical enactment declares at the same time the liberating of our intimacy with God, the creation of reconciled and unboundaried solidarity among human beings and the transformation of our perception of the world in the light of this decisive event of peacemaking. Liturgy discloses who we now are as human agents living in Christ, and so discloses – and reinforces – our witness to the unity of creation in the Logos. It ritualizes the new state of affairs, but in so doing opens us again to the divine activity that renews us; to act out and 'speak out' the pattern of the new world is in itself to accept and intensify our 'logical' receptivity to God's gift, not only to renew an *idea*. Liturgy is, in plain words, a moment of grace.

VI CONCLUSION

We began with the Pauline dichotomy between two sorts of solidarity: the negative solidarity that means we are all involved in *limiting* or undermining common human life, and the authentic solidarity of what God brings into being initially in the Covenant with the Jewish people and then in the universalized 'kinship system' that is the Body of Christ, the baptized community. Thinking through this transition has brought to light a closely intertwined set of insights about how we understand human possibility and human responsibility. The renewal and universalizing of our solidarity depends on the fact that Jesus' humanity is an embodiment of the divine self-communication or self-repetition; and a humanity re-created in the likeness of Jesus will thus be one that 'images' God as Jesus does, allowing itself to become a site for divine self-disclosure and divine response to divine gift. For the image to be fully at work, we need a doctrine of the human person rooted in the trinitarian mystery – not in a way that makes divine personhood an exalted version of finite cooperation but understanding what it means to say that there is literally *no* individual subject prior to relation and interaction; which means in finite terms, that there is no individual subject prior to history and culture. We are irreducibly historical and so also 'linguistic'; we exist in the medium of communication. Our mysteriousness to one another – a crucial element in our reverence for one another and our proper scepticism about the possibilities of total control over others – is not the inaccessibility of some deeply interior level of our being but the self-renewing and unpredictable working of mutual communication, constantly creating unprecedented situations and so unprecedented combinations of sound and symbol. But the most basic communication remains what God communicates to each active point of convergence in the human world, each historical subject – which is the invitation to intimacy and trust, the grateful acknowledging of dependence, and the exercise of a 'divine' freedom for reconciliation and re-creation. The divine image is realized in personal agency; and the full and free shape of that personal agency is the filial identity defined by the life, death and rising of the incarnate Logos. And the actualizing of this filial life involves a re-presentation of the transforming history at its origins and an effectual sign of human responsibility to create a unified and just meaning for the material world, a culture of reciprocal gratitude, receptivity and stability.

The often-cited phrase from Irenaeus, 'The glory of God is a human being fully alive', is a deeply Christological formulation – not simply a celebration of humanity in itself. God's glory, God's presence diffusing itself in beauty and illumination, is the presence in the material world of the active reality that mirrors its source in God: the glory of the God who makes covenant and accepts sacrifice (Exodus 24.17-18, 33.1-23, 34.29-35; 1 Kings 8.10-11, etc.), and who declares the divine identity in the face of Jesus and in Jesus' fellowship with the disciples (John 17.22, 2 Corinthians 3.7–4.6). Ultimately, a Christological anthropology is one that looks towards the *glorifying* of humanity though its alignment with the self-sharing and self-showing of God in the eternal Word and the Word made flesh. To be human is to be the site of glory;

reflecting God's illuminating beauty in a communion without condition or limit. And the life of Christ's Body, the Church, is therefore above all else defined as the life that gives space for a transformed humanity to recognize itself and be renewed by God in its energy and imagination for transformed action in the world. When the Church acts simply *as* Church, declaring to itself and the world what renewed humanity is like, it fulfils its calling – but that should never be taken to mean that the Church is no more than a static manifestation of an ideal condition for humanity, because the very act of showing what it is prompts and activates its labour in history, where the newly restored vision and liberty celebrated in the liturgy define every human engagement that believers now undertake. In other words, a Christological anthropology is also a *liturgical* anthropology; and we turn next to a fuller exploration of this.

PART THREE

DIALOGUE

6

LITURGICAL HUMANISM:
THE ANTHROPOLOGY OF
WORSHIP AND SACRAMENT

I

'I must say as strongly as I can that what held me back from becoming a Christian was what seemed to me to be the absence of a real theology of freedom and a real theology of the Holy Spirit and of the experience of the Holy Spirit.'[1] Olivier Clément, one of modern Orthodoxy's most distinctive and insightful thinkers, insists throughout his work that what is needed to address the spiritual poverty and banality of the modern West (and not only the West) is not more and better conceptual refinement in meeting atheist arguments, nor more and better programmes for self-improvement with a 'spiritual' gloss, nor more and better institutional solidarity. It is the experience of a distinct kind of humanness, in which the twin notions of liberty and personhood are credibly fleshed out. As he says elsewhere,[2] these twin notions are vital to any understanding of what *history* is; and he sees in much contemporary thought and practice what

---

[1] Olivier Clément, *L'autre soleil* (Paris, Stock 1975) (henceforth AS), p. 128.
[2] Olivier Clément, *La révolte de l'esprit* (Paris, Stock 1979) (henceforth RE), pp. 139ff.; cf. Clément, *Anachroniques* (Paris, Desclée de Brouwer 1990), pp. 76–7 (henceforth An), *On Human Being: A Spiritual Anthropology*, trans. Jeremy Hummerstone (London/New York/Manila New City 2000) (henceforth OHB); ET of *Questions sur l'homme* (Sainte Foy, Editions Anne Sigier 1986), chs 2 and 3.

amounts to a denial of history and a nostalgia for a timeless, organic life – whether in struggles for an abstract equality, or in the reduction of human aspiration to a set of needs that can be filled moment by moment without reflection or self-scrutiny. The Christian revelation – and this includes the Jewish revolution of understanding that underlies it – is what makes history possible, because it speaks of a world both interrupted by the Word of God and transfigured in all its living complexity by the Word of God. All Christian doctrine arises from the acknowledgement of that transfiguration. In that superb introduction to *The Orthodox Church*,[3] written by the young Timothy Ware (whose perspectives throughout his theological career have been so close to those of thinkers such as Clément), we read a quotation from the Anglican George Every about how Orthodox understand dogma as 'a field of vision wherein all things on earth are seen in their relation to things in heaven, first and foremost through liturgical celebration'. What is claimed by Christians is that human existence is addressed by an act that is completely beyond the categories of nature, of repeatable process; so that our humanity is in turn taken beyond repeatable process and made capable of responsibility in the strictest sense of the word – a capacity to *answer*, and so to be changed by a relation. 'The meaning of history,' says Clément,

> like the meaning of the human subject, is to be found beyond the limits of the world – but this is a "beyond" that has, in the Incarnation, become interior to history and humanity ... It is the death and resurrection of God made human that truly constitutes the End of history, or rather the End *in* history so that the word "End" does not signify some kind of closure but an infinite opening, a threshold of light. This is an End that judges history's totalitarian pretensions, its illusions and hypnoses; this End, we have argued, wounds history with the

[3] (London, Penguin Books 1963), p. 271.

142

wound of eternity and opens up in it the path of repentance and so of hope.[4]

The point is that revelation presupposes a God who is personal and free: if such a God engages us, addresses us, our human identity becomes something we don't control. We are who we are because we are spoken to by an agent irreducibly and unimaginably other; to be human is to be summoned to answer. But this also means that to be human is to be summoned to 'communion': there is no life for us without that awareness of and coming to terms with the call to answer to, and for, what is not ourselves. Every other person is the object of God's free address, and to look at the face of a human other is to look at a reality that is the focus of an infinite attention. In the light of revelation we see human faces for the first time.[5] The 'humanism' to which the Christian rightly lays claim is a vision of every human face as the focus of self-forgetting love; so that there is no conditionality about human worth or dignity, no more or less that depends on status, achievement, age, race or whatever. The invitation to engage with the act of love that has eternally engaged me is at the same time the invitation to engage with the human other who, like me, is already seen by God and addressed by God. Hence we can speak, as does Clément, of the 'sacrament of the brother/sister'.[6] To believe the Christian revelation is to be immersed (the word is deliberate) in this 'circulation' of attention and invitation; always invited to the contemplation of the divine in the face of the revealer, Jesus; always invited to the recognition and service of the human other – and, as Clément does not fail

---

[4]RE, p. 141; for one of Clément's fullest discussions of a theology of history, see his *Transfigurer le temps: Notes sur le temps à la lumière de la tradition orthodoxe* (Neuchatel, Delachaux et Niestlé 1959), especially Part II, and ch. 5 of Part III. ET by Jeremy N. Ingpen, *Transfiguring Time: Understanding Time in the Light of the Orthodox Tradition* (Hyde Park, NY, New City Press 2019).

[5]OHB, p. 55; cf. OHB, ch. 5 and RE, pp. 63ff., 369ff. on how this transforms our understanding of eros.

[6]E.g. RE, pp. 203ff.

to insist, the non-human other as well,[7] since the renewed human subject is also liberated to see the world itself as loved by God and inviting humanity to discover how to live in reconciliation with its processes, neither absorbed in them nor struggling to defeat them.

I have begun with this summary of themes highlighted by Olivier Clément not because they are unique to him[8] – though he often expresses them with unique beauty and clarity – but because the way he sets them out helps us to see how liturgical life and experience embody the new humanity – and how they throw light on the losses or errors of so much of the culture we are familiar with. The humanism to which Clément directs us is visible and effective as liturgy, specifically as eucharistic liturgy; and if we are concerned to engage persuasively with a world threatened with an immense range of dehumanizing forces, we must be explicit about the connection between Christian anthropology and Christian liturgy. Clément, in the autobiography from which I have already quoted, describes his pre-Christian frustration in terms of being 'hungry for the Eucharist',[9] hungry for a *practice* that would exhibit the new humanity he was gradually becoming aware of – a humanity characterized by royal authority, priestly mediation and prophetic showing of 'the End already present'. The royal role appears in witness and work for peace and justice in history, the struggle against slaveries of all kinds. Priestliness is a matter of 'the human being breathing in God, breathing the Spirit, and so making the universe and history breathe in God, sowing the seed of eternity in them: this prayer/breath, this power of "making Eucharist in all things", untiringly in love with the knowledge and power in human beings that makes for the

---

[7] OHB, ch. 7.

[8] For example, Henri de Lubac writes that 'Christianity is not one of the great things of history: it is history which is one of the great things of Christianity', *Paradoxes of Faith* (San Francisco, Ignatius Press 1987), p. 145.

[9] AS, p. 142.

communion of persons and the transfiguration of the earth'. And the prophetic vision is not only of the End in our midst, but specifically the vision of all human flesh and every human face with the amazed attention that arises from the fact of God having become flesh and face.[10] This is the humanity for which Clément yearns, the humanity that (in Timothy Ware's phrase),[11] 'finds [its] perfection and self-fulfilment in worship'; this is the eucharistic reality for which he is hungry; and, in case anyone should try to divide the sacramental from the contemplative, this is also the basis for understanding contemplative activity in the community as finding its proper rationale in what liturgy shows, and for seeing liturgy and theology alike as grounded in and oriented to contemplative attention – and the joy that arises in it.

II

So how does our eucharistic practice actually exhibit and realize all this? How does our anthropology become visible, tangible, in liturgy? One obvious place to begin is with the point about our humanity being engaged or addressed: the language of liturgy is essentially responsive. Liturgy fails in its purpose if it is repeatedly and obsessively talking to itself, i.e. explaining itself to a real or imagined audience; it is the speech of a community in answer to the proclaimed or recited Word and enacted presence of God, and so is primarily adoration, petition, thanksgiving. Its characteristic vehicle is the second person singular – occasionally and for very specific functions the second person plural, to exhort and invite the assembly. When liturgy is overtaken by the latter, however, by exhortation, let alone interpretation of what it is doing, it is in real danger of becoming simply a reflection to the community of itself, its aspirations and concerns, or else a code of artificially organized signs; it has ceased to *show* anything more than itself.

[10] Ibid., pp. 140–1.
[11] Op. cit., p. 272.

But when it is speaking in response to what it understands as an initiative from elsewhere, it may or may not persuade anyone that there *is* in fact an 'elsewhere', but at least it will not be mistaken for a mere exercise in corporate uplift, the polishing of a shared self-image. Words spoken to God acknowledging who God is, as in the Trisagion or the Sanctus or the Gloria, are also acknowledgements of who we as human speakers are – *recipients* of communication before we are speakers, and thus speakers who are always liable to be interrupted. This is a speech that is consistently hesitant even when it is extravagant in wording (like the Sanctus or Gloria), because it recognizes that what it says is a belated attempt to 'trace' the act that has given it birth. Liturgical language shows something of the meaning of the word 'grace' by its responsive and confessedly 'secondary' character. The liturgical scholar Thomas Pott has written of liturgical theology that 'it reflects and asks itself how the history of salvation, which consists of a dialectic between God's action and the response of his people, is incarnated in the liturgy of the Church'; and he goes on to argue that this means an exploration of the 'connections' that are made and/or witnessed in the liturgy, between God and humanity, between humanity as a whole and the liturgical action going forward – and, we might add, between human beings themselves and between humanity and the non-human environment.[12] Language embodies connections, relations; so to look critically at the language of liturgy is inevitably to look at how this language embodies and articulates connectedness with the action that is believed to generate it. And in this context, a theological liturgy will be one that challenges any human aspiration to 'speak life into being' in purely immanent frameworks – whether this be in a mechanistic understanding of material process, a closed picture of the human future in terms of satisfying determinate wants, an anti-realist epistemology in which it is the speaking and

---

[12] Thomas Pott, *Byzantine Liturgical Reform: A Study of Liturgical Change in the Byzantine Tradition* (Crestwood, NY, St Vladimir's Press 2010), pp. 107–8.

fantasizing will that is the ultimate focus of our attention, or any other refusal of the possibility of interruption.

Liturgical humanity is a humanity both preceded and overtaken by the abundant – even 'excessive' – communication of God. And this in turn means that the language and action of liturgy take *time*. Liturgy is not the same as ritual, the stylized performance of some function with a simple beginning and end. It is a period of time in which the transition from one world to another can be traced and enacted.[13] The various forms in which this transition is symbolically acted out include in Orthodox liturgy the two 'entrances' through the icon screen, as well as the emergence from the altar of the celebrant with the Holy Gifts; but Western traditions also have their ways of showing this, whether in the complex ceremonial of a High Mass or in the early Anglican practice (largely abandoned by the mid-seventeenth century) of inviting the congregation to move into the chancel stalls at the invitation to confession, receiving Holy Communion there and then returning to the body of the church. The humanity embodied or enacted in the liturgy is a humanity acknowledging its need to *be moved*, to be drawn from one world to another; a humanity acknowledging that the world it occupies habitually is 'in question' and in need of opening on to another comprehensive frame of reference. In more theological terms – and picking up a theme close to the heart of Clément's concerns[14] – this ultimately entails recognizing the power and pervasiveness of *death* in the world we occupy and receiving from elsewhere the assurance and in some sense the experience of a world not limited by death. Liturgy, when it is doing its proper work, involves an 'appropriation' of death, a confession of mortality, so that the transition that is worked through in the liturgical act is genuinely a passage into life – from a world

---

[13] My debt here to Catherine Pickstock's *After Writing: The Liturgical Consummation of Philosophy* (Oxford, Blackwell 1998), especially Part I, ch. 2 and Part II, ch. 4.2, will be obvious.

[14] E.g. An, pp. 111–12; RE, pp. 34–40; OHB, ch. 9.

whose horizon is lifeless isolation to a world whose horizon is inexhaustible relational exchange. The time of the liturgy is thus the time of passage: we recognize that we are living 'towards death', in the Heideggerian phrase, that our unredeemed time is marked by the intensifying of self-enclosure, the growing risk of a final refusal of communion, and we expose ourselves to relation with a life that has already embraced death – has made death part of a narrative of continuing relation. As Clément says,[15] death and hell are closely associated in the traditional language of liturgy and theology: we are living in the direction of isolation, in that 'fallen space, the space that separates and imprisons', where I am both at odds with myself and unable to escape from myself. The liturgical affirmation is that there is another space to occupy, in which distance is not alienation, and time is an unfolding of constantly fresh perspectives on the endlessly fresh abundance of God's act, because that act has always already put death behind it – not ignoring or trivializing it, but on the contrary passing through it in all its pain and gravity in the cross of Christ. As is often remarked, Eastern iconography depicts the resurrection of Christ by depicting the descent to the underworld, Christ raising up Adam and Eve and the saints of the First Covenant. This image is in a sense at the heart of 'liturgical time'; this is the pivot on which the world turns, and the transition through which liturgical action takes us is a journey into a life that is constantly *receiving* life. We are obliged to face fully the reality and the consequences of our mortality, the way in which the isolation of death can come to overshadow our acts and relationships. But when the fear of death is acknowledged and overcome in the light of the resurrection, something else becomes possible, and this possibility is what is enacted in the climax of the liturgical action.

This climax is the making present of the events of Christ's life and death, the release of the Holy Spirit that the resurrection enables and the sharing of transformed material stuff, food and

[15] OHB, p. 144.

drink. The food we share becomes the 'language' we share, it is what carries the meaning we acknowledge together. The material world as represented by (summed up in) the sacramental elements is neither an enemy to be overcome nor a storehouse of resources to be exploited, but a vehicle of relation, with God and one another. Thus the new world into which liturgy inducts us is not a disembodied world of ideals: it is shaped by specific physical actions – the literal assemblage of a community of listeners and the sharing of material food understood as itself having been moved from one 'world' to another. The humanity embodied in the liturgical action is constituted not only by an understanding and enactment of time, by a temporally extended passage from world to world, but by a renewed mode of relating to the material environment. Brought to God, placed in the hands of Christ, the elements of bread and wine are surrendered for transformation. Suffused by the Spirit of the Risen Christ, they are identified with his life; as such they act as instruments to unite the assembly. They are not possessed or deployed by anyone: they simply become the matter of a shared action, regarded as themselves active, as having an inexhaustible interiority. And this particular transformation speaks of possibilities for the material world when released from our struggles to possess and master. In this respect, the humanism of the liturgy is a vision that gives us a kind of distance from the material stuff of the world sufficient for us to let go of our aspirations to control it or manipulate it. We are identified in the liturgy as material beings, part of a material complex of agency in the world, who must find their way and plot their action in this world conscious of the fact that matter can bear the life of God, in and out of strictly 'sacramental' activity. We are pointed back to the 'sacrament of the brother/sister' and the recognition of the depth that underlies the human face.

Built into all this is also the acknowledgement of the significance of *memory* in human identity. Liturgical humanity is humanity conscious of, 'mindful' of, a context wider than that of the individual or even the community in this moment: to remember what has to be remembered in liturgy is to be aware that what is now happening for this particular group of people is inseparable from and unintelligible without, first, the events that generate liturgy in the first place, the historical events that make liturgical transition possible, and, second, the world of reference that in turn generates or animates those events. That is to say, liturgy is 'mindful' of the eternal life of God the Word and of that human life in which it is embodied once for all. But as with the other characteristics of liturgically formed human existence, this has implications that extend beyond the understanding of relation with God. We are led to see our humanity as always imbued with more than we can at this moment grasp or manage – and this involves both our past and our future: several Orthodox scholars have observed that the prayer immediately following the Words of Institution in the Liturgy of St John Chrysostom 'remembers' the cross, the burial, the resurrection, the ascension and the sitting on the Father's right hand *and* 'the second and glorious *parousia*'. Remembrance extends to past, present and future; to the entire context in which the praying assembly stands, including the final consummation that is prayed for and is already present in the liturgical act. So with respect to all our human business: what we are is shaped by what has taken place and, in some sense, by what is hoped for and anticipated, the direction that is seen and imperfectly grasped. Our humanity lives intelligently to the degree that it acknowledges its rootedness, not simply in the past, significant though that is, but in the network of interwoven actions and processes that form present identity, including the reaching-out of those actions and processes into an as yet unseen future. Liturgical humanity cannot compose and possess a final account of itself: it knows that what is immediate and accessible is partial and that it lives out of all kinds of 'otherness' – a point that is, of course, another way of expressing what has been recognized in relation to humanity's character as addressed and engaged from outside itself, as always cast in responsive mode.

Alexander Schmemann, an Orthodox theologian sharing much in common with Olivier Clément, writes of the remembrance that takes place in the liturgy that it is simply our awareness of 'the very *reality* of the kingdom ... because Christ manifested it and appointed it then, on that night, at that table'.[16] The kingdom of heaven is a material and social world entirely transparent to Christ, one in which every situation is, precisely, an occasion of recalling or recognizing Christ, an occasion of remembering. And this focus on the coming of the kingdom illuminates another remark of Clément's: 'Attachment to a liturgical time understood in itself, above and beyond historical (and even cosmic) time, is very typical of an attitude of sacralization closed upon itself.'[17] Liturgical time and liturgical remembrance must not become something enjoyed as an escape into some parallel universe where the tensions of what I have called the 'habitual world' are dissolved: rather, to quote Schmemann again,[18] it is a time in which each of the liturgical actions performed in this world is 'transformed by the Holy Spirit into *that which it is*, a "real symbol" of what it manifests'. Liturgical action is, we might say, 'saturated' with the meaning God gives to the material process of the world. Thus we must say that, instead of providing a route out of the actual world into a sort of religious virtual reality, these actions uncover meanings that are always latent in the world we know. We as agents and speakers, the material we handle, see, sense and eat, the physical environment of the church, all of these have their depths exposed when the Spirit is invoked upon them. The point of liturgy is that we should 'know the place for the first time', as T. S. Eliot says of spiritual activity in the *Four Quartets*. We are returned to where we actually are in God's eyes: in relation, in communion with God, with one another, with the creation.

III

Much of what we have been considering is, of course, the general heritage of liturgical Christianity, not only of the Orthodox

---

[16] Alexander Schmemann, *The Eucharist: Sacrament of the Kingdom* (Crestwood, NY, St Vladimir's Press 1987), p. 200.
[17] RE, p. 105.
[18] Schmemann, op. cit., p. 223.

world; but I have chosen to set it out in these terms because it seems that Orthodox theology – despite the fact that Orthodoxy has a history of liturgical development and change like other communions[19] – sees more clearly how and why the action of the liturgical assembly *is* the defining reality for the Church, not in what it articulates in word or concept but in its character as *manifestation*. It is a theology that expects to find an anthropology in the liturgy, in a way that Western theologies have not on the whole sought to do (with some notable exceptions, including the writings of the Anglican Gregory Dix, with his notion of 'eucharistic man' as a reality opposed to the 'economic 'man' or 'mass man' (*sic*) of high modernity[20]). To say this is not to propose a restrictive picture of Christian humanity as solely occupied in ritual activity – the caricature that all too readily comes to the Western mind. Rather, what we are looking at is how this activity specifies and incarnates a culture, which poses serious questions to aspects of our prevailing cultural scenes. Liturgy, especially though not exclusively the eucharistic liturgy, claims that certain human possibilities have been definitively realized and that these are the deepest, most durable and most universal determinations of our humanity. We discuss with agonized intensity how Christian identity is to be embodied in the world in such a way as to make it clear that it does not depend upon a political or intellectual legitimacy gained from some other discourse; but we have not explored with anything like the imagination of a Clément or a Schmemann how what we do in liturgical assembly constitutes a distinctive culture with a distinctive and critical anthropology.

Some of this comes more clearly into focus if we try to spell out what a liturgical anthropology makes or should make impossible as defensibly, intelligibly *human* behaviour. In the light of what we have been discussing, the fundamental and central affirmation of liturgy is that we are not self-created – that is, what is most important and defining about us is not our individual will and the

[19] See Thomas Pott, op. cit.
[20] Gregory Dix, *The Shape of the Liturgy* (London, A&C Black 1945).

agenda that flows from that. But this does not mean that human specificity, the uniqueness and liberty of the person, is extinguished either by a rival subjectivity in a relation of simple dominance, or by impersonal process. What and who we are is essentially defined by the gratuitous invitation from an unimaginable other into shared life – and to see the invitation of God in this way is at once to see that issues of dominance and thus of rivalry should not arise. This is not an other who competes with us; and to understand the nature of the personal liberty that so acts, through invitation and participation, is to understand radically different possibilities for our own understanding of liberty and the uniqueness of an active subject.

This is the first principle of what we might call a liturgical scepticism about certain human claims or fictions. Directly deriving from it is a scepticism about any approach to humanity that refuses or trivializes our location in time. This takes many forms: it is manifest in a popular culture that has limited understanding of the difference of the past from the present and a lack of concern with how ideas and ideals came to be out of dramatically different cultural situations. This is perhaps most painfully evident in a political rhetoric that treats the doctrines of liberal modernity as self-evident, oblivious to the theological debates (Christian and non-Christian) in which questions about rights and dignities first came into focus.[21] But it is also to be seen in refusals to see ourselves as in any way constrained by the futures we may be creating, in individual and global actions alike: if we cannot understand that we are affecting – not to say corrupting – our humanity now by indifference about the planet's future, as much as by self-centred individual behaviour, we shall be incapable of seeing how we might be defined by another sort of future: the kingdom, the reconciliation of humanity and

[21] For a fine corrective essay, see, for example, Larry Siedentop, *Inventing the Individual: The Origins of Western Liberalism* (London, Allen Lane 2014); and cf. also, Aristotle Papanikolaou, *The Mystical as Political: Democracy and Non-Radical Orthodoxy* (Notre Dame, IN, Notre Dame University Press 2012), especially ch. 3.

environment. Conversely, if we do live from such a future, we should be incapable of the short-term search for gratification and comfort that has so damaged our physical habitat. Liturgical humanism teaches us a deep suspicion of any such quest.

In the same way, it challenges any attempt finally to evaluate, judge or rank any person (in or out of the Church) on the grounds of achievement and status, or even natural capacity. Liturgical humanism, with its commitment to seeing the face of the other uncovered in the light of Jesus, forms us in the practice of unconditional attention to any and every other: it does not preclude difficult decisions, even confrontation, struggle for just relations, the naming of evil acts as such, but it requires all this to be set in the context of a recognition of worth that does not depend on a favourable verdict. The uncomfortable concerns of Christians about the unborn, the dying or the severely physically and mentally challenged have their roots here; and we might be more effective witnesses in these areas if we began by an insistent posing of the question: 'How, on any other basis than this claim to unconditional attention, can we prevent our judgement of the worthwhileness of human lives becoming dependent on circumstances?' This would not be to deny situations of extremity or to despise and condemn judgements made in situations very far from ideal simplicity; but it would affirm that the foundation of human respect lies in that liturgical conviction about the 'status' all share as recipients of a single gift and offer.

For a liturgical anthropology, there is no 'end of history' in terms of the triumph of this or that human agenda: we have to say both that history has ended, once and for all, in the manifestation of the kingdom through Christ's resurrection and the gift of the Spirit, and that history is an ineradicably real part of our human context, as a past that feeds and conditions us and as a future we must choose. Loose talk about the end of history will blind us both to the ways in which we are shaped by a past we cannot fully see and understand, and to the responsibility laid upon us to 'choose life' here and now, whatever the apparent direction of global affairs. The breaking-in of God's 'end' does not leave us with an indeterminate expanse of meaningless time to fill but gives form to our calling to act creatively, to work in and with our environment towards a future more transparent to God's purpose, without any guarantees except that of God's fidelity. The sacramental action gives flesh to a vision of what our humanity might be in a way that, without specifying a social or political programme, clarifies what is to be resisted – leaving us, quite properly, with a set of open questions as to the particular forms of common life, in family, community or state, that might best allow this humanity to develop and flourish. And it is important to ask those questions at every level: our choices are irreducibly to do with 'public' life as well as 'private', and the liturgical sceptic ought to have her critical acumen sharpened for what is anti-human in the public as well as the private sphere. A politics that fails to secure the vulnerable – nationally or internationally – and treats categories of people as dispensable; or that is systematically indifferent to the degradation of the material world; or that drains the lifeblood from education, undermining its necessary diversity and appeal to the imagination; or that shores up spiralling inequalities in the levels of human well-being and refuses critical engagement with a financial culture dangerously out of touch with social reality – any or all of these call for a critique from the perspective of the humanism defined by Christian liturgy.

It is in this connection that Clément, in a powerful phrase, calls for Christians to be the 'guarantors of the faith of others, of those also who do not themselves have faith but believe, often with real humility, in beauty and goodness'. They should be *guardians of an open humanity in an open society*.[22] It should be clear that this is not a commendation of some vacuous or value-free pluralism; the openness in question is the possibility of openness to the horizon of resurrection life. The believer is one who takes seriously all that keeps alive that kind of openness, in art, science or politics – someone who is committed to keeping alive a serious debate about

---

[22] Clément, An, p. 58 (italics in original).

the nature of the human at a time when trivial, functionalist and mechanical anthropologies are so often taken for granted. But the particular point of approaching all this by way of liturgical practice is that the Church does not proclaim a set of ideas about human being; it physically enacts the new world in a drama that is also a quite straightforward and literal event of gathering and feeding. And celebrating the liturgy is the primary way in which we are constituted guardians and guarantors, in Clément's words, of the faith of others; we show that the often obscure hope or confidence in human dignity that animates people outside the community of faith in Christ is not without foundation. Here, in this particular space and time, it is enacted, not simply as a humanly devised sign of what is hoped for but as a 'charismatic' event in which, so we believe, what is symbolized is itself present and effective.

> In every era, the divine liturgy can be the place and the mode by which the human being leaves behind the blind captivity of his or her normal conditions of life; the place and the mode in which he or she finds their prayers heard and receives strength for the realization of their hopes and desires. And if this emerges from reality not from a theoretical principle, why should our own age be deprived of a similar occasion for salvation?[23]

These words from a contemporary Greek bishop aptly sum up the offer and potential of a 'liturgical humanism' that defines something of how Christians configure their intervention in modern culture and politics. The perennial temptation of the North Atlantic mind is to believe that a mixture of gestures and programmes will solve long-term ailments; the perspective we have been exploring begins elsewhere, with the invitation to a communal event in which an alternative human reality is mapped out – and which, participants believe, actually enables

---

[23] Metropolitan John of Thermopylae, 'La divina liturgia: risposto all'inquietudine dell'uomo contemporaneo', in H. Legrand, Ch. Savvatos et al., *Nicola Cabasilas e la divina liturgia* (Bose, ID, Edizioni Qiqajon 2007), pp. 283–97, esp. p. 287.

that alternative to be a present reality, making a difference to them. A call to re-engage with contemporary culture on the basis of the liturgy is likely to sound precious and unrealistic if what people understand by liturgy is the enclosed world of ritual code criticized by Clément and Schmemann;[24] and we should not give house-room to any suggestion that this is some sort of safer alternative to other kinds of engagement, social and intellectual. But if what we most want and need to proclaim and to share with our world is the fleshly reality of the new community, the possibility of a transition into the new world that connects us with the depths of the familiar world, we need to keep liturgical action at the centre of our vision. As the Orthodox tradition represented by Clément and others insists, the question that we should be asking ourselves about liturgy in our churches is not whether it is instructive, even instantly intelligible, let alone entertaining, but whether it looks as though it is grounded in listening to the Word and event that has interrupted human solipsism; whether it looks as though it is credibly changing the vision and the policies of those participating, so that they are awakened to the active realities of person, liberty, communion and – ultimately – resurrection. The deepest problem with liturgical practice is a failure to make resurrection visible – and, in the context of our discussion here, this also means a failure to take death seriously, to be stuck in the banal present of the rootless, aimlessly desiring individual will. Jacques Maritain published many years ago a well-known book on *Integral Humanism*, seeking to show how Christian theology offered a more diversified and truthful account of human capacity than any secular ideology; the task of showing this to our culture remains – and perhaps what we most need at present is a clear locating of this in the liturgical context. This depends – to borrow a resonant formulation of Catherine Pickstock's – on registering 'the need to pray that we again begin to live, to speak, to associate, in a liturgical, which is to say the

[24] E.g. Schmemann, op. cit., pp. 44–7.

157

truly human and creaturely fashion'.[25] If the gospel is more than another ideology, another theory, this is where we must begin, conscious of the fact that the Christian 'interruption' does not offer solutions to discrete problems, or positive experiences to offset doubt and suffering. Clément quotes[26] a Russian Christian interviewed for a television programme during the Soviet era who, asked if Christianity made her happy, replied, 'You're not a Christian so that you can be happy, you're not in the Church to be happy but to be alive.' What is the liturgical embodiment of *that* recognition? If we can answer that, we shall have learned where to find integral humanism.

[25] Pickstock, op. cit., p. 176.
[26] An, p. 63.

7

TRADITION: THE MEMORY OF THE DISCERNING COMMUNITY

I

This picture of liturgically shaped and sustained anthropology has obvious implications for how the Christian believer and the Christian community are to act in human society. What would a political vision be like that was rooted in contemplative awareness and the recognition of the mystery of the personal or (in Lossky's and Sakharov's sense) 'hypostatic' dimension of human existence as a realm of uniqueness and resistance both to homogenizing external authority and to the tyranny of individualism? We shall be returning to this question in later chapters; but first we take a slight detour. The models of human and Christian living so far sketched have some obvious implications for how the ongoing life of the Church itself is to be understood, and we have already noted how a theologian like Lossky can locate authentic (Orthodox) Christianity as a point of balance between the excesses of collectivism and individualism alike. As we shall see in this chapter, he was not the first to use a typology of this kind. In the style of theology that developed in nineteenth-century Russia, informed both by the rediscovery of patristic spiritual texts and the impact of Romantic reaction against rationalistic and mechanical models of society, a very distinctive approach to the idea of 'tradition' emerges, which in turn shapes some of the major twentieth-century Orthodox discussions of the topic (as we noted in the Introduction in reference to Christos Yannaras's treatment of the 'ecclesial event') – connecting the way in which Christian theology is transmitted with the fundamental understanding of the human self and the character of human knowing that we have discussed in earlier chapters. It is worth examining these developments briefly to see how the actual conduct and ethos of life in the Church come to be treated in a more deeply theologically inflected way.

Prior to the nineteenth century, there had in fact been relatively little discussion in the Christian East of the relation between Scripture and tradition as 'sources of revelation' or criteria of the truth of the Church's proclamation. The rallying cry of *sola scriptura* had never been raised in the East as a programme for reconstructing teaching or liturgy, so that a defence of the Church's practice on the basis of an independently transmitted and unwritten teaching was not a priority; nothing like the Council of Trent's apologia on this subject was needed. Where the controversy about 'sources' seems to be referred to in Eastern texts, there is a clear Western influence, usually in terms of an attempt to align the Orthodox Church with one or the other side in post-Reformation controversies. But from the mid-nineteenth century onwards in Russia, there is a vocal refusal of these Western binaries, as three factors develop and interweave in Orthodox writing – an appropriation of new philosophical ideas about knowledge and community, a recovery of some of the central themes of classical Eastern Christian monastic teaching and practice, and a growing sense of the need to define the distinctive features of Eastern (especially Russian) Christianity over against the world of Western debates. Little of this writing is what we should regard as systematic theology: it is mostly found in pamphlets and essays, written for an educated but not on the whole theologically 'professional' readership. Rather than set out an ordered theory, what it does is to connect theological concerns with a range of questions around the nature of *religious ways of knowing* and so with questions about the human subject and human community as such. The provenance of so much of the earlier work on this in educated *lay* circles helps to give it its sometimes tantalizing and often richly generative character.

Behind it, as we noted above, lies the dramatic change in intellectual climate brought about by the beginnings of Romanticism in German thought in the early decades of the nineteenth century, which had fundamentally challenged the universalist rationalism of an earlier age. Enlightenment thought had typically emphasized the possibility of direct access to the truths of reason, independently of any history or culture of transmission, let alone any claims to an authority based in revelation. Post-Enlightenment discourse, in a variety of ways, posed afresh the problem of the *rootedness* of human knowing in communal practices and identities: concepts like tradition and revelation were deployed, if often in some highly untraditional ways, and the straightforward universalism of the eighteenth century gave way to a new interest in local, cultural and even racial belonging as a vehicle for contact with the truth, and in those aspects of human intellectual activity that did not fall under the rubrics of strict rational argument. Feeling and intuition become the focus of new kinds of speculation, and the apparent self-evidence of the priority of the solitary and autonomous mind is assailed on all sides. Novalis, Hegel, Schiller, Schelling and other giants of the new German intellectual and imaginative world – in their very diverse ways – all argue for a model of knowledge that does not take for granted a solitary or abstract reasoning subject; all understand knowledge as bound up with the discovery or recognition of the self as constituted in a web of communally constructed relations across both time and space.

But if this is so, then the knowledge of God above all is bound up with shared or communal experience. This new philosophical environment was assimilated enthusiastically by some Roman Catholic theologians in Germany, especially those involved in the new Catholic faculty of theology at Tübingen. As we shall see, this assimilation was an important element in the reception of German Idealism and Romanticism in Russia. But it converged with a very different development in the Russia of the first half of the nineteenth century: the recovery of the Eastern Christian contemplative tradition in its most sophisticated classical form. The publication of the *Philokalia* had exercised a strong influence on monastic life in Greece and the Balkans, and the version in Church Slavonic (not wholly identical with the Greek in its contents, but covering the same historical range) that appeared in 1793 consolidated its importance for the Russian Christian world. Communities like the famous monastery at Optina, rather more than eighty miles from Moscow, became centres both of patristic scholarship and of spiritual guidance. We have seen how the philokalic literature presupposes and sustains an anthropology; by the middle of the nineteenth century, this anthropology – a spiritual discipline that implied a subtle and comprehensive phenomenology of human knowing and willing, presented as a serious option for contemporary educated (and indeed not so educated) Christians – was increasingly part of a characteristic Russian response to interconfessional disputes and rivalries. The recovery of this monastic vision reinforced interest in the communal and liturgical context of Christian thinking, and the need to affirm the unity of doctrine with the life and practice of the spiritual community, and this was seen as a credible and necessary alternative to both Catholic authoritarianism and Protestant subjectivism.

An increasingly articulate Orthodox laity, dissatisfied with what many saw as the formalism of the piety they had been taught, were looking for new perspectives on the traditional faith of the Russian people that would help them defend it against the critiques both of Protestant pietists – very active in Russia in the wake of the Napoleonic crisis, as readers of *War and Peace* will recall – and Catholic polemicists who attacked the Orthodox Church's subservience to the state and apparent lack of any clear organs of doctrinal definition. The steadily growing conviction in some strands of Russian intellectual and literary life that the Westernizing reforms of Peter the Great had been a moral and spiritual disaster for Russia encouraged some to see pre-Petrine

Russian Christianity as a model of egalitarian, communitarian and spiritually sensitive culture, in which the unspoiled life of the peasant commune mirrored the virtues and graces of the ecclesial community. In other words, to understand why Orthodoxy was worth defending, one should look to the surviving traces of this culture as a lived example of what Orthodox identity really was. The Slavophile movement of the mid-century provided a very important seedbed for ideas about doctrine, tradition and authority in the Church.[1] Twentieth-century Russian theologians may have had a variety of reactions to the Slavophile heritage (often sceptical or hostile); but they do not dispute the significance of the movement in generating a distinctively Orthodox discussion of tradition and community.

II

Ivan Vasilievich Kireevskii (1806–56) stands at the fountainhead of this discussion. He had spent time studying in Germany as a young man, and had encountered both Hegel and Schelling. He came to regard their philosophies as a sort of manifestation or clarification of the limits of self-reflexive rational capacity: they had plumbed the depths of how we think about thinking, but had left open the question of how to understand the totality of the human subjectivity in its relation to comprehensive Truth.[2] This is where we need a 'meta-philosophy' of faith, which is the awareness of relation between the divine and the human person;[3] and such a meta-philosophy is nurtured in the monastic community above all. The basic shape of the holy life in monastic tradition does not

[1] Andrzej Walicki, *The Slavophile Controversy* (Oxford, Clarendon Press 1975), remains a good introduction; for a useful anthology of texts, see Aleksey Khomiakov and Ivan Kireevskii, *On Spiritual Unity: A Slavophile Reader*, ed. and tr. Robert Bird and Boris Jakim (Hudson, NY Lindisfarne Books 1999), which includes several of the texts discussed here.
[2] Ivan Vasilievich Kireevskii, *Pol'noe sobranie sochinenii* (*Complete Collected Works*), ed. M. Gershenzon, vol. 1 (Moscow, Put 1911), pp. 257–8.
[3] Ibid., pp. 274–5.

substantially change (it is a steady and unbroken practice, not a theoretical system), and so adjusting 'tradition' to contemporary needs is no great problem: there is simply a continuing *way of being* before God in community, which changes some of its externals from time to time but fundamentally remains the same.[4] The action of each particular agent within the community, whenever it is transformed by God's grace, is the action of the whole community, because in this context 'the building-up of each person builds up all, and the life of all animates each one'.[5] So it is not so much that there is a monastic teaching that remains unalterably authoritative *over* individuals in the community, but that a continuing transmission of practical wisdom shapes particular lives into a harmonious shared experience that opens the eyes of the heart to truths otherwise unattainable. Kireevskii admired Pascal, and the Pascalian idea of 'the heart's reasons' is reflected in his language, sometimes linked with the *Philokalia*'s language of 'keeping the mind in the heart'.[6] And it is this theme of what might be called the moral and spiritual conditions of knowing the truth that dominates the distinctively Russian account of tradition in the Church and allows Orthodox apologists to differentiate themselves from Protestant and Catholic rivals.

Kireevskii's near-contemporary and ally, Aleksei Stepanovich Khomiakov (1804–60), takes further the critique of Western rationalism (religious as much as secular). While Kireevskii had been strongly critical of Western Christianity, especially its failure in the sixteenth century to rediscover a true patristic perspective, he is less eager than Khomiakov to ascribe any unique charism to the Slavonic Christian world as such. Khomiakov's historical speculations are marked by the kind of racial determinism popular in many nineteenth-century writers, while Kireevskii's monastic focus means that he is far more at arm's length from the canonization of any cultural forms: even Byzantium has to die so

[4]Ibid., p. 257.
[5]Ibid., p. 278.
[6]Ibid., pp. 225, 249–52.

that true Orthodoxy may live.[7] Khomiakov sees the traditional Slavonic commune, the *obshchina*, as the perfect synthesis of person and community, and so as realizing the essence of the Christian vision of catholicity. In an important pamphlet responding to an attack on Orthodoxy by Ivan Gagarin, a Jesuit of Russian origin, Khomiakov argues that the Slavonic translation of *katholike* in the Nicene Creed as *soborny* – which Gagarin had taken as a weakening of the universal claims of the Church – crucially underlines the fact that the adjective 'catholic' is qualitative rather than quantitative in force. *Sobornost'* is related to words for 'assembly', 'council', a gathering for common discernment and decision. There are perfectly adequate Slavonic words for 'universality', Khomiakov points out; what the Creed's translators have understood is that 'catholic' denotes a habit of mind and heart, a transformed sensibility. The central sense of the Greek word is *kath' holon*, 'according to the whole', and so it refers to the *quality* of shared life, in each and every local Christian community. Every local church is 'catholic'; the adjective does not apply to the ensemble of diverse churches gathered under some centralized authority.[8]

Western Christendom has rejected this vision. Faced with the institutional egotism of the papal claims, concentrating the knowledge of truth in the person of a single hierarch, Protestantism sets up another form of ecclesial egotism in the shape of the individual believer deducing conclusions from the pages of Scripture. In both contexts, there is a search for something that will satisfy or pacify the unquiet individual, hungry for certainty. But this passion for externally assured certainty entails a separation between faith and reason, in which reason is drawn in to *make good the defects of faith*, so that faith is always in need of support from beyond itself.[9] In fact, faith is 'knowledge and life at the

---

[7] Ibid., p. 256.
[8] Aleksey Stepanovich Khomiakov, *L'église latine et le protestantisme au point de vue de l'église d'Orient* (Lausanne, B. Benda 1872), pp. 40, 398–9.
[9] Ibid., p. 51.

same time':[10] it is the actuality of participation in living truth and relationship. We are always already involved in knowing, and our greatest error is to try and think ourselves out of what we actually know in order to establish its possibility: in this sense, religious knowing is a paradigm of all knowing, and if we misunderstand what faith means, we are on the road to a general collapse of our intellectual and moral life.[11] We must abandon completely any idea that Christian language works by *drawing conclusions* from external data, let alone by establishing a system of checks and guarantees of its authenticity. The great apostasy of the Western Church – the introduction of the *filioque* into the Creed and the attempt to impose this on all the churches of Christendom – is a symptom both of a rationalist spirit, attempting to work out new implications from the data presented in Scripture and worship, and of a deep-rooted refusal of charity and mutuality, deciding without paying attention to the neighbour.[12] Kireevskii had also seen the *filioque* as representing the triumph of an arid conceptual system; Khomiakov goes further in seeing it as the repudiation of the specifically 'catholic' spirit. The claim that the Holy Spirit proceeds from the Son as well as the Father is the result of trying to make a deduction from the language of Scripture and liturgy simply on the grounds of abstract conceptual grammar (which is also why a doctrine like that of the Immaculate Conception of the Virgin cannot be acceptable to Orthodox Christians). Theories of doctrinal 'development' that imply this sort of approach to dogmatic language are a mistake; Khomiakov regards Newman on development as profoundly wrong.[13] But the worst offence is the attempted enforcement of this doctrinal deduction by an unaccountable absolutist papal authority.

In a famous formulation, Khomiakov insists that 'Neither God, nor Christ, nor his Church are an authority, which is something

[10] Ibid.
[11] Ibid., pp. 73–82.
[12] Ibid., pp. 33ff., 97.
[13] Ibid., p. 216.

external. They are truth; they are the life of the Christian, his interior life.'[14] In this light, it is clear why Khomiakov so emphatically rejects the separation of Scripture and tradition. Scripture is the voice and testimony of the Church: if it were proved that Paul did not write the Epistle to the Romans, the Church would simply say, 'It is from me.' The Epistle speaks from and to the common life of Christ's body. Khomiakov does not have a lot to say about the role of the hierarchy in the Church as guardians of tradition, since he is very wary of any suggestion that some charism of truthfulness belongs to one part of the Church only; for the same reason, he has no doctrine of the infallibility of ecumenical councils. Bishops in the Church are essentially qualified exegetes of Scripture rather than a *magisterium* in the Western sense;[15] and it would be fair to say that for the most part he makes no distinction between the teaching and the learning Church. Truth is what the entire body of the faithful experiences and inhabits *as* a body, through the integrity and intensity of its common life, the qualitative catholicity summed up in the word *sobornost'*. His response to the Western critique of Byzantine and Russian ecclesial life is basically that any theology which works with a dichotomy between 'sources' of revelation and the believing subject is undermining the very idea of faith as a comprehensive new disposition or habit of life, Christians finding their identity in mutual communion.

It is clear that Khomiakov had absorbed some of the arguments of the Catholic theologians of Tübingen – Johann Sebastian von Drey (1777–1853), for example, and still more clearly Johann Adam Möhler (1796–1838), who were strongly critical of the divorce between theology and the spiritual life and eager to restore a sense of *organic* life to thinking about the Church. They share Khomiakov's suspicion of claims to infallibility and insist on the transformation of the individual subject in the Church into an ecclesial self, living in unbroken mutuality and exchange and only as

---

[14] Ibid., p. 40.
[15] Sergei Bolshakoff, *The Doctrine of the Unity of the Church in the Works of Khomyakov and Moehler* (London, SPCK 1946), pp. 154–7.

such capable of knowing the truth.[16] Khomiakov's understanding
of the relation between Scripture and tradition is also very close
to what the Tübingen writers argued. Möhler has a good deal
more to say about the structures of the Church, however, and is
less wary of the language of doctrinal development – although the
substance of what he says is not that different from Khomiakov
in its insistence that there is no sense in which doctrine gradually
'grows' or advances; it is all always present in the common life
of the Church. Perhaps more surprisingly, Khomiakov shows
signs of having been influenced by two Swiss Protestant thinkers,
Alexandre Vinet (1797–1847) and Charles Secrétan (1815–95),
both of whom sought to develop a social philosophy and a theory
of the Christian community that held together the freedom of the
person and the irreducibly communal and cooperative nature of
human personhood. Khomiakov's French-language works were
published by Protestant houses, especially in Switzerland; but
his general failure to provide references or documentation in his
essays makes it hard to work out the exact degree of his familiarity
with either his Catholic or his Protestant interlocutors. We do,
however, have his correspondence with the Anglican Tractarian
theologian, William Palmer; and the insistence on the presence of
the whole Catholic Church in any one part of it may well owe
something also to Anglican apologetic of this period.[17]

The reception of Khomiakov's work by the leadership of
the Russian Church was mixed, though he seems to have had
an impact on the teaching in several theological schools. Filaret
(Drozdov, 1782–1867), Metropolitan of Moscow, and certainly
the most intellectually and spiritually weighty presence in the
mid-century Russian hierarchy, had reservations about aspects of
his vision, possibly connected with the fact that he had, in his
catechism of 1823, accepted the identification of catholicity with
universality that so aroused Khomiakov's ire; and he and others
were anxious about the lack of a theological understanding of the

[16] Ibid., pp. 220–57, for an overview of these influences.
[17] Ibid., pp. 77–80.

visible structures of the Church in Khomiakov. The epigrammatic comment of Fr Georges Florovsky in his history of Russian theology that Khomiakov 'replaced the Church with the "parish" (*obshchina*)'[18] reflects a common unease among Orthodox readers of Khomiakov. Yet, as Florovsky and others have noted, Filaret himself echoes Khomiakov in insisting that the guardianship of Christian truth belongs to the entire body of the Church, not to the hierarchy alone. And when he speaks about Scripture and tradition, he has much in common with Khomiakov in his refusal to see Scripture as anything other than the primary record of tradition and the credal definitions as anything other than a re-presentation of Scripture.[19] His emphasis on self-emptying as the essential characteristic of life in the Church, a theme constantly repeated in his sermons, where he regularly quotes Philippians 2 (on the self-emptying, the *kenosis*, of Christ in the Incarnation), provides a foundation for some of the twentieth-century developments of the theology of tradition, in that it gives central place to the dissolution of individualism in the life of the baptized community. And Florovsky notes elsewhere[20] that Filaret affirms something like a doctrine of 'qualitative' catholicity, the whole Church subsisting in each local community, and defines the guardianship of Christian truth as a charism of the whole Body of Christ, not the hierarchy alone (a conviction also found, though less clearly, in the 'Encyclical of the Eastern Patriarchs' addressed in 1848 to Pope Pius IX, a text to which Khomiakov and most of those who took up his approach appeal).

And although Khomiakov was never regarded with unqualified favour by the Russian theological establishment, it is clear that

[18] Georges Vasil'evich Florovsky, *Puti russkago bogosloviya* (*The Ways of Russian Theology*) (Paris, YMCA Press 1937), p. 251.
[19] Ibid., pp. 177–8; cf. Metropolitan Filaret Drozdov, *Slova i rechi sinodalnago chlena Filareta, Mitropolitana Moskovskago* (*Sermons and Addresses of Metropolitan Filaret of Moscow, Member of the Synod*), 2 vols, 2nd edn (Moscow, Tip. A. Semena 1848), ii, pp. 51a 57a.
[20] *The Collected Works of George Florovksy vol. 1. Bible, Church, Tradition: An Eastern Orthodox View* (Belmont, MA, Nordland Publishing Company 1972), pp. 40, 53.

his distinctive way of absorbing and transforming European philosophical themes that resonated with Orthodox ecclesiology continued to shape a lot of the more original theological discussions in Russia up to and beyond the Revolution. Yuri Samarin (1819–76), more consciously Hegelian than Khomiakov, developed the latter's model of the Church as organism and the interwoven relation of 'life' and 'faith' in the community,[21] and some of the theologians of the Theological Academy in Kiev in the 1880s, such as Silvester Malevansky (1828–1908), picked up aspects of this approach, though within a more rigidly 'systematic' structure. At the end of the nineteenth and the beginning of the twentieth centuries, Antonii Khrapovitskii (1863–1936), a very influential figure in Russian church politics and eventually Metropolitan of Kiev, produced a series of essays on the 'moral idea' (*nravstvennaya idea*) of a number of dogmatic subjects, including the Church, designed as a riposte to critics like Tolstoy who accused the Church of ignoring ethics for the sake of doctrine. These, especially the treatises on the Church and the Trinity, return regularly to the idea of the transformed consciousness of the believer, whose personal uniqueness is grounded and assured by incorporation into catholic communion, so that not only is the life of the Church an 'image of the Trinity', but the Trinity is known 'internally' in virtue of the nature of the common life of the Body of Christ.[22] Khrapovitskii is predictably more concerned than Khomiakov with issues around the visible structures of the Church, but his central concerns about the nature of freedom as actualized in communion and community and the way in which participation in the life of the Church is the source of doctrinal knowledge, needing no external criteria in infallible Scripture or papacy, is a clear development from Khomiakov's central contentions about qualitative catholicity. It is not an exaggeration to say that this cluster of themes had by

---

[21] Florovsky, *Puti russkago bogosloviya*, pp. 281–4.

[22] Metropolitan Antonii Khrapovistkii, *Pol'noe sobranie sochinenii (Complete Collected Works)*, 3 vols, 2nd edn (St Petersburg, I. L.Tuzov 1911), ii, pp. 16–18, 27, 65–8, 75–96.

the end of the nineteenth century become a standard trope in a great deal of Russian Orthodox self-understanding.

III

The most influential Russian philosopher of the later nineteenth century, Vladimir Sergeevich Solov'ev (1853–1900), makes the dissolution/transformation of individual consciousness one of the focal points of his system. Ecclesial life is a model or sign of the transfiguration of the cosmos by the radically selfless work of the eternal Word emptying himself of divine glory and power so as to form a new organism activated by the self-giving of the Holy Spirit.[23] Solov'ev does not distinguish universality and catholicity as sharply as Khomiakov, but, like the earlier thinkers we have discussed, he understands dogmatic definition and ecclesial tradition as the fruit of a qualitatively distinct form of life, a life free 'from self-esteem and particularism, whether personal, local, national or any other sort'[24] – which also means that Solov'ev is less willing than Khomiakov to idealize traditional Slavonic society as somehow a model of grace and communion. We know the unity-in-diversity of God as Trinity because of our growth in true self-knowledge, understanding the plurality and unity of the knowing subject as such (a surprisingly 'Augustinian' echo here) and the fundamentally interwoven and interdependent character of all finite reality. In this sense, the Trinity is known by 'contemplative reason' as much as by revelation;[25] but it would be a mistake to conclude that he is claiming that God can be known as Trinity independently of God's own action, since this is pervasive in all finite activity and all finite knowing.

---

[23] Vladimir Solov'ev (the surname is variously transliterated in Western European languages), *God, Man and the Church: The Spiritual Foundations of Life* (Cambridge, James Clarke 1938), pp. 115, 123, 138–40.
[24] Ibid., p. 159.
[25] Vladimir Solovyov, *Lectures on Godmanhood*, tr. and ed. with an introduction by P. Zouboff (Poughkeepsie, NY, Harmon Printing House 1944), p. 152.

The relation of this to Solov'ev's speculations about divine Wisdom, Sophia, is a major area of study in itself; but it is clear that, despite areas of significant disagreement, he shares the basic conviction of the mid-century essayists that the doctrinal language of the Church is the fruit of a certain quality of common life. As this theme is developed further in twentieth-century writers, the explicit identification of 'tradition' with the common life of the Church as such becomes more prominent. Sergii Nikolaevich Bulgakov (1871–1944), in his brief but very important summary of Orthodox theology written in the early 1930s for an ecumenical audience[26] actually entitles an early chapter, 'The Church as Tradition', affirming that 'Tradition is the living memory of the Church ... a living power inherent in a living organism':[27] Bulgakov echoes earlier writers in denying that tradition is any kind of an externalized scheme of criteria for the truthfulness of the Church's proclamation; and each believer, as well as the entire Christian body of believers, carries internally the fullness of tradition.[28] Scripture is itself a part of tradition in this wide sense. From one point of view, Orthodoxy has no quarrel with Protestantism in its recognition of the ultimate authority of the written Word; but that written Word is recognized by and interpreted within the ongoing life of the community: the divine life of the Spirit within the Church bears witness to the Spirit at work in Scripture.[29] The liturgical reading of Scripture is a dramatic instance of this, as it is an event in which the scriptural event happens spiritually in the Church today;[30] this is the paradigm for reading the Bible outside the liturgy – even when Scripture is being studied 'scientifically'. Bulgakov distinguishes

---

[26] Sergius Bulgakov, *The Orthodox Church*, revised translation (Crestwood, NY, St Vladimir's Seminary Press 1988). Many of the themes of this book are discussed at greater length in Bulgakov's longer treatise, the third in his major dogmatic trilogy, *The Bride of the Lamb*, tr. Boris Jakim (Grand Rapids, MI, Eerdmans 2001).

[27] *The Orthodox Church*, p. 10.

[28] Ibid., p. 11.

[29] Ibid., pp. 12–14.

[30] Ibid., p. 22.

the use of modern scholarship to clarify straightforward questions about text and history from a theological interpretation that always requires a 'responsibility' to the communal mind of the Church, to tradition. And this is not a matter of submitting to the judgement of past ages, but of entering more fully into a spiritual culture that is still evolving – but evolving as a shared reality that is inseparable from the way in which individuals are drawn out of their egotism in the Body of Christ.[31] Bulgakov is cautious about the language of 'development', noting that, while dogmatic utterance obviously becomes more complex and rich as time goes by, 'the Church is always identical with itself',[32] and the life of the Spirit in the Church neither grows nor diminishes. And the 'infallible' authority of doctrine cannot be thought of independently of the integrity and holiness of the Church's life: 'Unity of tradition is established by unity of life, and unity of tradition establishes unity of faith.'[33] Bulgakov goes on in the same book to draw heavily on the language of *sobornost'* in developing the idea that doctrinal formulation grows out of the sheer fact of common spiritual life and practice. A doctrine may be believed before it is articulated: 'The immediate and concrete experience of the Church contains the germ of dogma.'[34] Doctrinal formulation emerges from a process of 'conciliation', the sifting through open debate of contested questions; the formal and public conciliar process that finally determines the limits of what is to be said is not an authority acting from above or outside, but the embodiment of common discernment – which is why councils are not theologically essential to the Church's life, however practically useful; and also why even councils which appear to have sound canonical credentials have at times pronounced in error.[35] There is no guarantee of infallibility in a conciliar body,

[31] Ibid., p. 25.
[32] Ibid., p. 31.
[33] Ibid., p. 34.
[34] Ibid., pp. 67–8.
[35] Ibid., pp. 72–6.

only the continuing discernment as to whether a formulation is or is not a crystallization of authentic shared life and worship. This is the liberty characteristic of Orthodoxy, standing between the anarchic individual judgements of Protestantism (although it is important to recognize that there is a 'conciliar' tradition within certain kinds of Protestantism also) and the legalistic claim of Roman Catholicism.[36]

Bulgakov continues Khomiakov's legacy in connecting the question of tradition with religious epistemology overall, dissolving the duality of Scripture and tradition by understanding Scripture as itself an aspect of tradition, since tradition is understood here as for all practical purposes the actual worshipping life of the Church, which is the primary context for the proclamation of Scripture. He also – foreshadowing Lossky and other later writers – presents Orthodoxy as transcending the opposition of Protestant and Catholic (individualist and collectivist) identities in the Western Christian world. He has more to say than Khomiakov about the actual decision-making processes of the Church, but is equally reluctant to offer any set of identifiable external or institutional criteria for what counts as a true or valid decision by a canonically authorized body: he seems to be saying that a church that attends to its common life and nurtures its members in mutual selfless love will simply grow in doctrinal wisdom, and is not obliged to give any further account of how at any given moment it determines the validity of what it is proclaiming – simply because to raise the question of the validity of formulations is to raise the question of the authenticity of its spiritual life, and that is not a question that can be answered by any external guarantee. Tradition is a 'skill' that is learned, a habit of response to God that is inseparably intellectual and spiritual and is always exercised in the worshipping community, rather than a repository of doctrinal information. To accept its validity and authority is not the conclusion of a chain of argument so

[36] Ibid., pp. 80–2.

much as the decision to be a disciple whose personal identity is actualized in the liturgical life of the community.

Exactly these themes dominate the theology of tradition as it is developed by Georges Vasilievich Florovsky (1893–1979), briefly Bulgakov's colleague at the Russian seminary in Paris, and one of the most persistent and thoroughgoing critics of the older man's thought.[37] Despite their radical disagreements over Bulgakov's version of 'Sophiology', the two theologians converge to a remarkable degree on the subject of ecclesial consciousness and the definition of tradition. At much the same time as Bulgakov was writing *The Orthodox Church*, Florovsky was writing a substantial paper – also for an ecumenical audience – on the notion of the Church's catholicity,[38] which develops closely similar arguments about qualitative catholicity and about tradition as a milieu not a 'source' of doctrine. Florovsky follows Khomiakov in insisting that the *kath' holou* from which the adjective 'catholic' derives is distinct from *kata pantas*, which could refer to nothing more than what *happens* to be a universal conviction. Universality *follows from* the wholeness of true faith; it is not the foundation of true faith.[39] The capacity for loving self-surrender and for recognizing Christ in the other implies a transformation in human self-consciousness, and Florovsky draws on Khrapovitskii in articulating this. But Florovsky (again showing a striking closeness to Bulgakov) sees this more specifically in the context of a kind of sacramental telescoping of time, paradigmatically in the Eucharist: tradition is a victory over temporal succession, so that in the Church's worship we are contemporary with the events of Scripture and indeed with the entirety of God's saving

[37] For a comprehensive anthology of his work, see Brandon Gallagher and Paul Ladouceur, eds, *The Patristic Witness of Georges Florovsky: Essential Theological Writings* (London, Bloomsbury 2019), which contains several of the articles discussed here.
[38] Florovsky, *Collected Works vol. 1*, pp. 37–55, from an essay on '*Sobornost*: The Catholicity of the Church' (no. 18 in Gallaher and Ladouceur).
[39] Ibid., p. 40.

work.[40] For Florovsky, this is a corollary of belief in the Spirit's unchanging presence in the Church: 'Tradition is the constant abiding of the Spirit ... a *charismatic* not a historical principle.'[41] There can therefore never be a development of doctrine that in any sense *supplements* what is given in the events of the Church's beginning or in the scriptural record.[42]

This comprehensive overview is grounded in a couple of earlier essays – a 1929 piece on 'Eucharist and *Sobornost*',[43] in which there is a preliminary account of how the Eucharist creates 'a new catholic humanity' in the image of the Trinity, in which the 'impermeability' of human selves to each other is overcome;[44] and a broader account of the nature of revelation, first developed in an essay published in 1931.[45] A shorter version of this had also been given to Karl Barth's seminar at Bonn in 1931.[46] In this paper, Florovsky underlines the fact that revelation is fully given in the fact of the Church's foundation and the descent of the Spirit:[47] the heart of revelation is the new fact of God's 'closeness' (*blizost'*) to creation. Knowledge of God is thus more than a recollection of the past acts of God; it is an announcing of God's present agency, in which historical recollection is itself transfigured.[48] 'Dogma is a statement of experience, not a theorem of speculative thought'; it is a 'logical icon' of the divine reality that dwells in the Church,[49]

[40] Ibid., pp. 44–6; cf. Florovsky, *Collected Works, vol. 3. Creation and Redemption* (Belmont, MA, Nordland Publishing Company 1976), pp. 39–40, from 'Revelation, Philosophy and Theology' (no. 7 in Gallaher and Ladouceur).

[41] Ibid., p. 47.

[42] Ibid., p. 48; cf. pp. 73–5, from an essay of 1963, 'Creation and Creaturehood' (no. 1 in Gallaher and Ladouceur).

[43] Florovsky, '*Yevkharistiya i sobornost'*' ('Eucharist and *sobornost'*'), *Put'* 19, 1929, pp. 3–22.

[44] Ibid., pp. 8–9.

[45] Florovsky, '*Bogoslovskie otryvki*' ('Theological Fragments'), *Put'* 31, 1931, pp. 3–29.

[46] Florovsky, *Collected Works, vol. 3*, pp. 21–40 (no. 7 in Gallaher and Ladouceur); since this is a shorter and slightly different text, reference is here given to both versions, the Russian original first.

[47] Art. cit., pp. 5/23.

[48] Ibid., pp. 11/28–9.

[49] Ibid., pp. 12/30.

and so it makes no claims to completeness in its account of God's being and action. Just as Bulgakov[50] writes of the incompleteness of Orthodoxy as a system, so Florovsky contrasts the Church's doctrinal language with all philosophical systems and underlines its inexhaustibility:[51] what is not codified in strict dogmatic form may still be conveyed in symbols, and only at the end of time will there be a full manifestation of the truth embodied in the Church's life. Catholicity is again defined in terms of the transformation of the human self, the dissolution of a 'mine' and 'yours' mentality and the gift to the believer of the unity-in-communion of the Holy Trinity, in which each subject possesses the wholeness of divine life;[52] Khrapovitskii is once more cited, along with the familiar texts from Filaret and the 1848 Patriarchal Encyclical[53] on the gift of tradition to the whole Orthodox Christian body (allowing, like Bulgakov, a specific role for the hierarchy as expressing the common mind of the eucharistic community). And the Russian original of this essay concludes with a resounding denial, closely echoing Khomiakov, of the idea that authority in the Church can be external or imposed, since 'Authority cannot be the source of spiritual life.'[54] As in many other pieces, Florovsky underlines the 'charismatic' character of tradition – 'the charismatic or mystical memory of the Church'[55] – and the consequent need always to read Scripture within the catholic community, so that it is never simply an historical record. The trinitarian and pneumatological emphasis enables Florovsky to state clearly why the catholic consciousness is never a mere *collective* mind,[56] and why, indeed, catholicity means the emergence of a truly *personal* mode of knowing, delivered from the prison of individualism, yet still free.

[50] Bulgakov, op. cit., pp. 6–8.
[51] Florovsky, art. cit., pp. 16–18/35–6.
[52] Ibid., pp. 20–3/37–9.
[53] Ibid., pp. 24–5.
[54] Ibid., p. 28.
[55] Ibid., p. 23.
[56] Ibid., pp. 23–3/39.

This dense and very important essay – particularly in its original, slightly fuller, Russian form – draws together the main recurrent themes in the Russian Orthodox treatment of tradition, but offers a far more sophisticated and complex anchorage in both trinitarian and eucharistic theology, linking questions of religious knowledge and certainty with a fresh perspective on the implications for our understanding of personality and consciousness of the nature of the Church as a community that in some sense 'images' the Trinity. Later, mostly rather shorter papers by Florovsky repeat the same themes, sometimes almost verbatim (a habit of Florovsky's that is rather frustrating for the scholar is his recycling of material with minor verbal variations in different papers published in different languages). Articles from the 1950s and 1960s return to the topic of Scripture, requiring no 'supplement',[57] and of tradition as the abiding 'hermeneutical principle and method' in the Church, so that all doctrine is the product of tradition.[58] They thus also point to the need for a transformation of the Christian mind[59] into a scriptural shape in which the impress of the trinitarian life communicates itself as 'Human response is integrated into the mystery of the Word of God' as in Scripture itself and thus the sacred history continues in the Church.[60] Two significant papers of the 1960s[61]discuss the patristic basis for Florovsky's general approach, appealing to Athanasius on Scripture *as* tradition, *paradosis*,[62] stressing liturgy as the primary locus of tradition,[63] and discussing[64] the well-known passage in St Basil of Caesarea's treatise on

---

[57]Florovsky, *Collected Works, vol. 1*, pp. 73–5, from 'The Function of Tradition in the Ancient Church'.

[58]Ibid., pp. 75–9.

[59]Ibid., p. 113 (from 'St Gregory Palamas and the Tradition of the Fathers', no. 13 in Gallaher and Ladouceur.

[60]Ibid., pp. 21, 26.

[61]Ibid., pp. 73–92 ('The Function of Tradition') and 93–103 ('The Authority of the Ancient Councils and the Tradition of the Fathers').

[62]Ibid., p. 83.

[63]Ibid., p. 84.

[64]Ibid., pp. 85–8.

the Holy Spirit (ch. 27), which distinguishes *dogmata* from *kerygmata* – unwritten doctrine that is encoded in the Church's practice from proclaimed or defined teaching. Florovsky is clear that this cannot refer to esoteric 'traditions' in the plural, which are either not mentioned or deplored in patristic literature,[65] but simply recognizes the fact that belief is transmitted in usage and habit before it is formulated in definitions. And his (and Bulgakov's) point about the authority of councils is repeated: there is no formal condition for infallibility, and an infallibly truthful definition by a council depends on the infallibility of the Church as a whole insofar as it is faithful to Christ, the sole criterion of truth.[66] Once again, the idea of the 'charismatic' authority recognized in authentic councils is invoked.[67]

As we have noted, the convergence of thought between Florovsky and Bulgakov is striking, and Florovsky, especially in his earlier essays, is very evidently working the same ground as Khomiakov. Almost as striking is the regularity of his reference to Augustine on the idea of the *totus Christus* as summing up what he wants to say about the communal discernment of the Church as the site of Christ's present life and action,[68] though he is cautious about an excessively Christocentric model of the Church's identity that obscures the work of the Spirit, and identifies this as a weakness in Khomiakov and Möhler. But the theologian who most richly develops the theme of the interaction of Word and Spirit in the life of the Church is Vladimir Nikolaevich Lossky (1903–58), arguably the most creative Orthodox theologian of the twentieth century, who, in a number of interrelated articles written in the early 1950s, drew together the insights of the other theologians we have examined here and added some substantial contributions very much his own.

[65] Ibid., pp. 83, 99, referring to Irenaeus against the Gnostics.
[66] Ibid., pp. 96–7, 103.
[67] Ibid., p. 103.
[68] E.g. Florovsky, ibid., p. 16.

In his best-known work, *The Mystical Theology of the Eastern Church*, Lossky touches briefly on tradition as 'the life of the Church in the Holy Spirit',[69] in a passage that reproduces some of the familiar cluster of ideas deriving from Khomiakov – the impossibility of external criteria for truthfulness, the charism of truthfulness as bestowed on all members of the Church – but he adds the fresh point that, while the fullness of Orthodox truth is given to the whole Body in virtue of its life in the Spirit, 'the function of defining', the ability to formulate dogma, is part of the 'Christological aspect' of the Church, its rootedness in the once-for-all event of the Incarnation. It is part of a general thesis about the Church that is perhaps the most original and challenging feature of the book: the act and grace of Christ establish a set of structural possibilities for the renewal of humanity, but this renewal of human 'nature' in Christ has to become particular and internal to each unique believer in the life of the Spirit. The notion found in earlier writers that believers become most fully themselves as persons in the communion of the Body is here closely linked with Lossky's model of redemption as inseparably and complementarily the work of Son and Spirit (the 'two economies', in his terminology)[70]. But this analysis (which was and still is criticized by other Orthodox theologians as over-schematic) is much deepened and extended in the essays Lossky wrote in the last years of his sadly brief life. His study of 'Tradition and Traditions'[71] was first published – significantly – as a theological preface to a book on icons in 1952; and it should be read in tandem with a 1948 piece, 'Concerning the Third Mark of the

---

[69] Vladimir Nikolaevich Lossky, *The Mystical Theology of the Eastern Church* (Cambridge, James Clarke 1957), p. 188.
[70] Ibid., pp. 135–73, and cf. Lossky, *Théologie dogmatique*, ed. O. Clément and M. Stavrou (the second edition of a digest made by Olivier Clément from the unpublished courses of lectures on doctrine given by Lossky in Paris in the last three years of his life) (Paris, Les Éditions du Cerf 2012), pp. 159–69.
[71] Lossky, *In the Image and Likeness of God* (Crestwood, NY, St Vladimir's Seminary Press 1974), pp. 141–68.

Church: Catholicity',[72] a 1955 essay on 'The Theological Notion of the Human Person,[73] and a posthumously published (1963) study of 'Catholic Consciousness: Anthropological Implications of the Dogma of the Church'.[74]

The 1948 essay makes the case for 'qualitative' catholicity, and criticizes an unbalanced Christocentrism in ecclesiology that threatens to subordinate distinct persons in the Church to a kind of ecclesial 'superperson' and to present the ongoing life of the Church as a temporal transmission of powers from the first century onwards. This assimilates catholicity to unity; but they are radically different, since catholicity is the fact of unity *in diversity*. Lossky is careful to insist that the two 'economies' are always reciprocally related, and that there can be an imbalance towards pneumatology as well as a problem with undue Christocentrism, but the weight of this piece is directed against what he sees as a typically Roman Catholic stress both on historical continuity and on institutional cohesion. This is obviously influenced at some level by Florovsky's ideas about the compression or abolition of time in the Church, as well as by Khomiakov's formulations (quoted at the end of Lossky's essay), but is taken in a very different direction by its distinctive trinitarian argument. Similar points are made in the posthumous piece on catholic consciousness, once again resisting any model of submission to authority in the Church and proposing the idea of the Church as 'the unique subject of multiple personal consciousnesses':[75] each person in the Church genuinely becomes self-aware in and by virtue of the Church's shared life, and so understands and experiences himself or herself as constituted by the exchange and mutual gift of the trinitarian persons, and so also by the mutuality of the life of self-giving that characterizes the community of the Church. Interestingly, Lossky is critical

[72]Ibid., pp. 169–81.
[73]Ibid., pp. 111–23.
[74]Ibid., pp. 183–94.
[75]Ibid., p. 194.

here both of Tübingen Catholicism and of Khomiakov's theology of the Spirit as both being unduly influenced by a Hegelian structure that absorbs the particular into a universal movement of impersonal Spirit.[76] Thus Lossky's ecclesiology and doctrine of tradition are tightly linked with his very full and careful account of how the unique person is realized in the life of the Church precisely as the finite person becomes conformed to the self-emptying (*kenosis*) and self-transcending (*ekstasis*) of the Son and the Spirit, who live only to give their life and identity *to* the other and receive everything that constitutes their life *from* the other – themes that are worked out in the 1955 paper as well as in these studies in ecclesiology.

The essay on 'Tradition and Traditions' again reproduces some themes we have identified in Florovsky – notably the impossibility of thinking of doctrinal development as in any way supplementing or completing the single gift of revelation in Christ through the Spirit in the Church.[77] But two new themes appear here. Lossky defines tradition as 'the critical spirit of the Church ... made acute by the Holy Spirit'.[78] The life of the Spirit in the Church directs believers to question accretions and superstitions in the name of an integrity that has to be constantly renewed in fresh contexts – which is why 'tradition' as 'the unique mode of receiving Revelation'[79] is not to be identified with traditions or traditionalism. And the second new insight is in Lossky's discussion of the text of Basil on *dogma* and *kerygma*, in which he argues that Basil's distinction between privately or tacitly transmitted doctrine and publicly articulated teaching takes us only so far: *both* categories are expressions of the underlying fact of a tradition that simply *is* the hidden life of the Church. Liturgical habit

[76] Ibid., p. 191.
[77] Ibid., p. 157; it is worth noting that Lossky, like Florovsky, is critical of Newman's model of development in the light of this, as appears in some of Lossky's late unpublished lectures.
[78] Ibid., p. 156.
[79] Ibid., p. 155.

is nearest to this fuller reality of *lived* tradition, because it embodies the primordial gift of baptismal illumination and incorporation; but Basil's two modes of transmission are just that, two modes of articulating a deeper mystery that is the very identity of the community of Spirit-filled persons.[80] The essay forms a very complex and rich argument for a measure of flexibility and even plurality in practice within a continuing Orthodox identity that is always generating new forms and images, as well as new conceptualities, within a clearly bounded 'grammar' of common belief, hymnody and sacramental worship (hence the importance of this essay as an introduction to a study of iconography).

IV CONCLUSION

The continuity in Russian reflection on the role of tradition in the Church during the nineteenth and twentieth centuries is notable, and it is probably the most distinctive contribution made by Russian religious thought to the Christian theological spectrum during this period. In the context of this book as a whole, what is most important is the way in which it unites the definition of 'tradition' with a broader approach to both human identity and human knowing. Tradition is never a set of inherited beliefs to be apprehended by an individual consciousness; it is the climate of discerning receptivity that characterizes the life of the Christian community – a community in which the distorting lens of individual will and unexamined craving, and the myth of radical self-creating autonomy, are systematically challenged and exposed to the solvent acidity of grace. The Russian understanding of tradition as sketched here has thus been a vehicle for developing a theological approach to the human person; insights about the distinctive nature of religious knowing and the significance of communal practice

[80] Ibid., pp. 144–8.

in that connection; and a critical discernment around issues of authority and hierarchy is certainly something of relevance for conversations with the intellectual world of the twenty-first century – with implications not only for thinking about the Church, but also for thinking about the shape of Christian political vision and engagement as well.

8

JUSTICE, DISTANCE AND LOVE: A CONTEMPLATIVE STANCE IN POLITICS?

I

What might a liturgical and contemplative perspective of the kind we have been thinking about have to say in the unusually febrile atmosphere of national and global politics at the moment? One question that it illuminates is about what it is in political life that makes for what I shall call 'sustainable' justice – that is, a corporate habit of relation that allows a community to believe that the security of its members does not depend entirely on contingent relations of power at any given moment. To speak of justice at all is in fact to speak of what it is in human relations that is not settled simply by power: imagining this is the fundamental issue of Plato's *Republic*. For any social situation to be called 'just', it has to be capable of being presented as *more* than a just-about-bearable compromise between contending interests, arrived at by balancing potentially violent pressures. In the reality of practical politics, this aspect will regularly be to the fore, and it may reasonably be thought of as a search for *fair* settlement. But one of our problems is that, if the idea of what is 'just' is reduced simply to what is 'fair', the discourse never moves beyond a balance of the supposed entitlements each party begins with.

In contrast, we could point to an older and richer usage in which acts that are 'just' are acts that *respond appropriately* to reality – acts that from another perspective (thinking back to chapter 2) might be seen as 'truthful' responses to the reality with which they deal. The familiar words that follow the *Sursum corda* dialogue in the Roman Mass – *Vere dignum et iustum, aequum et salutare* – incorporate the language of justice into worship: what we do in worshipping God is what is appropriate to the reality that is God, and so is 'just and equitable'. The measure of justice, in other words, is not primarily about a balance of interests but about an act of recognition. What I believe (or any particular agent believes) about my interest, may or may not correspond to what actually requires recognition – in myself or in others. The real difficulty of 'doing justice' is the labour of recognition, the identification – always vulnerable and provisional – of what is due to the reality before us 'in itself', not simply in relation to the agenda of the moment. Understood in this sense, justice is inescapably a notion that recedes over the horizon of achievement, retains a critical and utopian edge to it, and is bound up with a sustained critical practice over time. To say that it is never 'arrived at' is not to make it a formally regulative idea only; the point is that in any and every specific situation, it allows the question to arise of what and who is and is not *acknowledged* in their actuality, and of what process and habits would be needed for that acknowledgement to be better secured or realized.

And this depends on 're-grounding' our language about what is 'just' in an understanding of *ius* that takes seriously the metaphysical hinterland of the word in an older theological context. What is just is what is 'aligned' to truth; this is what the etymology of the Greek and Hebrew words for justice suggests. It is in this sense that we can say that justice is an attribute of God. As we saw in chapter 2, God is, in the first place, faithful to God's nature, God is 'true' to God; the divine integrity never falters. And as a consequence, God's action in respect of all finite realities is to give them what is needed for their life and flourishing; we cannot imagine any distorting 'agenda' or self-interest where

God is concerned. The divine action is always one that respects the reality of what is made (which itself is shaped by the nature of the creating God and anchored in the eternal reality of the divine Word). God 'does justice' to God in the eternal act of self-knowledge and self-assent that is divine life, and so 'does justice' in and to creation in honouring what has been made and conserving and enhancing its life to the fullest degree. But for us then to 'do justice' in a mode that aligns with God's justice entails first and foremost a habit of fidelity to God and a perspective on God's works that will allow us to stand away from the definition of my own interest with which I begin my engagement with the world. This is not a search for the proverbial 'God's-eye view' of the environment, but a practice of critical detachment from any particular account of the world in terms of my interest, a practice sustained through time and renewed by repeated scrutiny and exposure to challenge.

In the background of such a view lies the Evagrian theme that has so often returned in these pages, the diagnosis of how knowledge is inflected by passion, and how our perceptions may become 'diabolical' when dominated by the question of what individual profit or satisfaction may be gained from the object of knowledge. If justice is a way of *seeing* before it is a way of *acting* – the attempt at a response to the environment that is fitting to what that environment actually is – then what is required is an *askesis*, a discipline that keeps us attentive to the ways in which our account of our interests may distort what we see and think we know: an education of the passions. The particular challenge we are considering here is how what is traditionally configured as practice for the individual may be reimagined as a political project.

A couple of points may be made straight away. First, it is important to clarify that this is not a merely general challenge – and therefore capable of being utilized to silence any protest from those whose interests are being actively denied by more powerful agents; it is primarily for those powerful agents, those who have the liberty to silence the interest of others in the face of their own. An appeal to the kind of justice we have been considering is disastrously misunderstood if it is seen as a commendation of political passivity: to accept the dominance of another set of interests that silence one's own is itself an act of *injustice* in the wider sense. Augustine's comment in the *de civitate Dei* that the spiritual health of the oppressor is the most serious casualty of an oppressive regime[1] can be developed to ground a critique of political passivity, since it leaves unhealed the damage the oppressor does to their own soul. And the injunction to scrutinize one's own account of one's interests (collective or individual) makes no sense if *any* account of those interests can simply be silenced in advance by another agent. Second, the possibility of some sort of political *askesis* is premised on the accessibility of institutions of open and public debate, and of dependable flows of information. To speak about a 'spirituality' of political life is emphatically not to direct attention away from institutions towards some kind of private self-cultivation; it is to work for the making and preservation of durable environments for genuinely *political* discourse – the articulation and examination of policies and projects in a climate where some significant equality of 'voice' is guaranteed. And such 'environments for political discourse' are essentially communities of *discernment* in which the goal is learning the skills of self-examination in the presence of those whom I or we are tempted to define in relation to our own supposed needs.

II

A contemplative political *paideia* is one in which we accommodate the necessary distance of love – a provocative statement, given that we assume love to be about commitment and solidarity. But in the light of the foregoing discussion, it should be clear that the investment of love, if it is to be more than an exercise of self-serving emotion, requires a particular kind of time-taking in which

---

[1] IV.3: the tyranny of unjust rulers injures them more than it does their subjects, making them slaves to their own passion.

we step back from our initial articulation of our interests and our initial account of others. We interrogate our own self-descriptions, beginning with the simple (or not) exercise of reimagining them as if they were not simply *ours*; that is, we learn to consider them as one element in an 'ecology', not as the factor that organizes the mapping of all others. We interrogate our initial account of others – i.e. other agents, complexes of circumstances, including material objects and conditions – seeking to imagine them not as they relate to or serve us but as products of a history that is not ours and may not be accessible to us; and ultimately in relation to their source in God. In the context of this *askesis* of distancing, silencing the voice of primary attachment or investment, we may be said to clear the path for love – if by love we mean a deliberate and (to use the word again) sustained attention to a reality not at our disposal.

This perspective is echoed in a somewhat surprising context by Dietrich Bonhoeffer in his fragmentary *Ethics*, where he invokes the idea of *das Wirklichkeitsgemässe*[2] as the basis of ethical action for the believer – 'what is appropriate/adequate to reality'. Bonhoeffer is still regularly misread as kind of 'situationist' in his ethics, but he is in fact concerned above all to dissolve the fiction of an isolated ethical subject facing a morally unstructured or uninterpreted set of facts. The moral agent is always already 'representative' of the selves with which s/he is involved; this agent is an *historical* agent, being who they are as a result of their involvement with others, given identity by that involvement. Discerning and responding to *das Gebotenes*, the requirement of the situation, means both recognizing the reality of one's own multiple connections and investments as an agent acting with and for others, and recognizing the constraints of the specific situation – *including*, above all, the fact that the situation is grounded in the acceptance and transfiguration of all things by God through the Incarnation. 'The most fundamental

[2] For example, Bonhoeffer, *Ethics* (*Dietrich Bonhoeffer Works, vol. 6*) (Minneapolis, MN, Fortress Press 2005), pp. 221ff.

reality is the reality of the God who became human';[3] 'to act responsibly means to include in the formation of action human reality as it has been taken on by God in Christ'.[4] This in turn means relinquishing the craving to know that one's action is just according to some pre-ordained set of criteria; we have to accept '[u]ltimate ignorance of one's own goodness or evil',[5] and this is what sets Christian ethical action in the sharpest contrast to ideology, which will always promise to assure us of our goodness and justification. What we do as believers is to release into God's hand, so to speak, the action we have undertaken, confident not that *we* have done justice but that God will continue to act so as to do God's justice. Yet this does not mean that we are absolved from attention and discernment; quite the opposite.

In a later draft of this section of his argument, Bonhoeffer spells out what he now calls *Sachgemäßheit*, 'suitability' or 'adequacy to the facts',[6] insisting that this incorporates a recognition of 'law' as an element in the world we engage with (hence my phrase a moment ago about not confronting a morally unstructured set of facts). But law is an inescapably analogical notion, whose clarity is less and less obvious the closer we are to a specific human situation; in political ethics, there may be a tension between 'the explicit law of a state' and the deeper question of what conserves the 'necessities of human life'[7] – the fundamental structures of human solidarity that Bonhoeffer elsewhere discusses in terms of the 'mandates' that bind us in family connections, in working collaboration and in broader political affiliations. The law of a state that effectively dissolves these solidarities in the name of a single political/ideological loyalty has to be resisted. But discerning when this extremity has been reached is a highly complex question – and by definition it cannot be resolved by

[3] Ibid., p. 223.
[4] Ibid., p. 224.
[5] Ibid., p. 225.
[6] Ibid., pp. 270ff.
[7] Ibid., pp. 272–3.

appeal to an abstract ideological criterion. There is always a debatable element remaining in any decision to cleave to law or to resist it. Coming to a decision is not a matter of applying a universally valid principle that can be abstracted from attention to the particular situation; attention to every detail, every aspect of the historical 'embeddedness' that we inhabit, is ethically imperative. And, in contrast to the facile resolution of situationism, the agent is not seeking for a new principle that will provide individual absolution for an unconventional moral decision, but attempting to see clearly both their own involvement/investment in a situation, all that makes them more than a free-floating agent whose decisions affect themselves alone, and the nature of the situation itself in respect of its relation to the widest horizons of solidarity – discerning (or trying to discern) what kinds of human solidarity are honoured or imperilled by this or that decision, and then acting in the trust that God will still be free to act, not through the correctness or effectiveness of our action but because we have given place to God's mercy on the basis of his embrace in the Word Incarnate of both our finitude and our complicity.

Bonhoeffer's ethical reflection here is shaped by his personal anguish over the decision to take part in active resistance to the government of the Third Reich; but it has a clear general import as well. His critique of an individualist ethic that seeks only to secure the innocence of an isolated agent connects – remotely but significantly – with the Evagrian critique of a perception dictated by the supposed needs of the ego for satisfaction and the Evagrian analysis of how passion distorts the possibilities of just and truthful knowledge. Bonhoeffer demands that we work on the givenness of our responsibilities and affiliations, in order to act 'representatively', taking responsibility for the well-being of all whose lives are linked with ours – a category that obviously widens constantly as we understand better our involvement in the actualities of history. And the related demand to scrutinize as patiently and carefully as possible the ways in which possible actions support or destabilize the fundamental forms of human solidarity is a way of articulating the older concern to see what is presented in its relation to God's purpose, that is, in the full range of its relatedness. What is distinctive in Bonhoeffer is the emphasis on the Word *Incarnate* as the context in which the world must be seen: the compromising interconnectedness of the world's history is already taken into the scope of divine action through the entry of God the Word into precisely those compromised connections. If the fullness of divine agency in the incarnate life is not diminished by this, then there are grounds for faith that our own ineradicable involvement with the tangles of history will not defeat the divine purpose and the divine mercy.

III

Contemplative practice for the tradition that Evagrios inherits and helps to mould is among other things a ceaseless vigilance in respect of the images we construct and entertain, images primarily of God, but also of ourselves and our unexamined desires. Putting together these unlikely partners, Evagrios and Bonhoeffer, what we find in common is an account of what discernment might mean in public as well as private contexts. Learning discernment is first learning how to identify and bring to stillness the urge to reduce the world to the terms of my desires; in other words, it is to do with learning to observe and question whatever forms of controlling power I possess. And second, it is learning how to read the various and complex situations of the historical world with an eye to how they serve or fail to serve fundamental human solidarities. From this perspective, a 'contemplative' political practice might be summed up as one that seeks to make room for the narrative of the other; one that does not begin by attempting to absorb this narrative into itself, and thus is willing to learn how it is itself seen and understood. Only a practice of this sort can ultimately ground a politics that works towards the difficult common ground on which majority and minority can negotiate together: the prevalent pathology of our political life seems to be the idea that majorities obliterate the interest of the minority and that political victory is – while it lasts – licence for a majority to enforce its agenda. And this in turn has a retroactive effect on political campaigning in that it encourages the idea that political disagreement is essentially and invariably a contest of absolute and incompatible loyalties, so that the opponent's victory is the worst outcome imaginable. In other words, the failure to factor in the critical space in which I am able to hear how I am heard and seen becomes a driver of the febrile absolutism of online polemics, and of the corruption of democratic politics into majoritarianism.

To say that we must learn to distance ourselves from our commitments in politics in order to arrive at both justice and love is at first sight a bizarre recommendation, suggesting a corrosive indifferentism. But the distance involved is not a refusal of commitment; it has rather to do with what it is that we are committed *to*. Bonhoeffer's commitment is manifestly a serious and ultimately costly affair, but it is a commitment neither to victory nor to innocence. It is a commitment to the *Wirklichkeit* he evokes – the reality both of a many-layered and historically complex acting self and to the precise demands of a particular context; as well as a commitment to a radical and all-powerful mercy beyond all planning and justification. Nor is this about a detachment from particular interests that allows an 'objectively' just outcome to prevail, as if justice were simply an abstract allocation of deserving. Justice as seeing, what is there and responding appropriately, in *Wirklichkeitgemässheit* or *Sachgemässheit*, is a task for imagination and intelligence directed towards the detail of a person, object or situation whose life is grasped as organized around a principle that may never be fully accessible but is certainly not one's own individual agenda. To relate it to our earlier discussion in this book, it is a form of proper rationality, a way of being *logikos* or indeed of living 'truthfully'.

Returning to the question with which we began this enquiry, 'sustainable' justice, a degree of social and legal stability that will guarantee that defence and redress do not depend on the contingent arrangements of power, requires something of the discernment we have here been sketching; which also means that it requires *communities* of discernment in which the habits of scrutiny described can be assimilated and transmitted. It is – to put it mildly – not wholly obvious that traditional communities of faith can be relied upon to provide such a setting; but this chapter has tried to suggest that at least those communities have resources capable of being put to work for this end. 'The more we attend to the world, the less we find ourselves wishing to control it', says Jan Zwicky in a recent and haunting essay on the role of spiritual practice in our thinking about politics and the global environmental crisis ('A Ship from Delos').[8] Attention, she suggests, takes us into mourning as well as wonder, the sense of dangerous loss and damage as well as the celebration of 'deep acknowledgement'; a contemplative politics will be one that is capable (as seems so unthinkable in public life at the moment) of recognizing and naming our own failure, the hurt done as well as received, and the perpetual slippage towards violence (once again, Bonhoeffer has much to say on this). And if this is truly the fruit of the sort of distance we have been thinking about, we can perhaps begin to understand why Evagrios can say that *apatheia*, our liberation from defensive and aggressive instinct, is the gateway to love – as well as to a justice that has some claim to be a little more transparent to the just vision that God has of the creation.

[8] Robert Bringhurst and Jan Zwicky, *Learning to Die: Wisdom in the Age of Climate Crisis* (Regina, University of Regina Press 2018), p. 65.

9

HOLY FOLLY AND THE PROBLEM OF
REPRESENTING HOLINESS

I

It will be clear by now – not least with Bonhoeffer's example in mind – that 'rational' action by Christians is not simply going to map on to the prevailing patterns of what is generally considered 'reasonable' – the patterns of behaviour, both self-defensive and ultimately self-destructive that are deployed to protect the illusory independent ego and its ambitions for security and control. On the face of things, it is ironic that a tradition for which *logos* is so significant a theme should also have generated a fascination with behaviours that display conspicuous, even theatrical, disregard for rational norms. Eastern, especially Russian, Christianity has long been interested in 'holy fools' – figures who defy convention so as to show something of the anarchic character of divine grace or the drastic opposition between divine and worldly power.[1] Throughout this book, we have been concentrating on how the theological discourse so decisively shaped by Evagrios and his disciples offers resources for rethinking and rebuilding our

---

[1] It is not an exclusively Eastern phenomenon, in that there are Western saints who exhibit some of the traits identified as holy folly in the East; and the idea of sanctity, especially monastic sanctity, as being a form of foolishness, inviting mockery, can be traced in figures like St Bernard and St Teresa of Avila. See the wide-ranging study by John Saward, *Perfect Fools: Folly for Christ's Sake in Catholic and Orthodox Spirituality* (Oxford, Oxford University Press 1980), and Rowan Williams, 'Teresa and the Scriptures' in *Holy Living: The Christian Tradition for Today* (London, Bloomsbury 2017), pp. 131–49.

understanding of rationality to bring in those elements of bodily 'embeddedness' and relational mutuality that are systematically sidelined by so many of the norms of Western modernity. But in thinking about the range of lives and behaviours made possible by all this, it is impossible to ignore the most dramatic examples of resistance to prudence and convention that have nonetheless been recognized as holy. Martyrdom itself is, from certain points of view, a spectacularly non-rational outcome for a human life; yet those who risk it do so in the confidence that they are being 'true' to a reality with imperative claims – and thus are being supremely *logikos*. Yet – as has often been recognized – there are forms of voluntary self-humbling well short of actual martyrdom, but reflecting the same subversive obedience to *logos*. In this chapter we shall be looking at how the category of 'holy folly' has been understood by a Church naturally preoccupied with canonical regularity and good order, but also by various imaginative writers in the Russian tradition for whom the image of the holy fool provides a starting point for some teasing reflections on the difficulty of speaking about and truthfully representing holiness.

But how are we to define 'holy folly'? As soon as we start looking at the various contexts in which reference is made to the figure of the holy fool – in hagiography as much as in literary studies – it is evident that the term is used in a wide variety of ways. Sergey Ivanov's rather idiosyncratic monograph on the subject[2] gives some indication of the range of uses acquired by words like the Greek *salos* – more or less the canonical term in the earliest literature, and borrowed in other languages – and the distinctive Russian *iurodivyi*. But he also makes it clear that the earliest

---

[2] Sergey A. Ivanov, *Holy Fools in Byzantium and Beyond*, tr. Simon Franklin (Oxford, Oxford University Press 2006). Rather like Ewa M. Thompson, *Understanding Russia: The Holy Fool in Russian Culture* (Lanham, MD, University Press of America 1987), this book tends to see the tradition of holy folly as an innately amoral and non-Christian phenomenon that can be seen as partly responsible for various troubling aspects of Russian culture overall. Ivanov, however, shows more interest in the 'interiority' of the experience of the *iurodivyi* and interprets it as protest against anthropocentric moral judgement (pp. 413–14).

texts to present the figure of the *salos* offer something of a focal cluster of characteristics. 'Folly for Christ's sake', *salotes*, insane behaviour *dia theon* or *dia Christon*, is the conscious adoption of shocking and unconventional styles of action calculated to provoke public disgust or mockery – ragged clothes, partial or complete nakedness, mixing with disreputable people, wild and uncontrolled behaviour in public, apparent irreverence towards holy persons and places. It is undertaken in order to conceal an inner spiritual purity or maturity – to *deflect* a reverence or admiration that would be spiritually dangerous to the person involved. As Ivanov argues, the logic of this is partly shaped by anecdotes familiar in the stories of the Desert Fathers and other early monastic literature, which describe 'secret servants' of God – people living apparently ordinary or even apparently compromised and disedifying lives, whose inner state is equal to or higher than that of ascetics in the desert.[3] There is something inherently paradoxical about holiness itself, it seems: once it has become the subject of publicly recognizable criteria, once there is a kind of 'science' of the holy life, it is rendered at best dangerously vulnerable and at worst false. In the 'secret servant' tradition, the point of the anecdote is regularly to remind the self-conscious and anxious ascetic that their highly public struggle for sanctity is shadowed by the corrupting effect of the *image* of holiness that is being pursued.

Holiness is, we might say, an essentially ironic idea in this connection: once brought into language, self-perception, culture, it is emptied of its radicality and integrity. The *salos* may not be able to resolve the dilemma entirely but sets out to limit the damage that might be done by the routinizing or commodifying of holiness; he or she will deliberately transgress the norms of conventional holiness and invite not reverence but contempt. It is true, as Ivanov notes,[4] that such a person will be acting out of a consciousness of their own advanced spiritual state; at the

---

[3] Op. cit., pp. 34–48.
[4] Op. cit., p. 48.

same time, that awareness breeds an awareness of intensified spiritual risk, the temptation to maintain a persona of holy and authoritative stability. The adoption of the role of a *salos* is itself an ascetical action, a detachment from the hunger for praise and status.

But it can also be connected with the need both to test and to display one's detachment: the *salos* who lingers in the taverns or is seen in the company of prostitutes is someone confident of their passionlessness, someone who trusts that their instincts will not be stirred by the proximity of temptation. Thus, from very early on, the exercise of holy folly can be *both* a kind of protest against pride in ascetic achievement and an extreme demonstration of it. As Ivanov says, whatever the historical recollections underlying the early lives of holy fools, the figure of the *salos* is a literary construct rather than a psychological portrait; if we treat these lives as portraits, we encounter just the tensions and contradictions we have noticed between the deliberate concealment of holiness and the conspicuous display of it. When we read the various official cautions and prohibitions directed against *salotes* by bishops and synods, we can see how readily the Church's authorities recognized these tensions: conspicuous deliberate eccentricity is identified as a form of individualism and ostentation; paradoxically but inevitably, holy folly had become a recognized style of asceticism and as such had become as ambivalent as any other style, as vulnerable to the corruptions of self-consciousness.[5] The hagiographical text is thus not to be read as recommending holy folly without reservation but as reminding the pious of the underlying point about the mysterious and often counter-intuitive character of holiness. And it is intriguing to see how the literature of holy folly picks up a specific strand of Middle Eastern and Indo-European folklore to spell out the nature of holy folly in a manner that directs us away from *salotes* or *iurodstvo* as an adopted lifestyle and towards the basic insight

[5] Ibid., ch. 8.

about discernment of the subversive and contradictory nature of the truth as seen by God. This folkloric strand appears in Talmudic literature, in the Qur'an, in medieval Western romance (first in the *Merlin* of Robert de Boron) and Russian secular narratives of the same period, and survives in fairy tales from the Caucasus to the Celtic world (it appears in variants of the 'fairy bride' story such as the Welsh 'Lady of Llyn y Fan'). In essence, it is about the capacity of a supernatural being to perceive what others fail to see, a capacity that is shown in incomprehensible and initially offensive behaviour, inappropriate tears or (more often) laughter. In a similar way, some holy fools are described as throwing stones at churches or at the houses of the devout, praying in taverns, laughing at funerals, weeping at weddings or baptisms and so on: the story of the angel who takes human shape and causes scandal by his incomprehensible activities is found in various forms from seventh-century Byzantium onwards, ultimately being recycled as a Russian folktale about an angel who takes service with a parish priest. But it is one form of a narrative featuring not an angel but some other sort of supernatural being: the Talmudic legend of Solomon's capture of the demon Asmodeus has the same features, and it is developed in medieval Russia as the tale of Solomon and 'Kitovras', the centaur.[6] Sura 18 of the Qur'an ('The Cave', *Al-Kahf*) has a similar story attached to the figure of Moses and an unidentified companion who must be a spirit or angel of some kind. Certainly by the sixteenth century in Russia, the standard narratives of holy folly routinely report stone-throwing at churches and houses as a feature of *iurodstvo*, and explain it as the result of the *iurodivyi* being able to see demons on the outside of these buildings, in a way that is clearly connected with the model of a supernatural visitant seeing what ordinary mortals cannot. This in turn connects with the increasing stress

---

[6] See, for example, Leo Wiener, *Anthology of Russian Literature from the Tenth Century to the Close of the Eighteenth Century* (New York and London, G. P. Putnam's Sons 1902), pp. 114–15. The story of Solomon and Asmodeus appears in the Talmudic Tractate *Gittin* 68, with varying detail in different manuscripts.

in the Russian material on the *iurodivyi*'s gift of clairvoyance concerning the future, not an aspect that is much to the fore in the Byzantine material.

Thus the figure of the holy fool develops, especially in Russia, as a complex mixture of the holy but unconventional ascetic, subverting popular veneration by pretending insanity, and the supernaturally endowed 'alien' who has the power of clairvoyance and spiritual discernment. As such, the Russian holy fool (more than the Byzantine prototype) is often shown as confronting royal authority and (usually) surviving; the aura of alienness and the expectation of clairvoyant insight confer a degree of immunity. And as the slightly unstable linguistic usage indicates, *iurodstvo* could sometimes describe the condition of the 'holy simpleton' as well as the holy fool – the genuinely challenged or disturbed person as well as the one who deliberately chooses the persona of holy folly; there is as a consequence a certain predisposition in Russia, particularly after the sixteenth century, to regard the 'simple' or even the manifestly insane as attended by an aura of sacred immunity, even to expect them to show signs of the folkloric gifts of discernment in some situations. The 'idiot' who appears briefly in Pushkin's drama, *Boris Godunov*, is, like some of the actual claimants to *iurodstvo* in the seventeenth century, almost certainly not someone deliberately adopting a style of behaviour for ascetic reasons but a genuinely simple or insane figure, although he is depicted with familiar signs of conscious *iurodstvo*: chains and a heavy iron cap. Seventeenth-century accounts of holy fools in Moscow, including those at the court of tsar or patriarch, suggest a real – if generally untroubled – popular uncertainty about where to locate particular figures in regard to real or assumed insanity. And the official enactments of the Church in this period struggle to discourage uncontrolled voluntary *iurodstvo* while recommending compassion and respect for the afflicted.[7] The situation was evidently complicated;

[7] Ivanov, ch. 11; cf. Thompson, op. cit., chs 2 and 3.

and the treatment of holy folly in later Russian writing will illustrate vividly some of the same problems in distinguishing between voluntary and involuntary folly. It could be said that this again shows how the convention of holy folly brings to light, deliberately or not, some basic paradoxes about holiness. The conscious refusal of conventional marks of holiness itself becomes a convention; transgressive inversions of piety acquire the same level of self-conscious or even self-serving ambiguity that attends the ordinary norms. Yet the phenomenon – even as a literary affair – of holy folly acts as a prompt to look for insight, spiritual discernment, in unlikely places, and to suspend judgement on apparently eccentric behaviour. Hence the Russian tolerance, up to the Revolution and beyond, for public displays of 'folly'. *Iurodstvo* cannot be a programme for holy behaviour – or if it becomes so, it is another form of spiritually dangerous self-advertisement; but it is still taken for granted that there is some underlying fact, some basic oddity about the nature of sanctity, that only such narratives and figures can capture.

II

Dostoevsky's fiction is often appealed to for examples of holy folly.[8] Sonya in *Crime and Punishment* could be seen as an extreme version of the tradition of mixing with and identifying with public and notorious sinners, as she turns to prostitution in order to save her family. Myshkin in *The Idiot* is sometimes cited as a *iuorodivyi*, and the figures of Semyon Yakovlevich and Bishop Tikhon in *Devils* and Father Ferapont in *The Brothers Karamazov* are gathered into the same discussion. Makar

---

[8] A good overview in Harriet Murav, *Holy Foolishness: Dostoevsky's Novels and the Poetics of Cultural Critique* (Stanford, CA, Stanford University Press 1992); also the recent and very comprehensive Nottingham PhD thesis by Philip Gorski, *Kissed by God: Holy Foolishness, Russian Literature and Christianity*. I am indebted to Dr Gorski's work for many insights, even though I have questions for some of his conclusions. Some portions of his thesis are included in his valuable collection, *Godseekers: Essays on Literature and Spirituality, East and West* (Nottingham, Alpha and Omega Press 2019).

Ivanovich in *The Adolescent*, Alyosha's mother in *Karamazov*, possibly Sofya Matveevna the wandering Bible seller in *Devils*, and even the murdered Lizaveta in *Crime and Punishment*, have been discussed in the light of the *iurodstvo* tradition; and, as we shall see, some of the actions of Father Zosima in *Karamazov* reflect aspects of the conventional narrative. But there is need for care here in distinguishing some significantly diverse themes. Thus Sonya's life as a prostitute is as much to do with nineteenth-century fictional conventions of the tragedy of virtuous girls reduced to disgrace as with a more ecclesiastical tradition – although her interaction with Raskolnikov has some faint traces of a *iurodstvo*-style reverence for the sinner. Myshkin is not helpfully understood in the framework of holy folly, even though his unselfconscious homage to the courtesan Nastasya has echoes of some of the classical stories.[9] He is more properly regarded as a holy simpleton, whose eccentric behaviour is not a deliberate choice; he does not set out either to shock or to instruct. And as has frequently been observed, his actions (and his failures to act) bring not only confusion but suffering and unredeemed disaster. Makar Ivanovich – who himself refers in passing to *iurodstvo*, though in a very loose sense[10] – is a figure of simple gentleness such as Dostoevsky depicts from time to time as a model of traditional Russian piety, a man who instinctively sees what is lovable around him and has behaved with reckless generosity and forgiveness in his personal life; but he is not someone who has deliberately adopted eccentricity as an ascetical strategy. When he says of a private tutor in a provincial town that he lived 'like a *iurodivyi*', what he seems to mean is that this figure, reduced to destitution by drink, has settled into a life of beggary and poverty that is at odds with his social status and education; once again, not exactly

---

[9] Thompson, op. cit., pp. 146–7, takes Myshkin to be a fairly straightforward example of *iurodstvo*, as does Murav, pp. 88–97. Both underrate Dostoevsky's complex ironizing of Myshkin's supposed sanctity.

[10] *The Adolescent*, in the translation by Richard Pevear and Larissa Volokhonsky (New York, Vintage Classics 2003), p. 392.

a case of voluntary asceticism, but a turn of phrase that gives us some insight into what Dostoevsky's readership would have associated with the term – dissonance around status, conscious if not quite voluntary eccentricity. Alyosha's mother belongs to a well-documented category of women who habitually screamed hysterically in public (including during church services); she is in some respects a holy simpleton, but not an example of *iurodstvo*; and the same holds for her quieter namesake in the Lizaveta of *Crime and Punishment*. Sofya Matveevna is a character like Makar Ivanovich, a gentle and compassionate pilgrim but not a holy fool.

The case of Semyon Yakovlevich in *Devils* is an interesting one. Semyon (who shares a patronymic with a quite celebrated and controversial historical *iurodivyi* of the mid-nineteenth century)[11] is identified explicitly in terms of *iurodstvo*, and the author calls him, with obvious irony, 'our saint and prophet';[12] our attention is drawn to the comfort in which he lives, to the credulity with which his most eccentric utterances are received both by the devotees who flock to him and by the monks who give him a home, and to his explosive oddity and even obscenity. What is left unclear is whether Semyon is a 'proper' voluntary *iurodivyi* or a mentally ill person encouraged to live up to the expectation of a holy fool of the standard kind – or something of both, which is probably the likeliest reading. The episode featuring him is embedded in a section of the novel in which the symbolism and the narrative signals are all to do with vacuity, the deceitfulness and fragility of false appearances and the absence of true (genuinely 'iconic') images of the good or the holy. We can take it that Semyon's violent eccentricity is part of this tragically vacant spiritual space at the heart of the book: instead of being a figure who prompts spiritual discernment or challenges prevailing accounts of spiritual integrity, he is part of a dramatically distorted and

---

[11] Ivan Yakovlevich Koreisha: see Ivanov, op. cit., p. 352, Thompson, op. cit., pp. 36 40.

[12] *Devils*, in the translation by Michael R. Katz (Oxford, Oxford University Press 1992), p. 344.

blinded culture, an ersatz version of the radicality of the genuine holy fool.

In fact, there are two characters in the novel who do prompt the unsettling questions associated with authentic 'folly'. Marya Timofeevena, wife of the dark and enigmatic Stavrogin, is again described explicitly in terms of *iurodtsvo*,[13] though it is very clear that she is more accurately identified as a holy simpleton; she ignores social convention and restraint, responds unselfconsciously to anyone and everyone, and reveals insight into the true nature of those she encounters. She is closely related to Myshkin, yet without Myshkin's damaging effect on those around him: where the Prince seems to be terminally irresolute as to whether or not he can occupy a place within the web of human social and sexual relations, and where this irresolution creates lethal confusions, Marya is both established in such a web and entirely detached from it. Poignantly vulnerable, she is also a figure of remarkable strength and consistency as portrayed in the novel. And in this blend of weakness and strength, she foreshadows the briefly glimpsed but crucially important figure of Bishop Tikhon, who, in the unexpurgated text of the novel, hears Stavrogin's account of the appalling evil he has been party to and (unsuccessfully) offers him a way out of his obsessive guilt and self-protection. He is carefully introduced as a man about whom confusing reports circulate: he is suspected (wrongly) of alcoholism, his neurotic sensibility has made him unfit to hold pastoral authority, he provokes contempt from more conventional ecclesiastics, and even his admirers speak cautiously about him, 'as if they wanted to conceal something about him ... perhaps that he was a holy fool'.[14] Presumably this means that his supporters want to conceal or divert attention from the fact that he is deliberately inviting hostility and contempt, in the manner of a traditional *iurodivyi*. Dostoevsky is in effect sketching a redefinition of what *iurodstvo* might mean in a context where it

[13] Ibid., p. 176.
[14] Ibid., p. 451.

has become another conventional style: Tikhon is a thoroughly indeterminate figure as far as those around him are concerned – neither a 'classical' holy fool, nor a conventional saint, but a man whose reputation is mixed and unclear. His status in the novel as the one figure who speaks something like the truth to Stavrogin gives him the position of the traditional *iurodivyi* as the speaker of unwelcome insight to those who are not otherwise challenged. But this position cannot be formalized, enforced or justified; Tikhon remains, in his context, an ambiguous character.

As such, he is clearly in some respects an earlier version of Zosima in *Karamazov*. The same slightly ambiguous reputation, the initially unimpressive appearance (*Karamazov* I.ii.2), the gossip about comfortable intimacies with wealthy ladies and luxurious gifts to ease the monastic routine (I.i.5), the apparent lack of interest in living a life of maximal ascetical self-denial, combined, in Zosima's case, with an alleged fondness for the company of sinners – these are the sort of thing that give Tikhon and Zosima something of the aura of holy disreputability if not exactly holy folly. And Zosima's act in bowing to the ground before Dimitri Karamazov in recognition of the great suffering and purgation that lie ahead for him is a gesture quite congruent with the behaviour of a *iurodivyi* – both unconventional and clairvoyant. The cynical seminarian Rakitin speaks mockingly to Alyosha after the encounter, imagining how, when disaster overtakes the Karamazov family, people will say that Zosima foretold it; and he directly compares Zosima's reverential bow to Dimitri (whom Rakitin identifies as a potential criminal) with the behaviour of the *iurodivye* of folk tradition: 'They cross themselves at the sight of a pub and throw stones at a church' (I.11.7). And just as Tikhon is implicitly contrasted with a conventional but ineffectual holy fool, so Zosima is contrasted with not one but two 'flanking' figures. One is the magnificently characterized Father Ferapont (II.iv.1), who, like Semyon in *Devils*, seems to be both a practitioner of voluntary asceticism (allegedly wearing heavy iron chains as many Russian *iurodivye* of an earlier age had done) and an intermittently disturbed and delusional personality. He behaves 'like a *iurodivyi*'; and the rather dim-witted 'little monk' from Obdorsk who tries to make sense of Ferapont's conversation has to remind himself of the fact that the words and acts of all fools for Christ's sake have been 'ridiculous' (*nelepye*) at times. Ferapont's profound jealousy of Zosima comes out later, when he interrupts the prayers over the elder's body and is implicitly reproached by Father Paissy for assuming that his extravagant behaviour is a guarantee of sanctity (III.vii.1). But the other figure with whom Zosima is contrasted is Fyodor Karamazov himself. It is a commonplace that Zosima is the positive father figure in the novel over against the destructive Fyodor; but the parallel and contrast is subtly deepened when we note that Fyodor in his first meeting with the elder (I.ii.2) fleetingly compares his clowning (*shutovstvo*) with *iurodstvo*: he clowns compulsively, he says, exactly like a *iurodivyi* (*vse ravno ... chto iurodivyi*) in order to make people like him – or, as he goes on to say, out of an inner 'shame' and the conviction that he will automatically be despised. Zosima responds by telling him that what he is actually doing is turning his own lack of self-love or self-respect into a cause of resentment against others; and Fyodor claims to recognize that the elder is speaking the truth.

The point of this second *iurodstvo*-related comparison in the novel seems to be that Dostoevsky acknowledges the way in which transgressive behaviour can be a tool of triumphant pre-emptive aggression; it successfully defies criticism and the ordinary disciplines of social exchange. Zosima sees it precisely as a weapon projecting self-hatred on to the other, and striking back at it *in* the other (a familiar Dostoevskian theme, classically laid out in *Notes from Underground*), it becomes the opposite of the original goal of 'holy folly' – which was designed to dissolve anxiety about the judgement of others, or at least to discipline oneself not to attend to it. The awkwardness, the faintly embarrassing characters, of Tikhon and Zosima with their uncertain reputations are, for Dostoevsky, a way of restoring something of the original constructive oddity of the *iurodivyi*; the nineteenth-century equivalent of the transgressive behaviour of Simeon of Emesa or Vasilii the Blessed is the willingness of figures like Tikhon and Zosima to live with the knowledge of their own compromised reputations and to risk, as Zosima does, a muted version of the eccentricities of an earlier age of *iurodstvo* – as Rakitin correctly reads his behaviour. But it is perhaps equally important for Dostoevsky that the tradition of respect towards the mentally ill or 'simple' allows the reader to look to certain characters identified in this way as possible sources of illumination: they are not compromised by self-consciousness and so their 'folly' is not caught in the games of aggression and self-modelling that Zosima identifies, and that are, as we have seen, a problematic element in the tradition as it evolves. In other words, Dostoevsky recognizes what we earlier called the basic oddity about holiness: if someone attempts to conceal a rigorous inner discipline by external eccentricity or laxity, or to divert reverent attention by inviting mockery and contempt, that will 'work' only so long as it has not become a recognizable convention. When it does become such a convention, it becomes an essentially literary matter: the narrative of the holy fool acts to remind us that self-conscious holiness can't be holiness. But how might one depict this in the context of an acutely self-conscious literary idiom like the nineteenth-century novel? Dostoevsky's twofold strategy is to refocus our attention on the holy simpleton, on the one hand, and to rework the idea of the compromised public reputation of the saint on the other, in a typically nineteenth-century manner in which gossip and rumour play a large part, and the holy person's eccentricities are a blend of social embarrassments and miscommunications. One way of summarizing it would be to say that Dostoevsky takes completely seriously the idea that *iurodstvo* must now be something constructed in writing or rather *reporting*. The holy fools of his novels endure the saving humiliation of being talked about, being the subject of narration, being characters in another's story; and this is the way in which Dostoevsky brings up to date the primitive model of the *salos* as someone who relinquishes possession of his own hagiographical and reverential representation, and hands over his 'performance' of Christian life to the perception of others in the most drastic way.

III

Holy folly features in a number of nineteenth- and twentieth-century works of Russian fiction; and it is significant that it not only continued as a visible presence in the Russian social scene up to and beyond the Revolution but even appeared in rather untraditional forms, as (most notably) in the group of female holy fools associated with the famous convent of Diveevo (founded by St Serafim of Sarov, himself a saint with elements of *iurodtsvo* in his story) in the second half of the nineteenth century. A good deal has been written about how the tradition enabled Grigorii Rasputin to gain access to the highest political circles – and also enabled his supporters to justify his extreme behaviour with reference to the hagiographical conventions.[15] Dostoevsky would certainly have had the imaginative equipment to analyse this novelistically. But one of the most interesting echoes of the tradition can be found in that greatest of post-revolutionary works (that greatest of twentieth-century novels, so it could be argued), Mikhail Bulgakov's *The Master and Margarita*. The overall framework of the novel, the activity of supernatural visitants in Stalin's Moscow and the carnivalesque bedlam they create, reflects something of the unsettling folkloric representation of *iurodstvo*: the diabolical visitors utter ironic and incomprehensible predictions about (and to) the humans they meet, and create profound confusion about where order, reason and authority lie. But the 'embedded' story of Christ and Pilate likewise draws on aspects of the tradition.[16] Yeshua, at his trial before Pilate, exhibits the traits of a holy simpleton: he addresses

---

[15] This is intelligently handled by Douglas Smith in his recent biography, *Rasputin: Faith, Power and the Twilight of the Romanovs* (New York, Farrar, Straus and Giroux 2016).
[16] Gorski's thesis (above, n. 7) argues plausibly that the character of Ivan Bezdomnyi in the novel is also meant to exhibit aspects of *iurodstvo*.

Pilate as 'good man', just as a Russian *iurodivyi* might call the tsar by a familiar name or diminutive, and describes his brutal Roman guard likewise as a 'good man'; he is also bewildered by the charges against him, and manifestly confused and at a loss. At the same time, he instantly and intuitively grasps Pilate's state of mind, to the extent that Pilate is left – in the mythical world of the novel – suspended in time, waiting for the conversation with Yeshua to begin again, as it was the only moment when he has been recognized as he is.

In a brilliant piece of subversive rewriting, Bulgakov has Yeshua answering Pilate's question 'What is truth?' with the banal but entirely accurate statement, 'The truth is that you have a headache and you miss your dog' – the verbal equivalent of a *iurodstvo*-style deflation of religious propriety.[17] Yeshua is not simply a holy fool or simpleton, and by the end of the book he has mysteriously become the disposer of human destiny; but this is a figure that would have been hard to imagine without the *iurodstvo* tradition. And in connection with our discussion of Dostoevsky's handling of holy folly, it is significant that Yeshua is a character in the 'secondary' text of *The Master and Margarita* – that is, he is a 'fictional' figure, a figure whose identity is the identity of a *written* character in someone else's story (in fact, as the novel advances, a character in several different people's narratives or dreams). His anxious bewilderment in the face of Pilate's questioning is itself the response of a person caught up in a drama written by another, never having seen the script. Yet the ironic distance this gives is the vehicle of a truth that could not otherwise break in to a controlled, overdetermined script; hence the convergence of the Pilate-Yeshua passages of the novel with the main story of the disruption of the controlling fantasies of Stalinist Moscow. Yeshua is endowed with both powerlessness and clarity, the one being a precondition for the other: where there is no power to defend, there is no impulse

---

[17] 'The truth is, first of all, that your head aches ... You can't even think about anything and only dream that your dog should come', in the translation by Richard Pevear and Larissa Volokhonsky, revised edition (New York, Penguin Books 2016), pp. 20–1.

for concealment. But this powerlessness can best be shown, in Bulgakov's world, by presenting the ultimately disruptive truth in the medium of an unfinished and unfinishable fiction-within-a-fiction, and showing the judgement of Pilate's/Stalin's power through a figure who is, as a fictional character, at the mercy of the writer, and yet – as a fictional character in several quite different people's minds, at the same time a figure who cannot be written off as invented. It is a very sophisticated reworking of the theme we have been reflecting on, the challenge of how the unsettling truth of holiness can be represented in a literary and imaginative world of enormous self-consciousness.

But a much more recent work of Russian fiction takes a different approach again. Eugene Vodolazkin's novel of 2012, *Laurus* (*Lavr*)[18] has been greeted as a new exploration of *iurodstvo*, and indeed a whole section of it ('The Book of Renunciation') includes two *iurodivye* and a certain amount of discussion around the theme of holy folly; there is also an early allusion in the novel (pp. 18–19) to the Solomon and Kitavras story – the centaur who weeps at a wedding and laughs at a man's unawareness of approaching death – as if to signal that the novel will be addressing the questions posed in this literary and folkloric tradition. The central figure, originally called Arseny, is a peasant healer, an innocent like Makar Ivanovich rather than either a holy simpleton or a *iurodivyi* in the strict sense. His anxiety and incompetence causes the death of his lover, Ustina, in childbirth, along with their baby, and Arseny embarks on a life of wandering and poverty, in the hope of somehow living Ustina's unfinished life for her and offering his sufferings for the sake of their dead child. The novel brilliantly mixes voices and registers, moving from more or less realistic historical narrative to subversive postmodern moments, from the archaic register of Church Slavonic to modern colloquialisms; it depicts without irony several miraculous or preternatural events: there are healings performed by Arseny that

[18] Eugene Vodolazkin, *Laurus*, ET by Lisa C. Hayden (London, Oneworld 2015).

are inexplicable on natural grounds, episodes of clairvoyance and visions of the future; and, in one finely understated passage, we see the two holy fools of Pskov, Foma and Karp, walking on the surface of the river that divides the town, watched with mild curiosity by the townspeople. Foma and Karp – and sometimes Arseny – do many of the things that classical *iurodtsvo* stories depict as typical of holy fools:[19] stripping or wearing rags in winter, throwing stones at churches, emptying drinks away in pubs, stealing bread from a baker and distributing it to beggars, sharing food with animals. In one episode,[20] Arseny warns a priest of his forthcoming murder by appearing to threaten him with a knife; the same threatening behaviour (though without the clairvoyant interpretation) is reported of the historical holy fool Prokopii of Viatka in the seventeenth century.[21] And Arseny's miraculous intervention to save a distant city from destruction by fire again echoes the sort of anecdote associated with some of the Russian holy fools.[22]

At one point,[23] Foma challenges the people of Pskov about their understanding of holy folly when Arseny has been beaten by an infuriated tradesman. 'Everyone in Rus' knows that you're not, like, allowed to beat holy fools', the townspeople say; but Foma replies that if holy fools are called on to suffer, there must be someone to beat them: 'he goes ahead and sins to supply him with that suffering. Somebody has to be the bad guy, right?' Russian people are 'senseless and merciless' as well as pious, so there will never be lacking those who will appropriately persecute the *iurodivyi*. But Foma implies that the ordinary people of Pskov – of Russia in general – cannot really tell the difference between the necessary guilt accepted by a man who beats the holy fool in order to give

[19] The walking on the water to engage in a territorial battle is originally a story about the fourteenth-century Novgorod holy fools Fyodor and Nikolai; see Thompson, op. cit., p. 85.

[20] Ibid., pp. 169–70.

[21] Ivanov, op. cit., p. 325.

[22] Ivanov, op. cit., pp. 279–80 on Prokopii of Ustyug.

[23] *Laurus*, p. 158.

him a chance of exercising holy patience and the one who beats out of senseless cruelty: in other words, both the holy fool's motivation and the violent man's motivation are equally obscure. It is a further twist to the recurring paradox we have noted in narratives of holy folly: if we cannot finally tell whether the person behaving oddly and transgressively is a genuine holy fool or not, if we cannot be sure that they are not either simply mad on the one hand or acting out of spiritual pride on the other, the same applies to the person who attacks or mocks the *iurodivyi*: perhaps he is acting out of piety. In such a confused world, holy folly will continue to be a teasing and paradoxical phenomenon, or so Foma seems to be arguing.

But in his earlier conversation with Arseny he has already in fact set out his basic definition of holy folly. He recognizes Arseny as a *iurodivyi* in some sense, when Arseny arrives, sick and disoriented, in the town: he is, as Foma says, already 'the realest of holy fools'. But his 'disowning' of his body is only part of the calling he must fulfil. He has already begun to call himself 'Ustin', as a sign of his commitment to living for the sake of his dead lover, but this, according to Foma, 'is only the half of it. "Do more", Foma whispered into Arseny's right ear. "Disown your identity."'[24] And this becomes the consistent motif of the story: Arseny lives under various names until he finally takes the monastic Great Habit with the name of Lavr or Laurus. The heart of his own particular *iurodstvo* is precisely this lifelong act of living the life of another; not simply an act of reparation or penitence for failure and sin, but also a positive transformation of his own life into a space for the lost other. Ultimately his holy folly is one way of disowning a secure identity, an identity that can be possessed and defended.

IV

This illuminates something about the entire complex tradition we have been looking at in hagiography and in fiction. In one

[24] Ibid., p. 146.

way or another, *iurodstvo* or *salotes* is from the beginning a way of stepping back from a clear public identity as a holy person; it is about the corrosion of the idea of holiness when it becomes a matter of public recognizability. At its simplest, it is about how a person guarantees that they will not be corrupted by public respect and religious celebrity. But, as we have repeatedly noted, the paradox is that once this has itself become a recognized strategy, the same problems arise. Hagiographical representations may continue as if this were not really a problem; for them the point is not to exhort others to a method of holy living, but simply to go on illustrating the simple message that God's ways are not ours, that holiness is not identical with rigorist ascetical devotion or conventional fervour, and that wisdom and insight may be gained from unlikely sources. But the more self-conscious register of fiction is bound to dig more deeply; hence Dostoevsky's exploration of the ambivalence of traditional *iurodstvo* and its possible re-emergence by way of the obscurely compromised or uncertain reputations of holy figures like Zosima or Tikhon. Bulgakov's carnivalesque Moscow and dreamlike Jerusalem exhibit ways in which the uncanny and uncontrolled, in the destructive shape of the diabolical visitors to Moscow or the compassionate helplessness of Yeshua before Pilate, may bring to light the spiritual wretchedness of a closed and pervasively dishonest society – as the *iurodstvo* of a sixteenth-century saint might have done in the Russia of Ivan the Terrible. He also shows how the absolutely and completely 'fictional' – that is, written or narrated – identity of Yeshua can become the moral lever of the whole book's denouement. This most dramatic form of powerlessness, being spoken of in the words of others, is revealed as a source of liberation: this figure has no ground to defend and so can be the agent of freedom for others locked in conflict and suffering. Vodolazkin's Arseny stays with this theme of displacement or dispossession – the disowning of identity as both an ascetical activity and an act of making space for the other whose life has been denied. This latter idea does not figure in the tradition, but Vodolazkin persuasively shifts his account of *iurodstvo* in the direction of such a creative reading of the conventions of holy folly.

The Russian literary treatment of *iurodtsvo* is thus, finally, not an antiquarian recreation of a set of ambivalent ascetical practices, nor an affirmation of the sanctity of postmodern transgressiveness. The texts examined here take seriously the spiritual difficulty of the traditional idea and use that difficulty to clarify and refine the notion of holiness itself. *Iurodstvo* begins in an acknowledgement that holiness is at once visible and invisible; it is a specific pattern of human life, yet as soon as it is recognized and characterized as such it becomes problematic. Because it entails a profound loss of self-regard, the dismissal of any idolized self-image, it will resist being made the object of analysis or regulation. The deliberate refusal of behaviour that might encourage reverence or admiration is a simple strategy for avoiding these spiritual traps, but brings its own difficulties. So holy folly is reimagined in the world of Russian fiction in a variety of ways – not least in terms of the acceptance of an identity that is spoken about, written about, gossiped about; the person who exhibits holy folly is the one who embraces or at least endures in spiritual freedom the identities that others create for them. And in refusing to join in the contest over who will most successfully create and maintain their own identity in the violent world we inhabit, the holy fool in these fictions not only shows others what is true about them in ways that no one else can (Bishop Tikhon and Father Zosima), but also helps to spring them from the traps in which they struggle and suffer (Yeshua, Arseny). And as Bulgakov's haunting narrative suggests, this constantly brings the theologically minded reader back to the central challenges of Christology – to the tension between failure and triumph in the life and death of Jesus, to the theological affirmation that in the 'hiddenness' of divine majesty on the cross, the divine glory is most fully revealed, to the figure of a saviour who renounces divine identity in the name of human solidarity – even to the irony that the living divine Word by whom all things were made (John 1.2), and on whom all act and speech is dependent, is regularly mediated in the Church's life by the written human word and the spoken human voice pronouncing sacramental formulae. Whatever else is involved in the literary and hagiographical tradition of holy folly, it functions at least to bring into sharper focus some of these issues and to remind any reader tempted to blandness or complacency in their faith and theology that the difficulty of recognizing and speaking effectively about holiness is embedded in the basic story of a divine action brought about through human passivity and even absurdity – precisely the insight that St Paul enunciates in those words in 1 Corinthians about the folly of God that have provided the vocabulary for talking about *iurodtsvo* through the centuries.

10

THE BODY OF CHRIST AND THE MINISTRY OF MARY

If there is one twentieth-century Orthodox saint who exemplifies both the 'canonical' holy folly of martyrdom and the more ambiguous side of *iurodstvo* that has to do with compromised behaviour and scandal to the conventional faithful, it has to be Mother Maria Skobtsova (Elizaveta Iurievna Pilenko, 1891–1945 – Kuz'mina-Karavaeva by her first marriage, Skobtsova by her second). She has already been mentioned more than once in this book. A pioneer in Orthodox social activism in her work with refugees and destitutes in France in the 1930s, and a recklessly courageous defender of French Jews during the German occupation of Paris, her stature in this respect has long been recognized; her execution in the concentration camp at Ravensbruck – allegedly as a result of voluntarily taking the place of another woman threatened with death – is widely acknowledged as a martyrdom, and she was canonized by the Ecumenical Patriarchate in 2004. However, it is only recently that attention has been paid to her own theological reflection on her vocation and witness. Natalia Ermolaev, in her very significant doctoral thesis at Columbia in 2010, opened up some of this theological territory and included in the dissertation a translation of material from Mother Maria's notebooks; more recently Katerina Bauerova has published an essay on Mother Maria and

216

the feminist theorist, Hélène Cixous.[1] As the complete Russian edition of Mother Maria's writings advances, there will be more material to fill out our understanding of her theology; for now, it may be worth offering an interim report on some of her more original insights.

I THE IMITATION OF CHRIST AND THE MATERNAL BODY OF CHRIST

The most fully developed theological reflection can be found in the texts translated by Richard Pevear and Larissa Volokhonsky in the 2003 anthology of St Maria's writings, especially the 1939 essays on 'The Second Gospel Commandment', and 'On the Imitation of the Mother of God'.[2] Two themes that immediately emerge as shaping theological priorities in these pieces are the inadequacies of a 'Protestant' analysis of the commandment to love the neighbour – an understanding of the commandment as addressed to an individual summoned to do her duty to God – and a recognition of what Mother Maria calls the 'terrible' aspect of this commandment. In exploring both these orientations, she produces a notably original theology both of the Body of Christ and of the Marian aspect of Christian love. The one thing we must

[1] Ermolaev's thesis is entitled 'Modernism, Motherhood and Mariology: The Poetry and Theology of Elizaveta Skobtsova (Mother Maria)'; see also her article, 'The Marian Dimension of Mother Maria's Orthodox Social Christianity', *Philanthropy and Social Compassion in Eastern Orthodox Tradition: Papers of the Sophia Institute Academic Conference, New York, Dec. 2009*, ed. M. J. Pereira (New York, Theotokos Press 2019), pp. 182–99. Bauerova's paper is 'Motherhood as a Space for the Other: A Dialogue between Mother Maria Skobtsova and Hélène Cixous', in *Feminist Theology*, January 2018, pp. 133–46. There are also brief but useful discussions touching on her theological ideas by Grigori Benevich in his 'Mother Maria (Skobotskaya): A Model of Lay Service', in *Religion, State and Society* 27.1, March 1999, pp. 101–08; also, Michael Plekon, *Living Icons: Persons of Faith in the Eastern Church* (Notre Dame, IN, University of Notre Dame Press 2002), pp. 59–80; and Paul Ladouceur, 'The Social and Political Theology of Love of Saint Maria of Paris', in *Sobornost* 40.1, 2018, pp. 60–74.
[2] *Mother Maria Skobtsova: Essential Writings* (Maryknoll, NY, Orbis Books 2003), pp. 45–60, 61–74.

move decisively beyond, in Mother Maria's understanding of the commandment to love the neighbour, is the reduction of this love to the individual's assumption of the (individual) selflessness of Christ, a taking of the cross by the individual disciple. In her discussion of the 'Imitation of the Mother of God', she sets out a sympathetic, intense and moving account of this spirituality: Christ calls us to absolute renunciation, the renunciation he himself undertakes, and all Christian morality is developed as an embedment of this basic imperative. 'In all these various paths Christ himself made legitimate this solitary standing of the human soul before God, this rejection of all the rest – that is, of the whole world.'³ The self moves forward in nakedness to Gethsemane, Calvary and final resurrection. In one sense, the cross, the anguish of solitude and death, is simply the fate of all human beings; but our embrace of this is what is distinctive for us as believers: 'To accept the endeavour and the responsibility voluntarily, to freely crucify your sins – that is the meaning of the cross, when we speak of bearing it upon our human paths.'⁴ This moment of self-renunciation is the decisive breach with the order of 'nature', the manifestation of true freedom; our imitation of Christ in accepting the cross thus becomes the supreme mark of our inheritance of the status of children of God.

Mother Maria does not simply reject this perspective, but she insists on its radical and even damaging incompleteness, on the fundamental ground that it leaves untouched and untransformed the fact that all this is cast in terms of my suffering, my choice, my cross: the theological rhetoric of freedom here obscures something else that is more primordial in the love of neighbour, something that has about it the flavour not of freedom but of 'necessity', the necessity of what is natural within the life of Christ's Body. If the basic reality is the individual's embrace of the cross, the moral action of the Christian is 'a sort of humanistic afterthought, a sort of adjusting of these basic Christian principles to those areas of life that

---

³ *Essential Writings* (henceforth EW), p. 63.
⁴ Ibid., p. 64.

lie outside them'.[5] And this, Mother Maria argues, is a dangerously rootless theology of compassionate action. In effect, what she goes on to outline, in some dense and quite speculative pages of the same essay, is an alternative model of understanding Christian love that does not pivot upon the individual act of embracing suffering but upon the already given solidarity in suffering that membership in the Body of Christ involves. She begins with a meditation on the similarity between sword and cross and the contrast between their significance. It is easy to think of the cross as the sign of passive suffering and the sword as the sign of active intervention; but this journalistic cliché is turned upside down by the gospel, in which the cross is voluntarily – actively – accepted and the sword is the infliction of what is not chosen. The Mother of God is seen as the paradigm victim of the sword (Luke 2.35); her suffering is unchosen in the sense that her solidarity with the agony of her son is bound up with her 'unavoidable' involvement as mother. From the beginning of her mothering at the Annunciation, she is exposed to the entirety of her son's fate; what he chooses or accepts, she is involved in, whether she chooses or not. And in this light we must also see her as involved in and with the suffering of the entire Body of Christ, the Church. Mother Maria does not fully articulate the argument, but it is clearly implied that this also means her involvement with human suffering in general, to the degree that all human beings, consciously or unconsciously, are somehow on the way to identification with the Body of Christ, perhaps in the sense that Christ's suffering is professedly an identification with human suffering as such.[6]

The implication drawn out is that the baptized member of the Body bears a double image, the likeness of the crucified Son and the likeness of the Mother of God,[7] and so is called both

---

[5] Ibid., p. 66.

[6] Ibid., pp. 68–9; for the sword and cross symbolism, cf. ibid., p. 58, from the essay on 'The Second Gospel Commandment'.

[7] Ermolaev, 'The Marian Dimension', p. 189, notes the dependence of some of her ideas in this area on the thought of her mentor, Sergii Bulgakov.

to accept the cross in freedom and to bear the consequences of human solidarity, beyond anything that could be chosen or understood, predicted or contained.[8] Love of neighbour, rather than being a chosen policy of personal behaviour, is grounded in the 'necessary' exposure of the baptized believer to human pain; we are unavoidably 'co-sufferers'. She had in fact sketched out something of this typology of voluntary and unavoidable suffering some years before this essay appeared, in a somewhat gnomic sequence of meditations and aphorisms published in 1927 under the title of 'The Holy Earth' (*Svyataya zemlya*),[9] where she speaks of the 'predetermined' nature of the suffering of the Mother of God (in contrast to the Son's embrace of Golgotha), and of the fact that the Son, in choosing the cross, is unable to spare his Mother the pain of the sword. 'The Sonship of Christ is simultaneously a sonship not only in regard to God but also in regard to the Mother of God';[10] and this profound solidarity with human flesh and materiality is inexorably the cause of unchosen suffering. The Son's suffering becomes the source of the transfiguring co-suffering endured by the mother, and this is what it means to think of the Mother of God as an image of the sanctified earth, the sanctified flesh, drawn into the free act of God on the cross.[11] It is because of this that the believer is committed to co-suffering, not simply suffering as a result of choice; our transfigured humanity is a transfigured earthliness and fleshliness, not simply a new kind of subjective liberty. The later essay drops the 'holy earth' language, but echoes closely this analysis of the transfiguring effect of a 'given' solidarity, conceived as maternal. As Mother Maria expresses it, this has to do with an ethic that is not about effort or even 'spiritual' attainment, not about duty or the willing assumption of some extra burden:

[8] Bauerova, 'Motherhood as a Space', p. 143, notes the echoes of Soloviev in her use of the androgyne image.
[9] *Put'* 6, 1927, pp. 95–101; reprinted in *E. Yu.Kuz'mina-Karavaeva:Izbrannoe* (Moscow, *Sov'etskaya Rossiya* 1991), pp. 245–57.
[10] Ibid., p. 252.
[11] Ibid., p. 253.

the Christian's response to the pain of another is as instinctive and non-negotiable as the mother's involvement in the child's suffering.[12] And in this light, sin becomes a refusal to be touched by the pain of others. This certainly makes sin omnipresent in the world of self-protection; if sin is the refusal of God, the refusal of the agony of humans made in God's image must be sinful, and as soon as it is defined in such terms we recognize sin's universality and power over us as never before and understand why love is 'holy folly'. The essay concludes with the acknowledgement that this is an alarming calling – but that at least in diagnosing sin in this way, we are less likely to rationalize it as natural, proportionate and justified behaviour, less likely to use the limits of our resources and powers as an excuse for turning away from any particular kind of pain.[13]

To summarize this aspect of Mother Maria's vision, we have to say that love of neighbour has both a Christocentric and a Marian dimension. We are called to take up the cross, certainly; but to take up the cross and follow Christ is, for the Christian, not a question of taking inspiration from a great teacher or exemplar but of sacramental identification with Christ. Christ's Body, into which we are baptized, is a body born of Mary, and as such it is itself, as a fleshly body, implicated in the interconnection of the material world, the 'holy earth', so that it is connected with all human suffering. Being in the Body entails exposure to all of this, not only a call from outside the ego to take up the cross as a spiritual enterprise, a *podvig*, in the traditional language of Russian spirituality (the word is used – critically – in this sense in the 1927 text). But there is more to say of the active effect of this 'maternal' love of neighbour as it is realized in the life of the Body. The recognition of our given solidarity brings with it the recognition of the image of Christ in all we encounter – 'the perceiving of God and Son in the other':[14] we see not only the image of God

[12] EW, p. 71.
[13] Ibid., pp. 72–4.
[14] Ibid., p. 70.

in the straightforward sense of what is given in creation, but also the 'filial' dimension of all human subjects, persons being brought to birth in their God-reflecting humanity. To live in the Body of Christ is to 'adopt' all others; each of us 'adopts the whole Body of Christ for itself'[15] and the calling of the believer is to bring Christ more fully to birth in every encounter or relationship. If we are unavoidably committed to sharing suffering because of our solidarity in the Body, we are equally committed to seeing in every other a potential child of God, and our solidarity can and will act so as to bring that filial reality to light. And in 'adopting' the other, we take on their pain and their sin, we make ourselves answerable for them, for their well-being and for their relation with God – not because our 'mothering' is a sign of our advanced spiritual standing but simply because we are all healed in and through this interpenetration of human suffering and need or failure. The solidarity re-created or newly intensified in the Body of Christ, the unsought and unplanned accompaniment in need, breaks open the isolation of both individual sin and individual pain and begins the work of transfiguration.

In the background is another piece of speculative theology, originally published in 1931, an essay on 'Birth and Creation'.[16] This essay is a riposte to Berdyaev's idealizing of the 'creative' as the supreme manifestation of human liberty. A creator, so Mother Maria argues, can make an 'essence' that is radically different from the creator, a reality that does not share the creator's natural and defining characteristics, but the act of creation does not as such constitute a 'hypostasis' different from the creator; birth, on the other hand, issues in a new hypostasis but not a new 'essence' or nature. Birth cannot help producing a new hypostasis; the mother cannot determine the personal uniqueness of the child, and so is always related to it as an other. Creation can manifest only its creator's hypostasis, and so is in fact unfree in one very

[15] Ibid., p. 71.
[16] *'Rozhdenie i tvorenie'* ('Birth and Creation'), *Put'* 30, 1931, pp. 35–47. See Bauerova, 'Motherhood as a Space', pp. 138–9, for a full discussion of this.

THE BODY OF CHRIST AND THE MINISTRY OF MARY

significant sense; it cannot reflect any personal will other than its maker's. But birth is the generation precisely of personal will and intentionality: it may not be a 'free' act in the sense of a sheer exercise of will, but what is mysterious and theologically significant about it is that it is a natural process that issues in liberty.[17] In this essay, St Maria is – very boldly – using the theologically familiar language of trinitarian and Christological definition (essence or *ousia* and *hypostasis*) to challenge, as she does in her Marian essay, an exaggerated stress on groundless choice and individual assertion, the kind of exaggeration deeply typical of Berdyaev – in fact, we might say, to challenge a strongly gendered understanding of freedom. The divine life knows nothing of creation in itself; the eternal Word is 'begotten not created', according to the Nicene Creed, and this implies, she argues, that the divine 'birthgiving' of the Word tells us something important about the role of the 'natural' in human life. As she is careful to say,[18] she is not identifying the non-freedom of divine birth (or human birth) with some sort of external constraint; it is not that birth is a mark of slavery, but that it is the unfolding of something that cannot be intelligibly cast in terms of slavery versus freedom. In earthly history as in the divine life, the paradox is that the repetition of sameness in essence produces difference in personal subsistence and thus a genuine relationality. If this argument is set alongside the Marian essay of 1939, we can see how the affirmation of unchosen (but not therefore simply 'unfree') solidarity is common to both: the event of birth issues in another exemplar of the same essence, humanity; yet it also issues in a radical otherness, 'hypostatic' otherness, which means that the mother and the child have a history of relation to fashion and negotiate. Humanity is 'repeated', but the human relation generated is unrepeatable, an image of the unrepeatable relation of filiation between the divine Father and the eternal Word. And so the 'adoption' of the human other, in all their terrifying and

[17] Ibid., pp. 39–41.
[18] Ibid., p. 41.

unfathomable difference, is the way in which a solidarity outside our control can be thought and enacted in the practice of concrete behaviours of compassion, service and shared risk.

II THE BODY OF THE WORLD AND THE SINS OF UNWORLDLINESS

The implication of Mother Maria's theological scheme is that our own 'mothering' of others into Christlike life by our adoption of their need and sin is in effect the generation of others capable of generating, mothering others into a 'mothering' discipleship. The continuity of human communities is the vehicle of transformation; and Mother Maria notes that this saving solidarity extends in time as well as space. The history of the First Covenant is in fact a story of the preparation, in this particular ethnic collectivity, of the 'divine birth'; which is why the solidarity of the Church with the Jewish people must be affirmed.[19] It is almost a throwaway remark on the essay, but it sheds light on St Maria's commitment to the Jews (as expressed in her poem on the subject)[20]; she goes further here than her mentor, Fr Bulgakov, despite his opposition to the pseudo-mystical racism of the Third Reich, and there is room for further reflection on the difference between them. But it is also one aspect of the way in which she consistently broadens out the significance of the solidarity of the Body of Christ. In her 1937 essay on 'The Mysticism of Human Communion', she distinguishes between the common and unhelpful understanding of otserkovlenie, 'churching', and the deeper and theologically appropriate sense of the term – differentiating between what she sees as an anxious sacralizing of ordinary life, and the habit of recognizing the divine image in the world as it is given to us, 'adorned with icons that should be venerated'[21] (human faces); a world that provides the material for Christ's own human self-offering and

19 EW, pp. 69–70.
20 Ibid., p. 33.
21 Ibid., p. 81.

its sacramental re-presentation.[22] Christ continuously unites the world with himself; or rather, in his fleshly humanity he is always already united with it. Fully to understand this is to grasp how our communion with the world in Christ simply is communion with God, not some deliberate working-out of the theoretical consequences of that communion with God.

On this basis, we are able to see that certain kinds of 'unworldliness' have the nature of sin – and that the most self-consciously 'worldly' individuals are in fact the most 'unworldly' in a negative sense. 'Worldly people are essentially separated from the world by an impenetrable wall':[23] worldliness is in fact the opening up of a lethal schism between the ego and the actual, material world – the abyss of human appetite on the one side and the endless variety of potential gratification and instrumentalization on the other, so that 'the most worldly man is the most separated and disconnected'.[24] The reduction of the world to a set of external objects for the ego is a denial of the basic insight that Mother Maria consistently works with, the theological significance of the unchosen connectedness with the materiality of the world's processes and with the alarming difference of material others that we have to recognize. The radically mistaken religious response to 'worldliness' is, she argues, a sort of replacement of the structure of 'worldly' desire and compulsion with a religious version of the same thing, in which the ego looks to God rather than finite things for satisfaction. The result is that a satisfactory relationship with God is put in the centre of the stage, and everything else is simply a task to be fitted around this focal commitment. She is in effect diagnosing two kinds of detachment from the material reality of the world: the detachment of the unsanctified ego, approaching the world as a store of consumer goods, and the detachment of a 'sanctified' ego, still isolated from the common life of creation but confident of a fulfilling communion with God: 'In this isolation

[22] Ibid., p. 78.
[23] Ibid., p. 76.
[24] Ibid.

of the "I" from the world, opposites meet'[25] – the isolation of the worldling and the isolation of the pious. For the latter – and Mother Maria regularly offers analyses of this kind of religiosity in her writings[26] – anything beyond this personal connection with God becomes a matter of duty or obedience, a 'job' that must be carefully monitored to make sure it does not disturb the stability and purity of spiritual communion. 'The world either simply lies in evil, or is the field where we exercise our virtues – in any case, it is outside the "I".'[27] Once again, the theological theme that comes to the fore in Mother Maria's analysis is the separation of self from world and the consequent denial of the solidarity she insists upon so regularly. The idea that the material world is simply the backdrop for our performance of religious duties or charitable 'jobs' is one that undermines what, for her, is a crucial element in Christian identity. Only as and when we see our compassionate service as something other than a *duty* do we grasp what it is to be in Christ. As she says, the 'charitable' work undertaken by monks in earlier ages and often described in classical monastic literature as 'an obedience' (*poslushanie*) is not in fact an extra chore on top of the main work of communing with God.[28] It is itself the stuff of communion with God.

There is an irony in the fact that her account of the relation between communion with God and the transforming love of the world to which we are called has echoes of Martin Luther, despite her repudiation of 'Protestant' mysticism, in that Luther's critique of medieval Catholic piety and ethics is centred upon the

---

[25] Ibid., p. 77.

[26] See, for example, EW chs 9 and 11.

[27] Ibid., p. 77.

[28] Again, Bulgakov's influence is in the background here. In his celebrated essay, '*Geroizm i podvizhnichestvo*' ('Heroism and the Spiritual Struggle'), first published in the *Vekhi* symposium in 1909, reprinted in the second volume of his collection *Dva grada* (*Two Cities*) (Moscow, Put 1911), pp. 176–22, he evoked the monastic ideal of *poslushanie* as a way of underlining the spiritual integrity and solidity of even the most mundane physical tasks (p. 207). For an English translation, see Rowan Williams, *Sergii Bulgakov: Towards a Russian Political Theology* (Edinburgh, T&T Clark 1999), pp. 69–112 (pp. 98–9 for the specific reference).

unacceptability of any idea that obeying the commandments is a task to be performed over and above the basic reality of our communion with God. The truth – as he spells it out in his treatise on *The Freedom of the Christian* – is that our 'good deeds' are the natural outflowing of something that has been created within us; they cannot be separated out as something to be achieved and itemized.[29] But St Maria is not primarily concerned, as Luther is, to rule out any notion that good works can be offered to God so as to win the divine favour; her concern is rather to make sure that the doing of such good works is the almost unreflective manifestation of living in the Body of Christ – and indeed of living in the world as touched and renewed by Christ. Luther sees charitable works as the consequence of our union with Christ; it is less clear that he sees this as the involvement of our baptized identities directly with the need and pain of others and the whole material world. But there is perhaps a little more possibility of dialogue across this gulf than Mother Maria seems to assume, to the extent that both repudiate the idea of a duty or 'job' that can be separated from the reality of union with Christ.

Mother Maria's observations on the world and the paradoxes of 'worldliness' are entirely of a piece with the emphasis she lays upon the prime theological necessity of displacing the myth of a humanity alienated from its material environment, literally its 'matrix', capable of relating, whether to God or to its material needs, only as an individual agent who 'owns' her story or her destiny. Her analysis of the sin of unworldliness illuminates from another angle her concern with love that is not achieved or even in any readily intelligible sense decided upon. Sin is willed isolation; and this isolation as a solitary desiring subject is what most erodes our reality; the pious adept and the greedy worldling are equally unreal, and cannot enter as they are into any truthful relations. Hence the formulation that Mother Maria uses in describing life in the Body of Christ as replacing false relatedness with true: at

---

[29] See Martin Luther, *The Freedom of a Christian,* tr. Mark Tranvik (Minneapolis, MN, Fortress Press 2008).

the end of her essay on the second gospel commandment, she speaks of the call 'to oppose the mystery of authentic human communion to all false relations among people'[30] – or rather, not exactly to oppose, as this might make the *sobornost'* of the Body simply another partisan human option, but to live the reality in a way that invites the recognition of its truth. The false relations she has in mind are those of 'class, national, and race hatreds', all forms of pseudo-sacred solidarity or 'mystical totalitarianism', and the passive homogeneity, the 'uncreative, imitative' spirit of 'secular democracy'.[31] These are, of course, distinct kinds of social unreality; what they show together is the way in which the falsity of all these relations boils down to their implicit assumption that solidarity rests on sameness. And fully to see what true relatedness means, we have to take seriously the other side of the coin in Mother Maria's unwavering insistence on the importance of unchosen connectedness, and that is her concern with the person, the unrepeatable identity of the human other.

III THE TERROR OF THE OTHER

We noted earlier how Mother Maria speaks about the 'terrible' character of the call to love the neighbour: 'In turning his spiritual world towards the spiritual world of another, a man encounters the terrible, inspiring mystery of the authentic knowledge of God.'[32] To encounter the neighbour at this level is to encounter more than flesh and blood, since the image of God in each human subject is not reducible to this historical and material reality, though it is, of course, literally nothing without it. If what we meet in the neighbour is God's mystery and self-revelation, the other I love is absolutely irreducible to any image of them I may form or any agenda I might wish them to serve. If my solidarity with them is something beyond my choice, my interaction with

[30] EW, p. 60.
[31] Ibid.
[32] Ibid., p. 57.

them is never going to be a battle for control: what is alongside me is a mystery in the fullest sense. St Maria's further thoughts on this are of particular value in clarifying what she means by solidarity. We approach the other without an agenda to promote and so without 'a certain curiosity' – that is, we do not relate to them as objects of vague interest, objects we can scrutinize from a distance; the other's experience is not a personal titillation for me. What we are summoned to is a 'strenuous' imaginative labour that will foreswear judgement and seek to see the world from within the other's point of view. This is not, though, to accept passively everything that happens to be true of the neighbour at any given moment: love is purposive, aiming at transfiguration. But this can only happen when we enter the 'inner atmosphere' of the other, so that what change I may seek to bring about is grounded in the logic, as we might say, of the other's actual history and temperament. 'Attention, sobriety, and love' should characterize our engagement – neither beginning from a fixed model of how change should come about, nor being 'sentimentally' affirming of the given state of the other.[33]

If we are to be tools in the hands of God for the transformation of the neighbour, the birth of Christ in them, love must be in the strictest sense disinterested. This resonates with the overall priority of dissolving the fictitious and dangerous role ascribed to the isolated ego with its own determined wants and goals. The love of neighbour is thus a radically kenotic affair: we are to struggle in our loving for the genuine well-being of the other, and so must struggle both with our own instinctive self-serving fantasies and also with the other's draw towards self-serving. The key tension is that in order to love disinterestedly, without 'mercenary' intent, we have to attend with all our energy to the particularity of the other: the last thing disinterested love can be is a blandly undifferentiated benevolence. Love bows down before the divine image in the other, before the unsearchable mystery

---

[33] Ibid., p. 56.

of personal uniqueness. Any love that leaves untransformed the ego's approach to love as a job to be done, as an individual achievement, is bound to stop short of a truthful recognition of the divine image, and so will never engage with the reality of the other: it will more and more 'de-realize' the other (to borrow a term Mother Maria does not herself use), and so will contribute to my own isolation from reality, my own de-realization. Thus a solidarity resting on sameness is bound to collapse into the logic of the unredeemed ego: it will seek to create a homogenized object for benevolence, the repeated, imitative 'selves' of a standardized multitude, and in doing so will solidify the separation of the ego from its objects. This is why it is essential to work on one's own 'inner world', scrutinizing and monitoring it for signs of false inwardness, the powerful impulse to protect and quarantine the soul. The adoption of passionate partisan views and tactics is always a mark of such an impulse, which is why this sort of partisanship must be so firmly resisted – not that our love should be (in the usual sense) 'dispassionate', but it should be free from the urge to determine and dominate the other's reality.[34] But in fact what Mother Maria is talking about is 'dispassion' in the classical Greek Christian sense of freedom from self-regarding and self-serving impulse; when this is purged in the soul, we are prepared for the encounter with the fathomless other. And this purgation is part of the 'terror' she points to in the obeying of the second great commandment, which is the terror appropriate when faced with the living God.

It becomes increasingly clear why she so insists on the unity of love of God and love of neighbour, and so strongly underlines the inadequacy and ultimate deceptiveness of thinking about love of neighbour as a duty performed to illustrate a general obedience to divine commands. Once again, we are reminded that the ego that has God as its desired object, the satisfaction of its individual longing and adoration, or the ego that is 'passionate' about its

[34] Ibid., pp. 55, 60.

own ascetical performance,[35] is exactly the same ego as the one that has earthly and physical gratification as its object; what is necessary is the transfiguration of the desiring subject, which happens only, so she implies, when the 'Marian' awareness of solidarity comes into focus. The true personhood of the other whom we love is generated and brought to birth by the kenotic event of our immersion in the Body of Christ, our being bound into solidarities far beyond what we could ever have chosen. Living in this condition, we are constantly giving place, giving space to each other. It is not that we have to renew over and over again some individual act of accepting the crucifixion of our passions and fears; more that we have to learn the habits that will unblock the reality that is always already at work in us, the connectedness into which we have been baptized, which is a connectedness with the entire human world and (consequently) the entire world of time and matter in which we live and out of which we ourselves are born. And the active undertaking to think oneself into the 'inner world' of the neighbour is the most serious element in our ascetical life; it is this which constitutes the active 'adoption' of the neighbour, with the goal of opening up the life of Christ in that neighbour.

To be, as Mother Maria says, 'more attentive to [our] brother's flesh than to our own'[36] means recognizing that we must see our brother or sister as involved in the world just as we are – that we must see them precisely as 'flesh'. The clear-minded discernment of the actual needs experienced at this level is the basis of asceticism – and Mother Maria grants that even theoretical analysis has its place here to the extent that it is free from our own ambitions and focused solely on those needs and the practical response to them. This attention to the sheer physical otherness, the toughness of embodied pain and privation, is the beginning of that more complex asceticism that strips us of our fascination with the story of our own passions, chastens our

[35] Ibid., p. 54.
[36] Ibid.

uninvolved curiosity about others, and readies us for imaginative entry into the standpoint of another. And in this many-layered accompaniment of the suffering other, the Christian genuinely reflects the many-layered work of Christ: 'He gave his flesh to be crucified, He suffered in His human soul, He gave His spirit into the hands of the Father.'[37] And at the same time, this is complemented by the Marian experience of standing helplessly under the cross: Mother Maria seems to be suggesting, as we have indicated earlier, that this Marian moment is in fact a crucial element in prompting our growth in the intelligent and deliberate attention involved in the conscious bearing of the cross with and for others; as if (though again Mother Maria does not say this in so many words) the Marian sense of being overwhelmed from outside by the presence of the other's pain is one of the things that displaces the ego and its self-oriented projects – including the self-oriented project of 'doing good' or 'serving the neighbour'. The 'terror of the other' begins in the simple invasion of our selfhood by the pain of the neighbour; but it is a necessary element in our learning what Mother Maria likes to call 'nonpossession'.[38] And only in that 'nonpossession' do we properly recognize the true sense of the personal, the inaccessible and impregnable dignity, mystery and elusiveness of the human other, and, ultimately, all others, sentient or not. That which claims attention at this depth or with this totality is 'functionally divine', acting towards us as a sign of God. When we have begun on the path of nonpossession we are able to see the world for what it is, not as a series of mirrors for the self. 'Terror' is an appropriate response to the extent that loss of control over our environment is bound to terrify. And if, as Rilke said, 'Beauty is only the beginning of terror',[39] Mother Maria implies that from another perspective, terror is the beginning, if not of beauty exactly, then of truthfulness.

[37] Ibid., p. 57.
[38] Ibid., pp. 104–6.
[39] From the first of the *Duino Elegies*: *das Schöne ist nichts / als des Schrecklichen Anfang*. Among many translations, see that by Patrick Bridgwater (London, The Menard Press 1999).

IV CONCLUSION

Mother Maria's theology of Christian social involvement is a complex creation; and its complexity is in large measure a function of the fact that she is determined to exclude – or at least eclipse – two major misreadings of the second great commandment. These misreadings may be characterized as the 'moralistic' or neo-Protestant error and the 'mystical' or ecclesiastical-Orthodox error. Love of neighbour is neither a programme to be taken up and implemented as the essence of Christian faith, nor is it an outward manifestation of our inner individual spiritual state. If it is the former, it is simply the act of a converted but not transfigured individual ego; if it is the latter, it is ultimately something accidental to Christian identity, a showing-forth of something deeper and more fundamental, and a showing-forth that would not be necessary in better circumstances. In reaction to these distortions, she argues that it is indeed in one sense a manifestation of the truth, but a manifestation that is utterly natural and inevitable. It is not – like, for example, a footprint that, given the right conditions, is evidence for someone having walked along this route – the sign, the trace, of something actually absent, and so only contingently related to its cause; it is rather – like the warmth emanating from a fire – a 'sign' without which the underlying reality would be unreal and unintelligible.

Thus far, Mother Maria's analysis is relatively straightforward. The complications come with her 'sword and cross' typology: here she seems to be saying two slightly different, though not contradictory, things. First, she is making the point that there is a major difference between a deliberate embrace of suffering and an unavoidable involvement in it. She consistently associates the cross with freedom (hence her argument in an earlier – 1933 – essay on 'The Cross and the Hammer-and-Sickle'[40] for the incompatibility of Christianity with any form of coercion); but she is clear that an overemphasis on imitating Christ by the voluntary acceptance

[40] EW, pp. 84–9.

of suffering results in a seriously unbalanced picture of Christian life and of the love of neighbour. It leaves untouched the root of sin and distortion, which is the illusion that each of us is primarily an isolated agent, relating to Christ as another isolated agent whose acts can be imitated. The implication is – as she spells it out in her essay on the Second Great Commandment – that we must understand our compassion for the other, our love and practical service of the neighbour as something organically arising from our incorporation in the Body of Christ, so that this incorporation is seen as intrinsically and necessarily productive of neighbour-love. But the second point is her proposal that an adequate analysis of this involves us in recognizing a Marian dimension to love of neighbour, in that our 'given' entanglement in the mutuality of Christ's Body, the absence in the Body of any secure boundaries between one subject and another, is analogous to Mary's 'entanglement' in the suffering of her son, the sword that pierces her soul. As the literal custodian of the flesh of the incarnate Word, she is involved whether or not she chooses to be in her son's agony: she is one flesh with him. And that fleshly solidarity is the best image we can have of that aspect of Christian compassion that is not about individual choice, that carries no suggestion of heroic moral self-determination. The ascetical discipline that goes with the learning of authentic love and effective response to pain is not the refining of a selflessly courageous will, so much as a steady and unsparing monitoring of the way in which the fundamental illusion of individual heroism finds its way back into our imagination.

So the 'adoption' of the whole Body, our mothering love towards each and every other, is not another version of the heroic venture out from the castle of the soul to embrace something alien, but the recognition of the full character of our prior relation with and 'investment' in the other. The other is already the bearer of the dual image of Christ and Mary: an agent capable in and only in the Body of Christ of bearing and accepting another's pain, with the hope that this solidarity issues in a fuller Christlikeness in lover and loved alike. 'Our soul', she writes, 'should co-participate in its neighbour's destiny'; and the salient word here seems to be 'destiny'. To speak of destiny in this context is to stress both the unavoidable nature of the suffering of human beings (not, presumably, in the sense that it is 'ontologically' necessary but in that a measure of vulnerability is intrinsic to finite agents) and the natural orientation of human beings to Christlikeness in virtue of their creation in the divine image. And this divine image supports and includes the Marian and maternal image of unsought and unchosen solidarity, the sharing 'in another's Golgotha'[41] that we are committed to as members of Christ's Body. The adoptive love that this embodies is a channel of grace that sustains and equips the conscious embrace of the other's need and the other's future in God.

Thus, in a convoluted but not incoherent scheme, the Marian ministry of solidarity, the ontological ground of neighbour-love, becomes a key to what relations in the Body of Christ and obedience to the commandments of Christ are and are not. If we begin with what I have called the 'heroic' acceptance of suffering or of the duty to love, we never get beyond the rootless isolation of the fictive self we habitually take for granted; if we begin with a solidarity that puts us at unplanned risk, that constantly surprises and shocks us, invades our supposed individuality, we can at least recognize that acts of conscious Christian asceticism and self-denial are grounded not in individual strength of will but in our prior incorporation in Christ. For St Maria, this understanding of Christian love, as something grounded in a supernaturally given solidarity that has nothing to do either with natural sympathy or with individual decision, is what is required by the belief that the Church is characterized by *sobornost'* and that the fundamental reality of human existence is universal responsibility – the great theological orientations of Khomiakov and Dostoevsky, who are both cited by Mother Maria as crucial sources of inspiration, and about whom she had written at some length in the late 1920s.[42]

[41] Ibid., p. 71.
[42] Ibid., pp. 58–9; 79–80 on *sobornost*; cf. *Izbrannie*, pp. 260–7, 280–6 on Dostoevsky (from an essay of 1929), and 320–49 on Khomiakov (another essay of 1929).

So for her, Christian love of neighbour is an ecclesiological theme, but also one that is rooted in the nature of finite reality itself and human reality in particular, understood as an interwoven system of mutual life-giving. What we call Christian 'ethics' is simply the tip of a metaphysical iceberg, so to speak.[43]

Katerina Bauerova, in her study of Mother Maria and Hélène Cixous, links all this with Mother Maria's own experience of the death of her children and with her haunting icon of the Mother of God with a crucified Christchild.[44] The mother living through a child's death is, Bauerova argues, a sort of inversion of the basic reality of motherhood, an 'antinomy': giving birth is a literal giving of space to the other, and experiencing the death of a child is witnessing and suffering the emptying of that space. In the poem written by Mother Maria about the death of her daughter Gaiana,[45] she seems to appeal to God to make her able to accept the entirety of God's world – an expansion of love – so as to release the dead daughter into her own future with God – a reconciliation with this particular loss or apparent reduction of living relationship. Bauerova writes that 'Motherly love which accepts the other means the broadening of the space of one's own self, and at the same time paradoxically, the diminishing of that same space' – also quoting Cixous on the 'endless' quality of the maternal body, in which desire is always flowing around in a movement that never simply 'returns to itself'.[46] This holding together of a simultaneous broadening and diminishing of the maternal subject captures something that does indeed express a theme in Mother Maria's thought, and the evocation of an endless – both 'purposeless' and inexhaustible – love resonates with much of what she says. But it takes us into a somewhat different territory from what Mother Maria explicitly discusses (though not by any means a wholly alien

---

[43] Cf. for a fuller argument on similar lines, Christos Yannaras, e.g. *The Freedom of Morality*, tr. Elizabeth Briere (Crestwood, NY, St Vladimir's Seminary Press 1984).
[44] Bauerova, 'Motherhood as a Space', pp. 139–41.
[45] Ibid., pp. 139–40.
[46] Ibid., p. 142.

one), to the extent that it misses the significance of the model of the Body of Christ as the ultimate ground of saving or life-giving involvement/investment/mutuality. It needs anchoring in some further Christological reflection. It is true that the unavoidable love of what is mortal – the love that cannot be escaped or denied because it rests on a prior solidarity in mortal flesh – is able to grow and deepen even or especially in absence. What the mother loves is what she is inextricably bound to, the child's flesh; but this binding becomes, crucially, an analogy for the deep binding of grace in the Body of Christ, which opens up again for us the solidarity in human fleshliness that we have lost or denied in sin; and such is the rootedness of this solidarity that the removal of the literal fleshly other through death cannot destroy the love but in some sense reaffirms it across the gulf of loss. Letting go of the fleshly other in the literal sense is not the end of love or of relation. Letting go of the fleshly Jesus, as understood in the Fourth Gospel (John 16.7, 19-22, 20.17), is in fact necessary so as to release something different and essential, the life of the Spirit of truth and communion; it is significant that the process is spoken of by the Johannine Jesus precisely as a birthgiving or mothering (John 16.21). And if we connect this to Mother Maria's language in her essay on the imitation of Mary, we could say that the 'adoption' of the whole Body in a maternal and Marian compassion is a radical letting go both of the isolated ego and of the fleshly other as an object of self-oriented desire – and so is capable of loving through or beyond death and loss. There is something here that is analogous to Simone Weil's challenging conviction that love for another should be love for them as if dead – that is, as if they could never reciprocate in a satisfying way.[47] But Mother Maria's perspective avoids the risk in Weil's language of a drastic denial of the mutuality of love, since it is grounded in the model of the irreducibly participatory involvement of the members of Christ's Body. It is not that the lonely commitment of a loving self is

[47] E.g., *The Notebooks of Simone Weil*, tr. Arthur Wills (London, Routledge 1956), vol. II, pp. 218–19.

untouched by the death of the other (which, in Mother Maria's terms, would be another relapse into the myth of the solitary and heroic ego), but that the loving self is part of a larger interweaving of gift and the transmission of life in which individual death cannot disrupt the flow of love given and received.

The practical implications of Mother Maria's theology of neighbour-love are best thought of in relation to some of the themes she develops in the wake of Dostoevsky. The novelist's insistence on 'universal responsibility', which she echoes closely,[48] is perhaps easily misread as a demand for some wholly unreal sense of unlimited empathy; but in the context both of Dostoevsky's novels and of Mother Maria's theology, the point is rather that our connection with others is never determined by our individual choice or individual feeling. We noted earlier the importance of the theme of 'solidarity without sameness': what matters is not that we deliberately assume a burden of imagined boundless compassion, but that we continually recognize that, confronted with the suffering of any specific other, we have no alibi. In that particular moment, we are accountable for the other in the sense that it is for us to seek that course of action that will open up for the sufferer whatever possibility there is of growth towards Christlikeness, whatever possibility exists of assisting the sufferer towards free responsibility. Thus there is a clear emancipatory dimension to Christian compassion; it is never exclusively a 'co-suffering', though Mother Maria makes it plain that this is always entailed. Even where our ability to make an emancipatory difference is severely restricted, the recognition that we are already involved in accompanying the sufferer is itself a manifestation of the reality of the Body of Christ and so a testimony to the healing circulation of divine act and divine love in the Body. And this becomes particularly significant and urgent where there is little or no 'natural' evidence of shared experience: so that the obligation for the settled professional in respect of

---

[48] A major theme in *The Brothers Karamazov*, echoed in EW, p. 59.

the asylum seeker, the US or European citizen in respect of the Pacific villager facing rising sea levels caused by climate change, or the Christian/Muslim/Hindu in respect of the Buddhist/Jew/ Baha'i is as urgent as that which is more obviously and directly felt in respect of the member of the same community. Mother Maria's own story is one that moves from the care of her own fellow-Russians to the support and defence of Jewish neighbours; and it is for this that she was arrested, and finally murdered in Ravensbruck. Her language about the various ways in which we rationalize our refusals of love on the grounds of what is reasonable or proportionate is certainly (as we have already seen) uncompromising: she recognizes that it is extreme, but challenges us to provide any theological rationale for these refusals, fully acknowledging that most of us fail dramatically and repeatedly. But precisely because this kind of compassion is not the result of individual effort but simply the showing-through (so to speak) of the underlying presence of solidarity in Christ, all we can do is continue to scrutinize the idle and selfish habits that obstruct such showing-through – not seek to force ourselves into heroism.

Mother Maria's vision of the Christian love of neighbour remains austere and intense; however, it is a radical interpretation of the implications of solidarity in Christ. Her thinking draws together with unexpected clarity and comprehensiveness most of the major themes of the theological and spiritual heritage explored in this book: the concern for an embodied theology, the Christological focus of all that can be said about our knowing and willing, the foundational significance of solidarity as a theological and moral lodestar, the awareness of liturgy as the motive force of practical service, ethical vision, and, ultimately, political wisdom – and the inescapability of a risk that can only seem irrational to any perspective other than that of the Body of Christ. She is undeniably unsystematic; theologically speaking, she does not completely clarify how solidarity in the Body of Christ carries over into solidarity with all. Like Dostoevsky, she takes this for granted, but does not theorize it fully. A more expansive theology of the universal presence and agency of the creative

Word of God, such as was traced in the spiritual and intellectual world discussed in our opening chapters, would be needed to fill out some idea of a sort of extended application of the language about Christ's Body that would help us understand that what is fully realized in the Body is always the deepest vocation and capacity of human beings as such. And – given her insistence that the entirety of Christian life and witness is 'an eternal offering of the divine liturgy beyond church walls'[49] – there is room also for a fuller theology of the liturgical action itself as the act of the Body of Christ and the act that continually reshapes the community of believers into their true 'form' as the Body, in which Christ may 'give those hearts of ours as food for the world, that He may bring the whole world into communion with those hearts of ours that have been offered up'. But this is simply to say that, like all serious theologians, she leaves the reader (and the believer) with more work to do. What she achieves is remarkable and novel enough: a fresh understanding of the command to love that radically separates it from individual moralism without losing anything of the comprehensiveness of Christ's claim on the life of his Body or anything of the hope for comprehensive transfiguration that life in the Body entails.

[49] EW, p. 185.

PART FOUR

EPILOGUE

I I

RETHINKING ESCHATOLOGY

I

When we think about this transfiguration, and when we name and enact it, both in liturgy and in active compassion and witness, we are (as we have already seen) performing work that has an eschatological significance; we are enacting what is promised as the final goal of creaturely existence. The fact and the activity of the Church is in no sense to do with memorializing a distant and inspiring past or transmitting a system of ethics or abstract doctrine. Among contemporary Orthodox theologians, Metropolitan John Zizioulas stands out as having consistently provided stimulus for the Church and the academy alike in his explorations of ecclesiology; and one of the topics that he has brought repeatedly into new focus has been precisely eschatology, most prominently in his insistence on the eschatological significance and context of the Eucharist.[50] Others have analysed and will continue to analyse the ways in which his eucharistic theology has developed in this regard.[51] My aim is simply to offer a few observations on the 'grammar' of eschatology and how – following through the

[50] See John Zizioulas, *Being as Communion* (London, Darton, Longman and Todd 1985), especially 2.IV, 3.II and 5.I and II.
[51] Paul McPartlan, *The Eucharist Makes the Church: Henri de Lubac and John Zizioulas in Dialogue* (Edinburgh, T&T Clark, 1993), remains a really valuable study; chs 4 and 11 are particularly relevant to the subject of this chapter.

logic of Zizioulas's thinking – it can be seen as pervading other topics in Christian theology in a way analogous to that in which it shapes eucharistic doctrine and practice.

The first point that has to be made about any theology of the Last Things is that eschatology obviously deals with that which cannot be imitated, repeated or narrated. What is eschatological is what has not happened; it is not an object, not an event (in the ordinary sense of something that has a before and an after), certainly not a process. And in all these ways, what I have just called the grammar of eschatology is strictly comparable to the grammar of 'God' and of God's presence in Jesus. What God does is never a process or an object for inspection; and while we may identify an event or set of events as divine action within history, the act *as such*, as related to God not to us, cannot be an item in any list, let alone an episode in the ongoing narrative of God's life. There are no such narratives, only the narrative of how God historically impinges on human narrative. Which is why the divine in Jesus is not an element, not identified with a series of specific episodes or even specific capacities (the characteristic error of extreme dualist or 'Antiochene' christologies): the narrative of God in Jesus is the narrative of Jesus, *tout simple*. It is not the drama of two agents working out a relationship.[52]

And accordingly – though this is to press the point – there is a sense in which what we say theologically about *grace* is also beyond narrative. The familiar debate about how (and whether) we differentiate between 'created' and 'uncreated' grace, often seen as one of the major differences of approach between Eastern and Western Christians, might be opened up in a new way if we began from the recognition that grace as such cannot be 'narrated', since it is the active God exercising God's characteristic mode of agency (self-forgetting self-bestowal on the Other); what we can speak of in terms of event and process (grace-giving moments, growth

---

[52] On the importance of Chalcedonian Christology for anthropology and our understanding of Christian hope, see ch. 7 in John Zizioulas, *Communion and Otherness: Further Studies in Personhood and the Church* (Edinburgh, T&T Clark 2006) – a seminal essay.

in grace and so on) is the world upon which grace impinges, transfigured and reshaped in encounter; which is very different from simply (as in the more tired varieties of scholasticism) speaking as though one 'level' of grace generated another, which could be analysed, apportioned and tracked in its processes.

In the light of all this, eschatology appears as that coincidence of historical happening and divine activity *outside which there is no possible perspective*. It is the coming-to-be in the world of a state of affairs in which the presence of God's act is as immediate and global as it is in the incarnate Jesus (though in a different mode): that is, a state of affairs in which the material world we know is rendered irreversibly transparent to the eternal act of God, when God is all in all, in the Pauline phrase.[53] That this entails judgement as well as theophany, or rather theophany experienced as judgement, is indubitable; but the point is that the eschatological consummation is a final and comprehensive 'saturation' of creation by divine act, without annihilating creation or absorbing it into the creator (which would be the same thing as annihilation).[54] The Christological logic of this should be clear. Whatever change or growth may then be imagined is beyond all that normally belongs to our language of change and growth. We cannot properly describe a creation united with divine action as in a condition of 'stasis', since that is the last thing we could say of God's action; but we equally cannot just extend our habitual ways of speaking about process or event. This is not just 'more history' – more narrative material. So that which gives us some raw material for thinking about eschatology must be whatever appears in the order of time that allows us to imagine the saturation of the world of matter and interaction by divine act – whatever conveys something of the sense of an action that is intense and relational, yet beyond change as we conceive it. Thinking about a range of doctrinal issues in relation to eschatology is thus thinking about how diverse areas of

[53] 1 Corinthians 15.28.
[54] Zizioulas, *Communion and Otherness*, pp. 259–63.

245

theology require us to identify aspects of our current experience of the material order as impelling us in the direction of this final coinciding of divine and created – or rather, not simply coinciding but manifesting the possibility of the coming-together of intense, unlimited act with a moment of worldly process; not exactly a vision of the 'timeless', as that vocabulary cannot but imply a *lack* in what is encountered, but the perception of a depth of activity and relation to which nothing could be added.

II

John Zizioulas is by no means the first or the only theologian to stress the eschatological context and meaning of the Eucharist.[55] To take only one fairly familiar example for English speakers, Gregory Dix's famous monograph on *The Shape of the Liturgy* traced (with – it must be said – some rather impressionistic historical tools) the way in which an originally eschatologically oriented celebration turned into a backward-looking action, understood not as an anticipation of the consummated future but as a repetition of the saving past.[56] Dix's eloquent contention that there is only one 'coming' of Christ, the one movement of the Son to the Father, perceived in the diverse moments of time that we call Incarnation, Ascension and Second Coming,[57] allows him to conceive of the eucharistic action as a moment in which the one supratemporal coming becomes an event in history, in the continuing history that is the narrative of a Church that is held together by the single event of the Son's gift to the Father. But what Zizioulas adds to this rich understanding of the Eucharist is twofold: first, he underlines the fact that it is

[55] Among modern Eastern theologians, see, for example, Alexander Schmemann, *The Eucharist: Sacrament of the Kingdom* (Crestwood, NY, St Vladimir's Seminary Press 1987), especially chs 2 and 11.
[56] Gregory Dix, *The Shape of the Liturgy* (London A&C Black 1945), especially ch. IX; see, e.g., p. 266 on the Eucharist as 'the contact of the church within time with the single *eschaton*, the coming of the Kingdom of God beyond time'.
[57] Ibid., pp. 247–55, 262–3.

through participation in this eschatological event that we have any theological knowledge at all (all theological knowing is in this sense eschatological, in that it works from a perception of the transparency of the world to the act of God); and, second, he makes it plain, in a way that Dix does not quite, that the eucharistic event is an event of ideal relatedness, of unlimited *koinonia*: what happens in the Eucharist is that the celebrating bishop convokes 'all in one place', *epi to auto*, to use one of Zizioulas's favourite patristic tags.[58] The event in question is one in which human persons, the inanimate matter of the world and the Spirit of the Incarnate Son are fully present to each other and in each other. And this co-presence means that we have in the midst of human history a state of affairs in which there is a clear manifestation of that global presence and co-incidence that we recognize as eschatological.

The Eucharist is of course what it is in virtue of the event of Jesus' passion and resurrection (properly called one event in that it is – in the Johannine terms echoed by Dix – a single 'going to the Father' through abandonment and death). And so the Eucharist is a state of affairs in which (i) the substance of what is being shown and spoken and shared as a common act and discourse is the Paschal event that manifests the Son's movement to the Father, (ii) this sharing, this common 'medium of exchange' in word and food, is what happens between persons who are gathered in freedom by the act of the Spirit as mediated in the charismatic convening act of the human celebrant, (iii) the pattern of the tangible action of the sacrament is a putting of material things wholly at the disposal of the incarnate Word. Because all those things are going on in the sacramental action, the nature of that action is 'eschatological': it is a state of affairs to which there is nothing to add. But when we have identified in our Christology and in the Eucharist what it means to claim that a happening in history has eschatological significance, it becomes possible to

[58] See, for example, n. 2 on p. 143 of *Being as Communion*.

see how other kinds of event in Christian practice may be read in the same way, with something of the same three elements we have just listed at work in them. In the remainder of this chapter, we shall be looking at two Christian practices that might be interpreted in this way, moving outward from the paradigmatic eschatological reading of the Eucharist to see a Christological/ eucharistic pattern in these other contexts.

III

Take first the practice of *reading Scripture*: because we so often operate with a highly individualized picture of what this entails in the Church – the devout reader alone with the text – we easily overlook the ways in which reading the Bible shows the marks of an eschatological happening. Scripture is a text for reading aloud, for proclamation: it is meant to be read in the assembly (think of the reading aloud of the Torah by Ezra and of St Paul's explicit instructions in Colossians 4.16; public reading is assumed by the rhetoric of all the Pauline letters). Human words are being presented to us as the 'convening' act of God, calling believers to a common faith and witness, constituting the shared speech of the new creation. Thus Scripture read in the Church is there as carrying the energy and meaning of the Paschal transformation: all scriptural reading is in some sense 'about' the resurrection, since it is about the living communication of Christ, upon whom all the record of God's dealings with our human world converges. Scripture shows the Son's movement to the Father: the drawing into one narrative of human history, gathered in the events of Christ's earthly course as it moves towards the Paschal transition, the passing over from death to life of Adam's seed renewed in the crucified and risen Lord. And Scripture is the setting-forth of a common story and speech: we are to shape our human language around these narratives and images, and to build common purpose and action through the language shared. The active communion engendered by reading Scripture in the assembly is a 'charismatic' reality – a response enabled by the Spirit who creates communion. And in case anyone supposes that the sharing of language is essentially the sharing of *immaterial* ideas or ideals, it is important to remember that language – in word and gesture – is a material transaction, the communication of bodies. If, in the Eucharist, bread and wine are placed 'at the disposal' of the Word of God, the charismatically proclaimed words of Scripture are, in an analogous way, put into the hands of Christ so as to become contemporary with him and transparent to him. Debates about the inspiration of Scripture are habitually skewed by a failure to see the essential character of scriptural address as eschatological in the sense we have been defining: to call Scripture inspired is not to ascribe to the written text a self-contained character of supernatural accuracy or whatever, but to say that when it is read, the Spirit of the age to come summons believers to reconciliation with God and communion with God through Christ. If we begin from the public and liturgical proclaiming of Scripture in the Eucharist – and in the *synaxis*, the gathering, of the Office as well – we are more likely to see inspiration as a word for what happens in the Spirit's address to the gathered community that shows forth the character of the renewed creation. Individual Bible study flows out of this: the believer reading Scripture 'in private', in personal devotion and study, is reading as part of the invisible assembly, reading in company, whether she or he knows it or not. For them to read in the Spirit is to read within the charismatic ambience of the community of the Last Days, the eucharistic assembly in which God and the world coincide.

In a similar way, we can say that *the life of prayer and holiness in the Church* at its most consistent and authentic is again an eschatological matter.[59] The unfolding of what contemplation entails – as described by the major teachers of the Christian East and the Christian West – is once again an enactment of the Paschal event, a process of growth in which the shape of the cross and the resurrection is 'inscribed' in

---

[59] See the final essay (ch. 8), 'The Church as the "Mystical" Body of Christ', in *Communion and Otherness*, for Zizioulas's own thoughts on how to theologize about Christian 'spirituality'.

the life of the believer. Loss and darkness, encountered in their full force and violence, issue in a homecoming to the place we inhabit, to life in communion, the Son's intimacy with the Father. The bodily actuality of the contemplative becomes a 'site' where reconciliation is shown, and so (to borrow the phrase ascribed to St Seraphim of Sarov) countless others find their salvation in proximity to the contemplative saint. Metropolitan Anthony Bloom would speak of the contemplative pastor as given for food to the spiritually needy, or of 'making one's soul a marketplace' for others. That is to say, the contemplative becomes a means of communion, a reality in the world that allows proximity to the eternal act of God and to that act in the reality of other human subjects. To the extent that *any* praying Christian becomes truly open to the act of God in Christ, they become a sign and foretaste of the end of things: they signify what happens when the material actuality of this world is given over to Christ. In this case, it is the bodily actuality of a person, the praying Christian, which is given over to be the embodiment of God's coincidence with human/worldly agency. The characteristic Eastern interest in the presence of divine *energeia* in the body of the saint (and in the iconographic representation of the saint) is not an assertion simply of supernatural power transferred to material objects (any more than scriptural inspiration is a doctrine about supernatural truthfulness transferred to the material text): it is to do with the saint's work of presenting the coincidence of trinitarian life, life in communion, with this specific human 'location', so that this life becomes something offered to and made possible for other human beings.

So the person who enters more deeply into the trinitarian mystery, through contemplative prayer or through sacrificial action and suffering (the martyr, for example), is someone who is not simply undergoing an individual transformation but is becoming a place where the Church 'comes to itself'. This throws some light on the regular insistence among spiritual teachers that a life of solitary contemplation is not only a gift given to the entire Church but is actually in itself a realization of deeper levels of communion – in no way a turning from communion but a further entry into it. As such, it is an eschatological mystery in the same sense as the Eucharist and the reading of Scripture. And those who have said of the monastic life that it has an eschatological character have understood the point. Here is a life in which a resolved openness to the action of God as revealed in the Paschal mystery is presented to Church and world in a 'sacramental' form of conduct, announcing the possibility – by the grace of the Spirit – of eucharistic coincidence between God and creation; here, then, is a life whose import is eschatological hope. Not every vowed monastic is a person of realized sanctity, but what matters is that the life itself declares an anticipation of the promised End. It is a life that has foresworn anxiety about the next generation, about provision for the future and the safeguarding of purely individual liberties: in celibacy and poverty and the promise of obedience to spiritual authority, it situates itself outside the habitual realms of human fear and defensiveness. It is this that has caused the monastic life to be called 'angelic' in the tradition – not because it is somehow less embodied than other kinds of human life, though that is a frequent misunderstanding of it, but because it places itself so firmly in a position where it does not try to own or master the future. It is 'angelic' because its rationale is really liturgical: it exists in the 'now' of work conducted worshipfully and worship conceived as intense and creative work.

And in an important sense, this throws into high relief the way in which every baptized worshipper seeking to move further into communion through sacrament, scriptural meditation and receptive prayer is involved in eschatological activity. These are not things undertaken in order to further ends beyond themselves; understood as, all of them, 'charismatic' events, they are events of encounter with the unbounded communion that is the life-in-act of God. We can say of them, to pick up a phrase used earlier, that there is *nothing to add*. We may say – and frequently do – that scriptural study and contemplative prayer are instruments towards our growth in grace or holiness; but any such phraseology grates on the theological ear. The Eucharist, the Scriptures and the life of prayer are already our inhabiting of holiness and of heaven, not means towards a distant and different end. Of course we might want to say that in order to be holy we live like this: but that is comparable to saying that in order to be musical we sing and play music. And the further implication is that for us to be eucharistic beings we must be in-formed by Scripture as charismatic encounter; for us to be readers of the Bible, we must be eucharistic beings; for us to be communicants and readers of Scripture, we must be contemplatives; for us to be contemplatives, we must be involved in Eucharist and Scripture. The eschatological framing of all these matters allows us to see the coherence of our discipleship as a life of manifestation, showing forth the End.

IV

In sum, then, the eschatological reading of the Eucharist so powerfully advanced and explored by Zizioulas provides a template for theologizing about other things. And we could extend the discussion still further if we began to ask what Christian ethics overall might look like if reimagined in the context of this eschatological perspective: Christian virtue, rather than being either a plain 'imitation' of Christ and the saints or a matter of obedience to divine instructions, becomes a manifestation of what is *hoped for* – a living-out of eucharistic reconciliation and transparency, in which the imitation of Christ is grounded in openness to the Spirit and our obedience in the sense of responding to the invitation to eucharistic relation (with God, each other and the material world). Zizioulas – like other major Orthodox thinkers such as Yannaras and Clément[60] – lays the foundations for a serious and far-reaching reconstruction of Christian ethics

---

[60] Christos Yannaras, *The Freedom of Morality* (Crestwood, NY, St Vladimir's Seminary Press 1984); Olivier Clément (with Stan Rougier), *La revolte de l'esprit* (Paris, Stock 1979); also the work of the Armenian American theologian Vigen Guroian, *Incarnate Love: Essays in Orthodox Ethics* (Notre Dame, IN, University of Notre Dame Press 1987), and *Ethics After Christendom: Toward an Ecclesial Christian Ethic* (Grand Rapids, MI, Eerdmans 1994); and the recent book of Aristotle Papanikolaou, *The Mystical as Political* (Notre Dame, IN, University of Notre Dame Press 2012), especially chs 2, 3 and 4.

in relation to ecclesiology and the sacramental life. But exploring this further would take us beyond the modest aims of this brief chapter, which has been simply to clarify some of the ways in which Zizioulas's eucharistic theology can structure our reflection on other topics, showing how fundamental to Christian theologizing the eschatological perspective is. While it would be misleading to say (in the manner of some twentieth-century European thinkers) that the only eschatology is realized eschatology, it *is* importantly true to say that the only way in which we can speak theologically about eschatology is by speaking of the epiphanic character of sacrament and sanctity. The only discourse we can have about the Last Things – given, as was said earlier, that we cannot by definition narrate or describe them – is one that seeks to display the ways in which eucharistic practice (including in that term the life of prayer and scripturally formed discipleship) embodies the ultimate coinciding of God's act and created happening; and, as we have seen, this will only make full sense if it is consistently rooted in our acknowledgement of the Paschal event as the definitive moment in human history of such coincidence.

Christians believe that in Christ – and most specifically in the defining events of cross and resurrection that establish once and for all Christ's full identity, divine and human – the end of the ages has been made manifest: here is that upon which all history converges. The work of the Holy Spirit is constantly to make us 'contemporary' with that end that is in Christ, and so to establish *our* identity within the Paschal mystery. When Christians assemble at Christ's invitation, and in and through the prompting of the Spirit, to pray Christ's prayer and receive the sacramental embodiment of Christ crucified and glorified, they stand at or beyond the end of the ages: 'Alpha and Omega, to whom shall bow / All nations at the Doom, is with us now.'[61] As they learn and struggle to inhabit that place, they become, unevenly and fleetingly but truly signs of the End, bearers of judgement

---

[61] The concluding couplet of hymn no. 307 in *The English Hymnal*, trans. J.M. Neale from the seventh-century *Sancti, venite*.

and hope. And so in this perspective the Church is neither the conservator of a fragile and threatened past nor the prophet of a utopian future, but the present witness of the possibility of a reconciliation leaving no created state of affairs untouched. If the Church knows that eschatological gift at its heart, it knows where its priorities are. It is not the least of the many blessings given to the Church by Metropolitan John's theology that this vision is presented with such energy and depth, a challenge alike to lazily traditionalist as well as lazily liberal pictures of the Body of Christ. As Metropolitan John expressed it in two of many luminous formulations in *Being as Communion*, 'the Spirit confronts the process of history with its consummation, with its transformation and transfiguration'; and the Church 'must both transmit history and judge history in the light of the eschata'.[62] Reconceiving eschatology in this light brings us with urgency and joy to the very heart of the gospel.

[62] *Being as Communion*, pp. 180, 181.

ACKNOWLEDGEMENTS

Several of these chapters have appeared in print in slightly different form, or have been revised after delivery as conference presentations.

Chapter 1 is a very lightly revised version of 'The Theological World of the Philokalia', in *The Philokalia: A Classic Text of Orthodox Spirituality*, ed. Brock Bingaman and Bradley Nassif (Oxford, Oxford University Press 2012); part of it was delivered as the Fr Alexander Schmemann Memorial Lecture at St Vladimir's Orthodox Theological Seminary, Crestwood, New York, in 2010.

Chapter 2 began as a seminar paper for a workshop at the Oxford International Conference on Patristic Studies in 2011, and an earlier version of the text appeared as 'Nature, Passion, and Desire: St Maximus' Ontology of Excess', in *A Saint for East and West: Maximus the Confessor's Contribution to Eastern and Western Christian Theology*, ed. Daniel Haynes (Eugene, OR, Cascade Books 2019).

Chapter 3 combines a lecture on 'The Embodied Logos' for the 'New Trinitarian Ontologies' Conference in Cambridge in September 2019 and a keynote lecture on 'The Renewal of Mind and the Transformation of Sense' at the 'Faith, Reason, Theosis' conference at Fordham University in June 2019.

Chapter 4 was originally a lecture entitled 'Deification, Hypostatization, and Kenosis', for a symposium on the theology of deification at the Catholic University of Leuven in 2014, and an earlier version of the text was published in *Rightly Dividing the Word of Truth: Studies in Honour of Metropolitan Kallistos of Diokleia*, ed. Andreas Andreopoulos and Graham Speake (Bern, Peter Lang 2016), and also in the symposium proceedings,

Theosis/Deification: Christian Doctrines of Divinization East and West, ed. John Arblaster and Rob Faesen (Leuven, Peeters 2018).

A version of Chapter 5 is due to appear in a special issue of *Perichoresis* (XIX.2, 2020), edited by Christopher Woznicki.

Most of Chapter 6 was delivered as 'Liturgical Humanism: Orthodoxy and the Transformation of Culture', the 'Orthodoxy in America' lecture at Fordham University in September 2014; a very slightly expanded version of this was published as a pamphlet by Fordham University Press and also appeared with a couple of small changes as 'Liturgical Humanism: Olivier Clément on the Anthropology of Worship' in *A Journey along the Christian Way: Festschrift for the Right Rev. Kallistos Ware on his 85th Anniversary*, ed. Elena D.-Vasilescu (Bern, Peter Lang 2018).

Chapter 7 is a lightly revised version of 'Tradition in the Russian Theological World', in *The Oxford Handbook of Russian Religious Thought*, ed. Caryl Emerson, George Pattison and Randall A. Poole (Oxford, Oxford University Press 2020).

Chapter 8 was originally a presentation entitled 'Justice, Distance, and Love: What Would be a Contemplative Stance in Politics?' to a session of the 'Leuven Encounters in Systematic Theology' in October 2019 on the theme 'Theos and Polis: Political Theology as Discernment'.

Chapter 9 was published as 'Holy Folly and the Problem of Representing Holiness: Some Literary Perspectives' in the *Journal of Orthodox Christian Studies* I.1, 2018.

Chapter 10 combines two lectures to conferences in Oxford on the life and work of Mother Maria Skobtsova (St Maria of Paris) in March and November 2019.

Chapter 11 began as an address for a study day in honour of Metropolitan John (Zizioulas) of Pergamum at Westcott House, Cambridge, in June 2014.

I am very conscious of my debt to the organizers of (and other participants in) the conferences mentioned here, particularly my friends and colleagues at KU Leuven and Fordham University, Elena Narinskaya in Oxford and Ryan Haecker in Cambridge;

also to Josh Heath, Michael Miller and Isidoros Katsos among research students past and present; to John Behr, John Chryssavgis, Brandon Gallaher, Simone Kotva, Nikolaos Loudovikos, John Milbank, Aristotle Papanikolaou and Michael Plekon; to the Epiphany Philosophers; to Paul Tyson and the other members of the 'After Science and Religion' project, who have helped shape some of the ideas sketched here; and to the magisterial figures whose thinking and witness have for so many decades continuously shed light for me on the theological path: Andrew Louth, Kallistos Ware, Christos Yannaras, John Zizioulas, and, among the departed, Donald Allchin, Antony Bloom and Olivier Clément. Eternal memory.

Rowan Williams
Cardiff, Epiphany 2021

INDEX

A NOTE ON THE AUTHOR

Rowan Williams is the former Archbishop of Canterbury and was the Master of Magdalene College, Cambridge, a position from which he retired in 2020. He was also Lady Margaret Professor at Oxford University. Williams is a contributing writer for the *New Statesman* and the author of dozens of books including *On Augustine*, *The Way of St Benedict*, *Holy Living* and *The Edge of Words*.

A NOTE ON THE TYPE

The text of this book is set in Linotype Sabon, a typeface named after the type founder, Jacques Sabon. It was designed by Jan Tschichold and jointly developed by Linotype, Monotype and Stempel in response to a need for a typeface to be available in identical form for mechanical hot metal composition and hand composition using foundry type.

Tschichold based his design for Sabon roman on a font engraved by Garamond, and Sabon italic on a font by Granjon. It was first used in 1966 and has proved an enduring modern classic.